The Human Equity Advantage

The Human Equity Advantage

Beyond Diversity to Talent Optimization

Trevor Wilson

A Wiley Brand

National Library of Canada Cataloguing in Publication Data

Wilson, Trevor, 1957-
    The human equity advantage : beyond diversity to talent optimization / Trevor Wilson.

Includes bibliographical references and index.
Issued also in electronic formats.
ISBN 978-1-118-45840-2

    1. Personnel management.   2. Human capital—Management.
    3. Employees—Rating of.   4. Organizational effectiveness.
    5. Leadership.   I. Title.

HF5549.5.M3W53 2013   658.3'128   C2013-900944-2

ISBN: 978-1-118-73076-8 (custom); 978-1-118-45851-8 (ebk);
978-1-118-45845-7 (ebk); 978-1-118-45849-5 (ebk)

Production Credits
Cover design: Adrian So
Typesetting: Thomson Digital
Cover image: stockcam/iStockphoto
Printer: Friesens

Editorial Credits
Executive editor: Karen Milner
Managing editor: Alison Maclean
Production editor: Pamela Vokey

John Wiley & Sons Canada, Ltd.
6045 Freemont Blvd.
Mississauga, Ontario
L5R 4J3

Printed in Canada
1 2 3 4 5 FP 17 16 15 14 13

To Donnette, Alex, Briana and James. My inspiration and my life.
Thank you for your understanding and unconditional support.

Contents

Foreword
By Lamarr Lark

I first met Trevor Wilson over 16 years ago at a diversity conference in California. At the time I was a divisional vice-president for human resources at Abbott. As with most multinational organizations diversity was very important to us, however, for years we had been wondering what would come after diversity and inclusion. I now realize we were exhibiting the early signs of what Trevor calls "diversity fatigue."

Trevor was one of the keynote speakers at the conference, and his approach seemed very unique. It was an approach not focusing on correcting the historical wrongs of equity-seeking groups but something much wider and more profound. He appeared to have done some breakthrough thinking on the issues of diversity and inclusion in the workplace and the requisite leadership strategies for the future. What really captured my attention was the term "human equity." I really wanted to learn more about it, so I stood in his line along with everyone else, waiting to have a discussion with him. When I finally met him, he not only seemed to be a leading-edge thinker, but his challenge to move beyond the old concept of diversity seemed to resonate with everyone.

After spending over 20 years in the field of HR, it is very refreshing to finally have some truly breakthrough, enlightened thinking as it relates to people strategies. Organizations have emphasized for decades that "people are our most important asset," but they have lacked a clear road-map as to what this really means. Human equity brings this platitude to life, introducing the reader to positive psychology-based leadership and management approaches. These new approaches are designed to show you how to maximize on the inherent talent inside your organization and help each person reach his or her full potential, not just because it is the right thing to do, but because it also creates better business results.

I firmly believe that human equity is the management philosophy of the future. It picks up where diversity and inclusion leave off and holds up a mirror to management and leadership. It identifies the specific leadership competencies required to move forward and provides a framework for authentic leadership accountability. And it provides a clear path for leaders to achieve the goal of putting their people first.

I'm sure after reading this book that you will agree that human equity will allow you to optimize on the unique differences of each individual, which is the secret to creating a sustainable competitive advantage for your organizations.

Lamarr Lark
Former Divisional Vice-President, Human Resources
Global Abbott Nutritionals
Abbott Laboratories
Partner WPM LLC (Where People Matter)

Foreword
By Gerry Bouey

During the early 1980s I had a job as a senior quality assurance officer within a large commercial bank. My main role was to help train senior managers and associates all over the organization on what it takes to become keenly client focused. I loved the job! It provided me with a great opportunity to work with all types of senior executives, all over the country. My background was in statistical process control, a concept and practice that I was able to perfect in a previous role as an operations manager. This experience afforded me the knowledge and genuineness to effectively "enroll" individuals on basic quality concepts, and servant-leadership. My job as a senior quality assurance officer was my first opportunity to work in a role that could influence organizational culture on a very large scale. The activities I was involved with were sanctioned by the CEO of the bank, which afforded me access, influence and the power to get things done without going through a lot of red tape. It was an amazing experience.

From my standpoint, my career was at its zenith: I had a dream job with all the perks I had always wanted. As in all life endeavors, though, my so-called happiness was just going through a cycle.

One day, my boss came to me and asked me to participate in a "diversity project" as part of the quality initiatives I was spearheading. My immediate cynical reaction was that the organization was just looking for an individual of color—a "poster boy"—to represent this initiative. After all, I had experienced all types of overt and covert "racism" throughout my career, which at the time was around 20 years.

I had developed a coping mechanism, an emotionally calloused approach. And I had developed a jaded opinion of "diversity" as a narrow approach to management, driven by compliance with laws and regulations rather than by any real, fundamental change in "heart" or culture within the organization. It appeared to me that most companies that implemented diversity initiatives approached them from a "have to" rather than a "want to" perspective. Regardless of what was said publicly, the diversity initiative I was being asked to spearhead in my own organization only reinforced my apathy and cynicism. A certain type of "fatigue" set in.

So I was not surprised that I rebelled against what I perceived as yet another "diversity" initiative, wasting my time and the resources of the organization. I told my boss that I was too busy to participate in such an effort. I felt that my plate was too full with implementing the current client-focused initiative to participate in such an effort.

My boss insisted—in fact, he said, "This is not a suggestion, this is an order!" Well, I do not like being told what to do, so I went into "compliance mode." "You can buy my hands, but not my heart," I thought, and reluctantly went to the kick-off meeting.

There I demonstrated, through my body language, all the outward signs of an individual not wanting to be there. I didn't bring a note pad or any writing materials, my arms were folded, and I did not participate in any constructive way.

Over the course of a year, what happened surprised me. This small team investigated what diversity was, and was not. We traveled all over the country, visiting large organizations that had had some success and others that had failed miserably. Our small think tank got a chance to explore the key ingredients of a systemic cultural change, which is a process that few organizations are willing to go through.

To my chagrin I found that I knew very little about diversity. This shocked and troubled me. I learned that diversity is actually an extremely complex subject, rooted in accessing human potential. I learned that it means far more than simply being treated fairly and giving certain groups equality; it requires a high level of consciousness that most organizations have little motivation to take on. What's also amazing is that my learning in this domain took place in the 1980s, whereas most businesses even today struggle with the topic, and still relegate diversity to a regulatory or compliance initiative, rather than seeing it as the basis for understanding and appreciating how to lead others, or for being led.

From my standpoint, I believe that the so-called conversation around diversity is usually only a superficial conversation within most organizations, and that the true conversation is around how you can get full engagement out of the individuals you work with. For most organizations, as long as the short-term demands of Wall Street are met, there's no problem. In a sense, I get that. However, a progressive organization might want to ponder: what was not realized? What was never actualized or accessed? What human "equity" was hidden and not exercised?

Daniel Pink, in his book *Drive: The Surprising Truth About What Motivates Us*, makes the case that individuals who work in a "social field" that facilitates autonomy, mastery and purpose will be the new winners in the marketplace. I happen to agree with that premise. But how do you attract and retain talent for new innovations and creativity for projects, services and other things that the market doesn't yet know it needs? The answer, for me, is in finding the "extra" that an individual brings to the party—or as my good friend Trevor Wilson would say, their human equity.

What is human equity? For me it's the organizational or individual ability to engage the best that a person has to offer, for the present and future success of the enterprise. Most often this potential, or "equity," is left on the table and never actualized. It is something that the individual will contribute voluntarily if and when the organization welcomes that contribution, not because the organization is trying to satisfy some compliance initiative. Going beyond compliance is a difficult task for most managers and supervisors within our modern organizations. Most do not have the training or the wherewithal to access the level of potential, or equity, that individuals have within themselves (and, to be fair, that most of us do not even realize we possess). So most leaders play small and safe in managing their people.

I believe Trevor's new book *The Human Equity Advantage* will address how you can best realize the maximum potential of this equity that is inherent in every individual. For those individuals who believe in the sacred stewardship of leading others, and those who desire to be led in an extraordinary way, the insights Mr. Wilson brilliantly presents in this book offer a significant opportunity to "up" their game, play at a different level, and achieve amazing results in the marketplace.

One word of caution: this is hard work. This is not for the faint of heart. This work requires an extraordinary amount of commitment and fortitude. Most organizations do not have the character or the extrinsic motivation to take this to its full fruition, although I am optimistic that there are some—the amazing few—that are willing, that want to leave planet Earth as a far better place than what they found. That's the audience, from my humble perspective, that this book is best suited for. If you are looking for a quick fix, a set of tools, a set of recipes, this book could satisfy that appetite. However, if you want to gain the full benefit of what Mr. Wilson is putting forth, I challenge you to put his wisdom and thinking into practice, based as it is on more than 30 years of experience in the conversation of inclusion, diversity and human potential. He has studied these concepts thoroughly, consulted on them around the globe, and has a track record of helping organizations be their very best.

As a final thought I am compelled to share and offer this observation. I believe that the true practitioner of developing human potential and human equity are individuals who actually believe in the people they lead. It almost seems that these types of leaders readily sense that there is much potential that is left un-used. As a way of operationalizing and accessing this "potential," a higher level and sophistication and conscientiousness needs to be acquired.

I would challenge readers of this book to think about the people they lead, and how are they inhibiting full actualization? Is it possible to access a potential that the individual themselves, might not even be aware of? If so, what tool might be used?

However you answer those three questions will give you the insight, and the where-withal, to perform in this new age of valuing people, and engaging the equity that we all bring to the table. We do not want this insight to be wasted or squandered away or, worse yet, buried with us as we leave this existence here on planet Earth!

Gerry Bouey,
Lewis University,
Leadership & Executive Coach,
TBG Leadership & Consulting, LLC

PART ONE

BEYOND DIVERSITY TO HUMAN EQUITY: THE REQUIRED SHIFT

Chapter 1

DIVERSITY FATIGUE AND THE UNFULFILLED PROMISE OF DIVERSITY

A couple of years ago I met with two dozen leading diversity practitioners to identify some of the toughest challenges they were facing. Among the usual responses, such as lack of leadership buy-in, no effective outreach strategies and challenges empowering employee network groups, there was a new theme. It was a theme that eventually seemed to dominate the entire discussion, yet none of us could quite put our finger on it. Finally someone said, "Our organization is facing diversity fatigue." That was it: *diversity fatigue.*

What, you may well ask, is diversity fatigue? It encompasses several things, including the Herculean effort required by diversity practitioners to keep the momentum going amid the toughest economic crisis since the Depression. It is trying to repackage and sell the business case for diversity by showing specific return on investment at a time of limited dollars for any corporate imperative. It is trying to figure out how to creatively communicate diversity in an extremely time-scarce environment when people struggle to do more with less. It is maintaining the gains with front-line managers (the so-called frozen middle) who ask, "When will this diversity thing end? Have we not handled it by now?" It also involves the endless task of breaking down silos among groups that have interest only in their particular dimension of diversity. All this is what we call *diversity fatigue.*

In July 2007, a leading North American human resources publication called *Profiles in Diversity Journal* ran a fascinating series of essays entitled "The Pioneers of Diversity." I was honored to be asked to join the group of 30 leading thinkers to comment on the state of the diversity industry at that point. Each pioneer was asked to write a short essay on where diversity came from, where it is now and where it needs to go next.

Not surprisingly, the pioneers agreed on where diversity came from—that is, when the concept first arose: the 1987 Hudson Institute's study *Workforce 2000*, which accurately forecast several dramatic changes to the North American workforce. Interestingly, most of the pioneers also agreed on where we are right now: most felt we are at a stalemate, one we've been stuck in for at least the last decade. At the very least, diversity needed a face-lift, if not a transformation. The most intriguing aspect of the essays, however, was the question of where we need to go next. There was virtually no alignment on this important question.

I decided to use this opportunity to formally introduce and write about human equity, which I had started thinking about in 2001. I called the pioneers' essay "Diversity: Ready to Evolve." I argued that it was time the conversation about diversity evolved from a preoccupation with superficial variations of gender, race and sexual orientation, to focus on the many characteristics that make every person unique. I argued that while the demographic dimensions of diversity could inform who a person is, they could never define that person. I concluded that it was time for human equity, a concept that focuses on maximizing the diverse talents of your total workforce.

It was just recently, on a coffee break from what, until that point, appeared to be a typical diversity executive briefing, that a senior executive of one of the most powerful global Fortune 100 companies turned to me and said: "Diversity is dividing our people. We've got blacks over here, Hispanics over there, gays in one corner, lesbians in the other. It's not working! And we don't know how to fix it. How do I get everyone on the same page when they're only concerned about their own issues?"

Being in the diversity consulting field for over two decades, I might be expected to be frustrated by the executive's comment. *Au contraire!* I was encouraged—and relieved. Finally, someone in a corner office was waking up to the fact that something is broken in the diversity arena. Two or three years ago, you would not have heard this level of candor, even in a private conversation—political correctness would not allow it. Diversity was a sacred cow, and any criticism of it by executives had the potential of leading to accusations of not being committed, not "getting it" or, heaven forbid, being one of those old boys from the white, privileged, sexist, racist, homophobic power network. Thankfully, it would appear that things are changing and some courageous executives are finally willing to move beyond political correctness and confront the brutal truth about corporate diversity.

More and more, C-level executives are asking those responsible for diversity and human resources, "Are we really making progress?" "What has been the return on investment of all this activity?" and "What difference have you actually made?" The truth is, anyone who has been in the field for more than 20 years has quietly been asking himself or herself the same questions and wondering what we should be doing next.

The best leaders know that in today's demanding market they will have to reinvent their organizations at least every three years. In 2010, the IBM Global CEO study found that almost 70 percent of global CEOs think their current business model is sustainable for only another three years; the other 30 percent believed it may be usable for as long as another five years. As the bestselling author Jason Jennings says in his excellent book *The Reinventors*:

> Today a combination of stagnant Western markets, former third world nations embracing technology and becoming manufacturing powerhouses with middle classes larger than that of the US, technology that makes everything increasingly transparent and customers who believe that they can get exactly what they want when they want it at a price they're willing to pay[,] all add up

to a game changing business environment. Anyone who thinks that they'll get a free pass and that they don't have to constantly reinvent their business has their head in the sand.[1]

After three decades of diversity, important lessons have been learned about how to do it the wrong way. We are now at a critical juncture in the journey and need to make some tough decisions about which road to take. The diversity industry has clearly hit a wall and needs to reinvent itself. It needs a breakthrough if it is going to be relevant to the business agenda over the next decade.

What are the current problems with diversity? Let's borrow from the David Letterman School of Analysis, counting down from 10.

THE TOP 10 PROBLEMS WITH DIVERSITY TODAY

10. Diversity cannot be achieved simply by focusing on improving the representation of women.
9. There is a hierarchy of inequity in diversity that breeds inter-group competition.
8. Success in diversity cannot be measured simply by tracking cosmetic changes in demographic representation.
7. Diversity has been dominated by an American-specific agenda and mindset, despite it being a global issue.
6. Diversity is too focused on "superficial" differences such as race, gender and sexual orientation.
5. Diversity in practice is about equity for some, rather than equity for all.
4. Diversity virtually ignores the importance of leadership behavior.
3. Diversity has not moved beyond awareness education about race, gender, culture and sexual orientation.
2. Diversity is based on a deficit paradigm.

---

1. Jason Jennings, *The Reinventors: How Extraordinary Companies Pursue Radical Continuous Change* (New York: Penguin Group, 2012), 4.

And the last—and most significant—problem with diversity today (drum roll, please) . . .

1. Diversity focuses on groups rather than the individual.

Let's take a closer look at these problems.

Problem 10: Diversity cannot be achieved simply by focusing on improving the representation of women.

In 1962, research scientist Felice Schwartz created Catalyst, which soon became the leading not-for-profit gender research think tank in the United States. Today, this impressive organization works globally with offices in the United States, Canada and Europe, and has more than 400 preeminent member corporations looking to Catalyst for research, information and advice about women in the workforce.

Catalyst is based on a hypothesis Schwartz put forward, also in 1962. She believed that the reason women had not made it to the executive positions in the Fortune 500 multinational corporations was not rooted in mal intent. Rather, it was simply an issue of ignorance. Maybe, she hypothesized, the leaders of these organizations were unaware of the appalling state of affairs surrounding gender representation. That is, they just didn't have all the facts.

In 1993 Catalyst conducted the first census of women in board positions and three years later introduced the Census of Women Corporate Officers and Top Earners. These annual counts are based on the belief that if a credible census of the executive boardrooms and positions were conducted and the numbers were shown to the male executives, they would surely act. These leaders of conscience would be "shamed" into fixing the problem if it was indubitably proven to exist. Thus, the annual Catalyst Census of Women Corporate Officers and Top Earners, which will soon celebrate its 20th anniversary, was born.

I first attended the very prestigious Catalyst dinner about a decade ago as a guest of one of our international clients, who joined almost every other Fortune 500 company at this impressive event.

I had the pleasure of listening to the then global president of Catalyst present the data from the think tank's latest census. She explained that really what she was about to present was the report card on gender issues in the North American corporate world over the past three decades.

"Let's start with the CEO office," she began. "How many women are currently CEOs of a major Fortune 500?"

I thought to myself, "By now it's got to be over 10 percent," so 50 women, I figured.

"One!" she announced with relish. "Not 1 percent," she emphasized. "One. Carly Fiorina at HP."

She continued by asking about the level just below CEO. "How many women are direct reports to the CEO?" She was referring to those at the executive vice president level.

Okay, this has to be about 10 percent, I reasoned.

"Four percent!" she announced. She continued to work her way down level by level—5 percent, 7 percent, 9 percent . . . not reaching double digits until the director level, and not reaching close to gender parity until the senior manager level. At this rate, she noted, it will take us 250 years to get to gender parity in the executive offices of the Fortune 500 companies.

If I wasn't already totally shocked by her research, I was by what she said next: "We've just got to work harder." My head began to spin, and all I could hear was Dr. Phil's voice in my head asking, "How's that working for you?"

"You're telling me that after more than 50 years of researching this issue of gender representation in corporate America and almost 20 years of presenting the representation numbers, the best answer you've got for us is *Do more of the same, but just do it harder?*" I thought about Einstein's wonderful definition of insanity: doing the same thing over and over and expecting a different result. "Don't you get it, lady? Something is broken!"

In the diversity field, gender is considered the crucible. It was reasoned that if organizations could overcome the attitudinal and systemic issues that lead to the gender representation disparities illustrated by the

Catalyst numbers, then they could apply these solutions to all the other underrepresented groups in the workforce. So here we sit, 50 years after Schwartz hypothesized that women were underrepresented at executive levels simply because of ignorance, almost 20 years of credible, comprehensive, bulletproof Catalyst research and almost nothing has changed. In fact, at a recent Canadian Catalyst dinner, I heard the global CEO and president make a virtually identical presentation—only this time she had it recorded on video.

Improving gender representation was always the hope for other underrepresented groups in organizations. If the glass ceiling was broken for women, it would not be long before it was broken for other equity-seeking groups. However, as we can see from the annual Catalyst numbers, progress has been glacial and it may be time to look to another strategy to diversify the workforce.

Problem 9: There is a hierarchy of inequity that breeds inter-group competition.

Years ago, when I was in government pushing for the kinder, gentler Canadian version of Affirmative Action, which we called Employment Equity, I watched an impressive presentation about the discrimination faced by gay men in the workforce. The group presenting had done an admirable job of collecting enough data to prove that homosexuals were in fact facing as much discrimination in the Canadian workforce as any other equity-seeking group. Thus, they argued that they too should be considered a designated group under the proposed employment equity legislation.

Now, this was more than two decades ago, so the likelihood that any politician in his or her right mind would make homosexuals a designated group under affirmative action was "snowball in hell" territory. It was a compelling presentation nevertheless. Yet, I sat in the audience, having a different conversation in my mind.

"You know, that's mildly interesting about homosexuals," I said to myself, "but frankly what they have to say doesn't affect me. Women have got theirs and I want mine. You gay guys will get yours right after my group (i.e., visible minorities). If it's between your group and mine—mine comes first."

Years later, my hero, Nelson Mandela, would name this interesting condition "the hierarchy of inequity," whereby my inequity is more pressing or more important than your inequity—a very human but counterproductive mindset. More on that later.

Many of the leading Fortune 500 corporations have created internal networking groups for women, ethnic minorities, gays, people with disabilities, Aboriginals, and so on. At least one major global corporation boasts more than 100 internal advocacy groups, including one for straight, white, able-bodied males (SWAMs). What, you may ask, are these groups up to? Are they working on improving the bottom line of their company? Maximizing shareholder value? Identifying productivity inefficiencies? Nope. By and large, these groups are concentrating on their own agendas and how to get the corporation to pay more attention to their issues—which ultimately means paying less attention to the issues of the other groups.

Recently, an "inclusiveness change agent" in a major Fortune 500 company confided to me that she had been chastised by her head office's executive champion for gender issues about losing focus because of the time and effort she spent on inclusiveness. "You are watering down our progress on gender by focusing on these other groups," she was told.

I actually think this is a very human response. Self-interest always trumps the interest of the collective. There are few purely altruistic acts, if any. The view is usually "What's in it for me?" and people ultimately will focus on issues on the agenda that most concern them. The establishment of diversity networking groups was a promising phase a decade ago, but now we have to ask what these groups are doing to improve the capacity of the organization to attract, excite and retain the very best talent regardless of gender, race, culture, sexual orientation, nationality and so on. In a study of more than 800 companies in the EEOC (U.S. Equal Employment Opportunity Commission) data base over a 30-year period, diversity affinity groups and networking programs did little to improve the position of underrepresented groups into management or executive positions. Despite that fact, these networks continue to be one of the most popular diversity interventions.[2]

Problem 8: Success in diversity cannot be measured simply by tracking cosmetic changes in demographic representation.

This is a lesson I wrote about almost two decades ago in my book *Diversity at Work* and it is still as valid today as it was then. Most people think diversity is just about fixing the numbers. Demographic changes in representation may be signals that attitudinal or systemic barriers are being removed, but the focus on cosmetically changing demographics will not lead to the promise of diversity, which has always been improved business outcomes.

Long before Clarence Thomas became the lightning rod for sexual harassment, he was equally despised as a vocal opponent of quotas and using numerical representation as a measure of success. In 1980, he was appointed to chair the U.S.-based Equal Employment Opportunity Commission, and equity-seeking groups across the country shuddered when he announced an embargo on quotas. His intention was to reduce the government's reliance on numerical representation as the primary focus of affirmative action. He argued that the reliance on numbers was a "weak and limited weapon" against inequity in the workplace. In his words, "The numbers distort the real issues surrounding discrimination. This approach fails because it allows an employer to hide continued discrimination behind good numbers."[3] Although I don't consider myself a fan of Thomas, I think he may have had a point.

Indeed, a quick review of the latest trend in the U.S. multimillion-dollar discrimination class action lawsuits indicate that Thomas may have been on to something. Look for the pattern. Those organizations that sign the most expensive anti-discrimination settlements one year magically make it to the top of the Best Diversity Employers list the next year.

---

2. Frank Dobbin, Alexandra Kalev and Erin Kelly, "Diversity Management in Corporate America," *American Sociological Review* 6, no. 4 (2007): 21–27.

3. Quoted by Thomas Sowell in *The Quest for Cosmic Justice* (New York: Free Press, 1999), 40.

They have a deathbed conversion, somehow managing in one year to significantly improve their representation of women, minorities or other groups within the organization. These are numbers that did not shift for years, yet now the progress is so remarkable that the employer can actually move to the head of the class in the numbers-conscious diversity industry—with a little help from some well-placed advertising investments in the website or publication that features the award.

This is not to say that organizations should ignore representation. Representation is one of several measures of progress, but it is not the most important metric. Despite being the focus of the diversity industry, demographic representation has proven itself to be a lagging, non-predictive and often imprecise metric.

Problem 7: Diversity has been dominated by an American-specific agenda and mindset, despite it being a global issue.

A number of years ago, I was asked to speak at a major corporate social responsibility conference in Brussels. It was one of my first times speaking about diversity outside North America. Just before delivering my speech, I met the gentleman who was to introduce me. He was a European managing director of a large U.S.-based multinational. He had a copy of my bio in his hand, with portions highlighted so that he would be able to read it more easily from the podium. He looked confused. "Mr. Wilson," he said, "I've read your bio, and I'm still trying to figure out what you actually do."

"Oh, I'm a diversity consultant," I offered, assuming that would clear everything up.

"Diversity?" he queried. "This is Europe! We don't have diversity here. We don't have African–Americans here. We don't have Hispanics here. Diversity is not relevant to us."

A few years later I was working on an assignment for a French bank in Bahrain. The CEO was a French national who had spent more than 30 years in the United Arab Emirates. He was a fascinating leader whom people described as being as much Arab as he was French. He was the perfect bridge between the two cultures. He was the type of leader that really "got" human equity the first time he heard about it. He immediately became a vigorous champion for the introduction of a human equity intervention, starting with his direct reports. He asked me to meet individually with his 15 executives to explain human equity to them.

Fourteen of the meetings were routine and finished within days of the CEO's request. The fifteenth meeting was next to impossible to schedule and then even more difficult to confirm. I assumed this particular leader was simply extremely busy, so I decided to "camp out" at his office in case he found a few spare minutes in his schedule. After being announced, I sat in his waiting room for most of the afternoon. His assistant was very apologetic and explained that her boss was always very busy. She offered me several alternative dates, but as I was leaving the next day, I continued to wait him out.

Finally, after his assistant had left, he surfaced from his office. He invited me in, saying, "I only have a few minutes, but I understand you are here to talk to me about diversity. That's the American stuff about women and minorities, right?"

"Well, it used to be," I said. "It has evolved a bit over the past 20 years."

"Evolved to what?" he asked suspiciously.

"To human equity," I responded.

"What is human equity?"

I proceeded to try to cram 20 years of evolution into the space of two minutes. I spoke to him about the distinction between diversity, inclusion, human capital and human equity, giving him a crash course on optimizing human potential.

He clearly was engaged and within 20 minutes we were in deep conversation about human equity. Ninety minutes later he confessed that he had had no intention of meeting with me, despite his boss's request. He had no intention of supporting some American consultant bringing an American idea of affirmative action that did not fit his company's corporate culture. He indicated that while he still had no interest in diversity, he was very intrigued by this idea of human equity.

These two incidents confirmed for me one of the biggest problems with diversity: it is perceived as an American issue based in American civil rights history, a history that has been dominated by issues of gender and race and, more recently, sexual orientation. These are issues that will not resonate in countries where differences in language, class or religion are far more relevant to the diversity conversation. For example, the French/ English debate, one of the most enduring issues of difference in Canada, rarely fits into the American diversity agenda.

From September 2011 to December 2011, the Conference Board asked almost 800 global CEOs to rank in descending order the top challenges they anticipated their companies facing in the coming years. The resulting list for European CEOs is:

1. Innovation
2. Human capital
3. Global political/economic risk
4. Government regulation
5. Global expansion
6. Cost optimization
7. Customer relationships
8. Sustainability
9. Corporate brand and reputation
10. Investor relations.

In light of the continued labor shortages caused by declining fertility rates and the social issues caused by immigrants brought in to meet these shortages, it is quite amazing that diversity has missed the European CEO list. I believe it is because this issue is still seen as an American one—and not relevant to the European business agenda.

The European managing director who was to introduce me at the Brussels conference was not an ignorant man. He was well read, educated and business savvy. How was it, then, that he had come to the conclusion that this diversity thing was only relevant in America? My guess would be because he was asked to implement a diversity program created by his American head office, by Americans, to deal with American issues. Now, don't get me wrong, I love Americans.

Some of my best friends are American. But I have seen many "global" organizations that simply don't get it. You can't sit in a head office in New York, Washington, Dallas, Seattle, Atlanta or wherever and design a global diversity strategy without including others in the world. It's not only illogical, it's irresponsible.

Recently, one of our U.S. clients took over a major technology company in India that has more than 20,000 employees. These 20,000 people will not become Americans just because their head office has shifted from Mumbai to Chicago. Their cultural values will remain the same and, more importantly, so will their corporate cultural values, unless the new head office makes a concerted effort to integrate this new acquisition into its culture. Our consultancy, TWI Inc., spends a lot of time on helping our clients understand the impact of being a truly global organization. As we tell our clients, the guiding rule of dealing with culture is this: what seems reasonable and logical in one culture may be totally irrelevant in another.

Most failed mergers and acquisitions happen not because the numbers are wrong but because the corporate cultures clash. And that is when both are within the same hemisphere. Global acquisitions, outsourcing, offshoring and supply-chaining will generate some of the most challenging diversity issues we have ever seen. As such, most existing diversity strategies designed for the U.S. domestic market will prove insufficient in this challenging new global environment.

We will come to see that this is where the promise of human equity comes in. Human equity evolves the diversity discussion about groups into the critical area of human capital—the second most important anticipated challenge of the Conference Board study. CEOs in Europe, China, India and the United States wake up at night in a cold sweat worrying about the lack of qualified talent to meet their innovation and future leadership needs.

It turns out that moving this message beyond America relies a lot on the terminology. While diversity and sometimes inclusion are seen as U.S. concepts, human equity does not have the same baggage. While there is a relationship between diversity and human equity, these are quite different concepts. At the end of this book is a glossary of terms to help readers understand fully what we are talking about as we move beyond diversity into the lesser-known area of inclusion and the brand-new area of human equity.

Problem 6: Diversity is too focused on "superficial" differences such as race, gender and sexual orientation.

One of the most exciting projects I have worked on in the past 20 years was for NASA. At one of the strategy sessions, I had the good fortune to listen to a scientist who had worked on the human genome mapping project. He explained that one of the first things scientists had to do was figure out the various possible combinations of human DNA. He explained that in the old days, the conventional wisdom was that there were infinite combinations of the billions of molecules of the double helix. But this imprecise estimate needed to be quantified in order to precisely map the full genome. He pointed out that roughly 3 billion pairs of biochemicals make up the double-stranded DNA commonly known as the double helix, but that there are a multitude of variations to these combinations. He pointed out that it is this multitude of variations that makes everyone unique. Upon doing the math, the scientists estimated that there are 10 to the power of 2.5 billion possible combinations of human DNA. He went on to say that if you divide this number by the current population in the world (7 billion), you will see the diversity of the human family.

I almost fell off my chair. I knew this was the next step in the journey. In *Diversity at Work*, I attempted to explain that this discussion was not really about how many women, minorities or LGBT (lesbian, gay, bisexual or transgender) people you have in your workplace. This discussion is really about talent. If you have 5,000 employees, then what you have is 5,000 individual units of talent. If leadership could figure out how to tap into each unit of talent and unleash that talent for the mission of the organization, that would substantially impact on any business outcome on the leadership agenda anywhere in the world.

Not long after hearing about the impressive DNA combinations, I was reading an excellent article by Marcus Buckingham entitled "What Great Managers Do." Buckingham writes: "Differences of trait and *talent* are like blood types. They cut across the superficial variations of race, sex and age and capture each person's uniqueness."[4] Wow, I thought. Talent comes in all packages—precisely 10 to the power of 2.5 billion. However, my talent is not defined by my race. My race does not define who I am, nor does my gender, age, nationality, sexual orientation or any other diversity dimension. These superficial characteristics may *inform* who I am, but they do not *define* who I am. Just as they didn't define me 100 years ago, they do not define me today.

Over the past 20 years, diversity has devolved into conversations about how many women, minorities, gays and lesbians you have in your workforce. This totally misses the point. What this conversation is really about is tapping into the 10 to the power of 2.5 billion possible combinations of human DNA globally. And since no single demographic group has a monopoly on any kind of talent, you will inevitably see a change in demographic composition simply by properly harnessing total human capital. Diversity's traditional focus on changing the demographic composition of the workforce has been putting the cart before the horse. If you focus on truly identifying and leveraging talent, the long-awaited demographic changes will come. This thought of leveraging total human capital is far more exciting than simply changing the demographic composition of the workforce.

Problem 5: Diversity in practice is about equity for some, rather than equity for all.

I argued in *Diversity at Work* that one of the most valuable lessons we have learned from years of legislated and now litigated fairness is the need to include all employees in a diversity program, including SWAMs (straight, white, able-bodied males). I attempted to argue that you can't pursue equity for one, two or even 10 groups. You are really striving for equity for all. I asked, "If discrimination against my black grandfather was wrong 100 years ago, then how can discrimination against my neighbor's white

---

4. Marcus Buckingham, "What Great Managers Do," *Harvard Business Review* 83, no. 3 (2005): 70–79, 148.

son today be justified? In order to create total equity in our society, all discrimination must be attacked."

Over the past 17 years, this is the area where I have had the most battles. One of my many critics is quoted as saying, "I don't know how he can justify his position . . . how can he compare a white man's parenting needs and the needs of people of color? There is a huge difference between them and the problems and barriers that exist to people of color getting and staying in the work force."[5]

Maybe, but let's at least check in with the white, single dad before jumping to this conclusion.

Recently, I was invited to speak at an internal diversity conference where the audience was made up of the company's eight employee resource groups (ERGs). As mentioned above, establishing employee resource groups is a common diversity practice where groups are organized to represent the interests of various components of an organization's workforce based on demographic identity. Each ERG was asked to make a presentation on its progress to date and plans for the future. I was suitably impressed that the organization had ventured beyond the usual constituencies of gender, race and sexual orientation to create several other non-traditional employee resource groups. For example, there was an ERG for English as a second language employees, an ERG for new and young employees and even an ERG for faith-based employees. From the outside it appeared as if the organization's diversity strategy was inclusive and the established, sanctioned ERGs covered all bases. However, upon closer inspection, I saw that one very important group was missing—the straight, white, able-bodied male (SWAM).

It turned out that I was not the only one who had noticed this "oversight." In fact, I was informed that a new employee resource group dedicated to SWAMs had organically formed in one of the company's regional plants. The group was called WOMEN. This was an acronym standing for "White, Original, Men's Employee Network."

---

5. Speech by Antoni Shelton, Executive Director of the Urban Alliance on Race Relations, 2007.

The organization's leadership and other employee resource groups were not amused. The possibility of sanctioning this upstart group was not even considered.

I thought this was an interesting take on diversity and inclusion. This particular company was in a resource-based industry that has been dominated by straight, white, able-bodied males for the past century. So how was it that this group was not seen as worthy of being part of the organization's well-developed and long-standing ERG network? The unarticulated and somewhat politically incorrect answer is that this group apparently faces no employment barriers, no discrimination and no unfair treatment, which is the reason SWAMs have held power positions in most organizations for so long. In other words, "They had their turn, and now it's our turn." It's an approach that has never been successful, whether you are talking about Kosovo, Rwanda or legislated equity. I would suspect that this model of SWAM exclusion is prevalent in most organizations pursuing diversity today.

I was amused to see that every resource group at this ERG conference had an almost identical mission statement. The mission of the women's group was "to help the company become the employer of choice *for women*." The minority group's mission was "to help the company become the employer of choice for *people of color*." In fact, other than the target group being different, all eight ERGs had exactly the same mission.

In my opinion, this created a zero-sum approach to diversity. For every member of my group that "wins," one member of seven other groups must lose. Earlier I mentioned a condition called the hierarchy of inequity referred to by Nelson Mandela. This is the notion that the exclusion or bias I face as a black man is somehow more important than the inequity my fellow white male employee may face because of his age, education or historical group membership. The hierarchy of inequity breeds the insidious and destructive mindset that, until you are finished dealing with the unfairness facing *my* group, you should not start dealing with the inequity facing any other group. As I mentioned above in the discussion of Catalyst, this may be a counterproductive perspective. One inequity cannot take precedence over another in any system. We must be willing to take on inequity when we find it even if does not impact directly on our personal group.

In cases like the company cited above, a good place to start may be with the group that has traditionally been excluded from the diversity strategy—that is, straight, white, able-bodied males. My last words of advice to the leaders of the organization were to fully sanction the WOMEN group and make it a part of the solution rather than a resentful example of an exclusive diversity strategy.

Problem 4: Diversity virtually ignores the importance of leadership behavior.
The diversity industry's lopsided focus on representation has led to its missing one of the most important variables in the creation of an equitable and inclusive workplace. After years of examining interventions that make a real difference, I am convinced that if an organization has not properly handled leadership behavior it will not succeed in changing the corporate culture.

In 2004 Robert Sutton's widely read *Harvard Business Review* article "More Trouble Than They're Worth" and his follow-up book in 2007, *The No Asshole Rule*, introduced the idea of a relatively small group (i.e., about 10 percent) of mean-spirited leaders who have enormous impact on the work environment. This group of leaders, now commonly called boss-holes, abuse their power and authority to get their way, using fear to motivate or manipulate workers.

In one blog post, Sutton explains his use of the not-so-politically-correct term *asshole*:

> I was determined to use the word asshole in the title because, to me, other words like "jerk," "bully," "tyrant," "despot," and so on are just euphemisms for what people really call those creeps. And when I have done such damage to people (indeed, all of us are capable of being assholes some of the time), that is what I call myself. I know the term offends some people, but nothing else captures the emotional wallop.[6]

6. Robert I. Sutton, "Why I Wrote *The No Asshole Rule*," *Harvard Business Review Blog Network*, March 17, 2007.

In my experience, the typical diversity programs that focus on representation and tactical group initiatives pay little attention to identifying and dealing with the boss-holes. This may be because it is much more uncomfortable to confront the behavior of this group who are generally unconsciously incompetent (that is, they don't know what they don't know) about their behavior. While their behavior may be transparent to them—they don't even notice it—it is never transparent to the people who work for them. However, because of their level in the organization, it could be a career-limiting move to tell them about their behavior. Another problem is this 10 percent are the most hopeful that they are leaders in these areas. In fact, we will see that these lowest 10 percent leaders mark themselves perfect scores on behavior related to dignity and respect, equitable opportunity, and ethics and integrity, while their colleagues mark them substantially below the norm (more on this in Chapter 7). Because of their unconscious incompetence, members of this group feel that the problems related to equity and inclusion rest anywhere but with them.

There is a famous merger in the legal industry that occurred more than a decade ago that people still talk about. A leading Canadian law firm looked to merge with an established American law firm based in New York City. At the celebration event for the merger, a founding partner of the New York firm sexually harassed nine female partners from the Canadian firm. The next day these nine women jointly took their complaint to the CEO and gave him an ultimatum—"It's either us or him, and if it's us, we will not be going quietly." Within a week, the partner's letter of resignation appeared on the front page of one of the largest newspapers in the country.

The firm had accepted his resignation, acknowledging that his behavior was inappropriate and violated the firm's policy against sexual harassment. But there are many organizations that tolerate this type of behavior because of the leader's high-level position or because that person is a valued or tenured member of the leadership group. This leads these organizations into a common trap: when individuals reach positions of influence where few employees have the power to tell them about their unacceptable behavior without fear of reprisal or retribution, the unacceptable behavior continues and possibly even escalates.

Psychological studies have shown that boss-holes such as the partner of the New York law firm reduce productivity, stifle creativity and cause high rates of absenteeism and turnover. Research also shows that 25 percent of bullied employees and 20 percent of those who witness the bullying will eventually quit because of it or "quit" by staying in their jobs but essentially checking out—something known in organizational psychology as *psychic absenteeism.*

Diversity practitioners have spent a lot of time looking at the representation of women and minorities, putting employee resource groups together and improving policies on outreach and selection, yet the group encompassing the lowest 10 percent of leaders has remained virtually untouched. Finding and helping the boss-holes move out of their unconscious incompetence is the most important thing an organization can do to move toward equity. Chapter 3 further discusses this idea of the lowest 10 percent, and the importance of good leadership—and shifting leadership behavior where necessary.

Problem 3: Diversity has not moved beyond awareness education about race, gender, culture and sexual orientation.

Over the past 20 years, many organizations have offered diversity awareness training programs designed to help their organization move toward a more equitable and inclusive work environment. Diversity awareness education generally moves people from a state of unconscious incompetence (where they don't know what they don't know) to a state of conscious incompetence (where they know what they don't know).

Organizations that are further along in their journey to an equitable and inclusive work environment understand that awareness training is only a first step in the education process. These organizations adopt an integrated approach that leads people beyond awareness to understanding, and then beyond understanding to behavioral change. We often remind our clients that a workplace environment does not change because people begin to think differently, a workplace culture changes when people begin to act differently, that is, when they become consciously competent.

Although diversity education has focused on improving awareness about race, gender, culture, sexual orientation and so on, sustainable organizational change is the result of behavioral change, especially that of managers and leaders. Our firm's experience is that progress toward an equitable and inclusive work environment is more likely to happen when key opinion leaders move beyond awareness and understanding to exhibit actions and behavior that demonstrate the commitment to equity and inclusion. To do this, the organization needs to move beyond a course in diversity to create a full human equity curriculum that will involve employee skills transfer, including the introduction of new management tools designed from a positive psychology perspective.

Stages of Commitment to Change—Fostering an Inclusive Environment

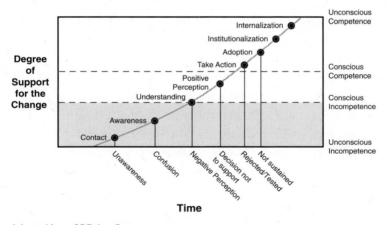

Adapted from ODR, Inc.©

In an integrated approach to education, a critical mass of managers and leaders move beyond awareness and understanding to the point where they take action to operate with conscious competence. With the requisite skills and competencies, managers and leaders can effectively create sustainable organizational change and move beyond the group focus of diversity.

Problem 2: Diversity is based on a deficit paradigm.

One of the biggest problems with diversity is its focus on righting the historical wrongs of certain groups. Diversity, like most of today's management paradigms, is deficit-based, dealing with what is wrong with certain groups in the world of work. Notwithstanding the platitudes about celebrating differences, a scan of the academic research related to diversity will uncover less than inspiring titles such as "Issues in Managing an Increasingly Diverse Workforce," or "A Field Study of Diversity, Conflict and Performance in Work Groups" or "The Relationship Between Race, Organizational Diversity and Absenteeism." While there is no doubt that there is value in this type of research, it cannot help but create the feeling that diversity is something to be fixed, managed or handled. This, more than anything else, fuels the problem of diversity fatigue.

In this book we look to the relatively new science of positive psychology as a way out of this dilemma. In 1998 Dr. Martin Seligman was the chair of the American Psychological Association. He confronted the psychological establishment with a challenge. Seligman's challenge was based on the premise that the existing model of psychology was unbalanced. He argued that since the Second World War, psychology had been dedicated to what was wrong with people and the work of psychologists had been focused on trying to fix their patients; in his words, "trying to bring people from minus 200 to zero." Seligman evidenced his perspective with a review of the academic literature. He found a startling 21 to 1 ratio between deficit-focused articles and those aimed at the positive. There were 5,584 articles about anger, 41,416 about anxiety and 54,040 focused on depression. On the other side of the equation, there were only 415 articles related to joy, 2,400 related to life satisfaction and a measly 1,700 related to what some call the ultimate reward, happiness.

As Seligman put it: "The science of psychology has been far more successful on the negative than on the positive side; it has revealed to us much about man's shortcomings, his illnesses, his sins, but little of his potentialities, his virtues, his achievements, his aspirations or his psychological height. It is as if psychology had voluntarily restricted itself to only half its rightful jurisdiction and that the darker, meaner half."

I believe the same could be said of the field of diversity. It has been far more focused on the negative side of differences in the workplace rather than looking at how to optimize on differences at an individual level. Looking to the strengths-based work of positive psychology pioneers such as Seligman, David Cooperrider and Chris Peterson, and referencing Gallup's early research on strengths-based management, the evolution to human equity promises the first management paradigm approached from a positive psychology perspective.

Problem I: Diversity focuses on groups rather than the individual.
In 1999 Dr. Janet Smith was asked to create a task force on diversity for the Canadian federal government. She pushed back, saying diversity was not the issue but inclusion was. When she was asked to define inclusion she used a definition that in an inclusive environment each person (not each group) is valued because of his or her unique difference.

Up until that point the diversity conversation had focused on groups, for example, my group of men, your group of women, my group of minorities, your group of lesbians, etc. This is where the diversity conversation has been for the past two decades. This has led to each group fighting for its rightful place in the organization and has led to concerns regarding tokenism for some groups and accusations of reverse discrimination against others. And yet, not much has changed in who runs the most powerful organizations today.

According to Catalyst, women CEOs represent less than 4 percent of the Fortune 500 companies today. One of the most influential African–American networking groups, the Executive Leadership Council, has pointed to the fact that the percentage of African–Americans in senior executive positions has actually decreased over the past decade. The vast majority of Fortune 1000 corporations' leadership positions are still dominated by one demographic group, that is, SWAMs. According to the Equal Employment Opportunity Commission, SWAMs represent a majority of managers, with white females barely making 30 percent and blacks, Hispanics and Asian–Americans each representing less than 5 percent. Organizations have experimented with hundreds of diversity measures focused on improving the conditions of selected groups and it is time to move beyond the group focus of diversity.

I am more than my group. While my group identity may inform who I am, it cannot define me. The fact that I am a black male over the age of 55 does not mean I cannot master the use of social media or become an effective president. The same stereotypes we talk about fighting in diversity have raised their head again but in more politically correct garb. In order to access the full promise of the diversity of talent in the workplace we need to evolve beyond the group conversation of diversity, using whatever you now know about a particular group to apply it back to the individual.

In my earlier book, *Diversity at Work*, I called for a shift from the "Age of Equality" to the "Age of Equity," where people get treated equitably and differences are recognized not just because it is the right thing to do but because it will directly impact on the productivity and competitiveness of the organization.

Today I call for yet another shift, a shift that moves beyond the conversation about diversity into the conversation about human equity, where differences are not just recognized but are seen as critical for organizational success. This shift uses positive psychology strategies to focus on job/talent fit. Most importantly, this shift moves beyond the group focus of diversity toward the individual focus of human equity, which allows for talent differentiation, differential investment in high performers and the opportunity to discover and play to the strengths of each employee.

The Required Shift

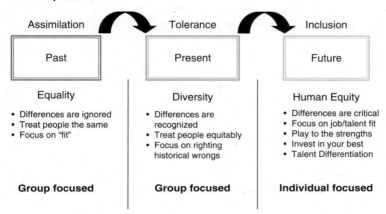

Assimilation	Tolerance	Inclusion
Past	Present	Future
Equality	Diversity	Human Equity
• Differences are ignored • Treat people the same • Focus on "fit"	• Differences are recognized • Treat people equitably • Focus on righting historical wrongs	• Differences are critical • Focus on job/talent fit • Play to the strengths • Invest in your best • Talent Differentiation
Group focused	**Group focused**	**Individual focused**

Source: Trevor Wilson, *Diversity at Work: The Business Case for Equity* (Toronto: John Wiley & Sons Canada, Ltd., 1996)

In the next chapter we will look at the evolution of this conversation by reviewing a measurement tool called the Equity Continuum. That chapter will further trace where we have come from, where we are now and where we need to go to move toward human equity.

Chapter 2
THE EVOLUTION OF THE EQUITY CONTINUUM

The original idea of rating companies on a five-point equity continuum was included in a book published in 1992 by Felice Schwartz entitled *Breaking with Tradition: Women and Work, the New Facts of Life*. Schwartz found that the companies she worked with followed a pattern of being motivated to develop women. In 1996 I built on the Schwartz model, creating an adapted version that moved beyond issues of gender to look at why organizations pursue any type of equity initiative. The new model was called the Equity Continuum and described the highest level organizations as Equitable and Inclusive. Schwartz labeled Level 5 organizations as True Equality, which she felt was utopian and unreachable in light of where most organizations were at the time. When I first wrote about Level 5 organizations they were presented as an ideal vision to give context to the entire journey along the continuum.

Since my first book, our firm has been using the concept of the Equity Continuum as a way of visually mapping the journey to a totally equitable and inclusive work environment. The continuum captures the various motivations behind organizations' efforts in the areas of diversity, inclusion and now human equity. As with anything else, the continuum has evolved over the past two decades as we learn more and more about these stages. The original continuum looked like this:

The Equity Continuum (1996)

Source: Trevor Wilson, *Diversity at Work: The Business Case for Equity* (Toronto: John Wiley & Sons Canada, Ltd., 1996), 41–46.

The arrow between levels 2 and 3 shows the emphasis of my first book, that is, the moment when organizations move beyond looking at these issues from a corporate social responsibility perspective and begin to reframe them as business issues.

The focus of this book is to move organizations beyond the group focus of diversity toward the individual focus of human equity. I believe that when the idea of inclusion began to appear in 1999, the opening for this transition was created. Today the continuum looks like this:

The Equity Continuum (2013)

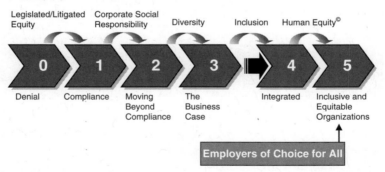

Let's review each level of the continuum and see what has changed over the years.

LEVEL 0: DENIAL

Organizations at Level 0 have not changed much since I first wrote about them. These are the organizations whose leaders believe they are at Level 5 and contend that there really is no problem in their work environment that will not resolve itself. These organizations are in a state of bliss and denial about any issues related to difference in the workplace.

LEVEL 1: COMPLIANCE

A Level I organization seeks compliance as a way to meet its legal or other obligations and thus avoid the negative consequences of noncompliance. These are organizations that focus on equality or treating people the same, rather than equity where difference is acknowledged and people are treated fairly. In a Level I organization initiatives generally stop if the law or lawsuit falls away since it is this external force that is pushing the change. As such the organization is taking a reactive approach to any change initiatives rather than a proactive strategic approach. The other distinguishing feature of the Level I organization is that success is primarily measured by way of changes in demographic representation of selected target groups in hiring and promotion. We will come to see that tracking representation is only one way to measure progress in moving along the continuum.

Legislated Equity

This stage is referred to as "litigated and legislated equity." Legislated equity includes laws and regulations related to human rights, civil rights, affirmative action, equal opportunity and employment equity depending on the jurisdiction. The intention of legislated equity is to remedy the effects of past discrimination against selected target groups. If we look at the history of affirmative action in the United States and India, equal opportunity in Europe and the UK and employment equity in Canada and South Africa, for instance, we may find different histories but a similar justification for these pieces of corrective legislation.

Thus, organizations at Level I are simply trying to comply with the external motivation that is "forcing" them to pay attention to the "target groups" that are believed to have faced unfair treatment for an extended period of time. Judging the success of a legislated equity program is primarily based on the hiring and promotion of the selected target groups.

In the early days of legislated equity programs, such as affirmative action in the United States and employment equity in Canada, there was considerable hope that government edict could change the hiring and promotion practices of organizations. It did not take long to realize that these types of legislated equity programs had failed to create any noticeable change. Some believed the legislation was flawed, others felt it lacked teeth but most agreed that it had not accomplished what it was designed to do, i.e., improve the representation of selected target groups. Even for organizations supplying goods and services for governments, who theoretically could lose their right to bid for federal government business, the exercise of compliance devolved into a bureaucratic paper chase. Most would agree that, regardless of the jurisdiction, legislated equity has created few jobs for so-called target groups compared to the mountains of reports it has generated.

Litigated Equity

By the mid-nineties a new form of compliance started to occur, especially in the United States, by way of big-dollar class action lawsuits. We refer to this development as "litigated equity." This new type of compliance certainly had more impact on organizations than government regulation and for a while caused quite a stir. Two of the most noteworthy cases of litigated class action suits happened at the Texaco and Coca-Cola corporations.

The Texaco and Coca-Cola settlements encouraged other litigated equity claims. Many were filed in Atlanta, which was seen as a Mecca for African–Americans and had intense competition for top-paying jobs. The fact that African–American employees had been successful with Atlanta's premier corporation, Coca-Cola, was also noteworthy. African–American employees at Home Depot filed a lawsuit in

2000 claiming the company fostered a "pattern of discrimination against African–Americans" and showed "reckless indifference" to a hostile work environment. African–American employees also filed discrimination lawsuits against Lockheed Martin, Waffle House and SunTrust Bank. The accusations ranged from discrimination in job responsibilities to retaliation for filing discrimination complaints.

How Is a "Target" Group Selected?

Interestingly, how a disadvantaged group becomes a so-called target group may not always be objective. Several decades ago, I participated in a project for a certain government that was considering which target groups to include under its legislated equity program. The consultation was meant to be a totally open, transparent process in which disadvantaged groups from across the nation were invited to present their cases for discrimination.

It was an amazing process. Literally every advocacy group for the disadvantaged diaspora were invited to participate in the process to convince the committee of politicians that they deserved to be a target group under the planned equity legislation. A true race to the bottom.

I have long forgotten most of the presentations, but one will always stay with me. It was by a group of gay men who had conducted painstaking research to demonstrate that homosexuals were facing discrimination in the workplace. Given that it was 1985, the year the World Health Organization announced there was an AIDS epidemic, with its ensuing anti-gay backlash, there is no reason to assume anyone was surprised by the conclusion. However, everyone in the room was amazed by the evidence.

This group had done an admirable job of demonstrating the impact of discrimination against gays and lesbians. They had the facts, the logic and the illustrative, heart-tugging anecdotes. Once the advocacy group had finished its presentation and was excused, the politicians considered their next steps.

"Are we seriously going to make homosexuals a target group under this legislation?" one asked, wringing his hands.

"Are you out of your mind?" responded the chairman (who, it turned out, was then an in-the-closet homosexual).

Remember, this was 1985. I doubt any politician would have had the courage to make gays and lesbians a target group under legislated equity, regardless of the jurisdiction. And yet, in the end, francophones were included as a target group, even though they had not even made a presentation. The point is, the process through which a group becomes a target group under legislated equity may not necessarily be "color blind."

This leads to another, more recent development, that of deselecting a target group. *Deselection* refers to the process by which a group loses its status as a target group. In 2009 the same government that had chosen to exclude gays and lesbians decided that women no longer qualified as a target group. Women had "arrived" and so no longer required the protection of legislated equity. The government justified this stance by pointing to the ample number of women in positions of power throughout its offices. In other words, the issues related to gender in the workplace had been resolved, and women could now rest assured that they were finally equal to men.

This is quite a lofty claim, regardless of the number of women in leadership positions. If gender issues were as easy to solve as shifting the number of women in the senior boardroom, we could have dealt with this a long time ago by simply placing more chairs at the executive table. Certainly the issues have proven to be more complex than that.

LEVEL 2: MOVING BEYOND COMPLIANCE

Level 2 organizations believe in the value of going beyond compliance. These are organizations that aim to support various disadvantaged groups, rather than the historically disadvantaged groups targeted in legislated equity programs. A disadvantaged group usually falls outside of government legislation and can include disparate groups such as LGBT (lesbian, gay, bisexual and transgender), new immigrants, parents with special needs kids, etc. Since Level 2 organizations have chosen to move beyond compliance, the list of groups the organization may seek to support can be extensive and usually quite subjective.

The aim of the Level 2 organization is really to be seen as doing the right thing. In other words, these are organizations motivated primarily by corporate social responsibility. As such, as leadership or public interest in topics change, the organization's interest may also change. In these organizations there is no plan in place to integrate diversity initiatives into the larger organizational culture. This means that although the organization may have one or more initiatives in place, these are isolated, tactical initiatives, unrelated to the strategic business imperatives facing the organization. In some Level 2 organizations, initiatives are pursued because the CEO may have a daughter with ADHD, or a son who is openly gay or a spouse suffering from clinical depression.

Not too long ago, the chairman of the board of a large international organization had a son come out of the closet. Up until this revelation, the leader had shown some mild interest in LGBT issues, but after his son's coming out he became a passionate advocate, forcing the firm to become a sponsor for the largest, most vocal LGBT advocacy organization.

The problem with this type of approach is that it's not reliable. A change in leadership or even a change in mindset could cause the program to be put in jeopardy. The program exists at the whim and pleasure of leadership. A loss of interest or even changes in external economic conditions could jeopardize the program.

Some would argue that approaching issues of equity and inclusion from a corporate social responsibility perspective is superior to approaching things based solely on legislation or litigation, as in Level 1. Our experience is that there is virtually no difference in terms of organizational change because the intervention is not designed to be strategically integrated into the larger organizational culture. The Level 2 initiatives are tactical, isolated efforts that certainly garner public attention but are not designed to shift the organizational culture. Level 2 organizations also rely primarily on changes in representation of certain groups as evidence of progress but the implementation of the corporate social responsibility initiative is the real evidence because it is simply the "right thing to do."

Over the years we have witnessed hundreds of Level 2–type initiatives. The list below is a sample. Notice that most concentrate on members of selected groups and do not appear to have any long-range strategic intent. The list was compiled from an annual event to find best practice diversity initiatives.

- Meetings to advance the careers of Aboriginal and visible minority employees
- Providing BlackBerrys to staff who are deaf to help in their communications with coworkers
- Providing internships to disabled workers
- Dedicating a budget for tools and services to help disabled employees in the workplace
- Helping women employees advance their careers by addressing barriers and promoting leadership development, mentorship and peer coaching
- Linking job postings to relevant community agencies to recruit employees from diversity groups
- Establishing a community network to recruit and retain LGBT employees
- Offering flexible work options and programs for older employees.

LEVEL 3: THE BUSINESS CASE

Level 3 organizations understand that diversity initiatives can impact on desirable bottom-line outcomes such as efficiency, retention of best talent and improved employee engagement, among others. In *Diversity at Work* I postulated a business case for equity, based on the substantial demographic changes in the North American work environment. The prime argument was if you could show leadership the link between a desired business outcome such as profitability, productivity, improved customer satisfaction, improved retention of best talent and increased shareholder value, then issues of diversity would move beyond the tactical corporate social responsibility identification. Over the years we have worked with various organizations to articulate various business cases. The following list is a sample of business cases where organizations have proven links between diversity and desired business outcomes.

- Reducing costs and improving ROI (return on investment) of human resources
- Improving client satisfaction and value
- Enhancing market positioning
- Improving workforce contentment and effectiveness
- Building leadership capability
- Improving ROI of workforce learning
- Identifying and matching best talent to business strategy
- Attracting best talent
- Retaining best talent
- Relieving headcount pressures
- Increasing return on direct compensation
- Measuring human capital contribution to business performance
- Managing talent globally
- Coping with an aging workforce
- Managing human capital during transition
- Reducing human resources risk management and compliance costs
- Improving knowledge management
- Responding to evolving client needs
- Maintaining and enhancing competitive position in changing market conditions
- Enhancing community partnerships
- Succession planning
- Increasing public confidence and satisfaction.

In our experience the most compelling business cases are linked to current organizational or business imperatives and aligned with the organization's core values. The best business cases are also quantifiable, that is, the organization can prove how much it will lose by not pursuing diversity or how much it will gain by implementing an effective diversity strategy. The other criteria of an excellent business case is that it is concise and can be spoken in minutes to the most skeptical critic.

One of the toughest organizations we have worked for was a police service organization looking to move beyond the Level 2 approach to diversity. The police chief wanted to create a bulletproof business case that would "shut up" his worst critics, who saw the whole diversity program as a waste of time and money. Working with his direct reports he created the business case below, linking it to key organizational changes that had been spoken about for years in the policing industry. What is noteworthy about this example is that the business case was reduced to one page, succinctly answering the question: "Why are we doing this?"

BUSINESS RATIONALE FOR WORKFORCE DIVERSIFICATION

1. Meeting Operational Requirements

Population growth, particularly among new immigrants, is challenging the efficient and effective operation of the police service. Rapid technological change, the rise of terrorism, new trends in criminal behavior and continuing demand for community policing are also testing the operational capacity of our organization.

To ensure that we have the skills, knowledge, experience and awareness to meet new operational requirements, we must diversify and grow our workforce. Operational requirements now include new language skills, knowledge and understanding of newly settled ethnic groups, ability to gain the trust of victims who are reluctant to pursue complaints and ability to encourage participation of diverse communities.

2. Competing for Talent

Our police service is operating in a highly competitive labor market, which is expanding rapidly. Demand for qualified law enforcement professionals is exceeding supply. The Canadian

Professional Police Association and the Canadian Chiefs of Police Association have both recognized that this dynamic affects all police services today.[1]

This is a significant trend for our police service, which is facing a complete turnover of senior officers and the need to grow at double the normal rate over the next five years.

Passive recruitment is no longer a viable strategy to supply the qualified recruits we need to meet growth and operational requirements. In this labor market, we must actively attract and recruit new employees and ensure retention of current employees who have more law enforcement career opportunities than ever before.

Our police service needs new skill sets to meet its operational requirements. This means we must recruit from groups that have not considered a career in law enforcement before.

Police Officers in Canada

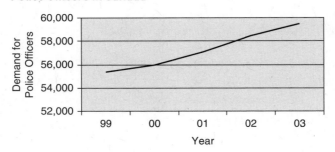

3. Becoming Employer of Choice for All

Now more than ever employers recognize that their greatest asset is their workforce. This is true for our police service, which relies on the skills, experience and judgment of its employees to deliver its law enforcement mandate.

(continued)

1. Strategic Human Resources Analysis of Public Policing in Canada, 2002.

Building a workplace atmosphere where all employees are valued and respected will deliver significant cost savings in improved productivity, lower turnover and minimal disruption of succession and promotion planning.

Retention is as important as recruitment. Employees have more career opportunity than ever before. When faced with a choice we want them to choose to stay with our police service.

4. Increased Effectiveness

Increased effectiveness delivers cost savings, especially in the area of crime prevention.

Reflecting the complete demographic characteristics of the city will enhance working relationships and trust between the police service and all communities, thereby leading to more effective crime prevention and investigation.

5. Achieving Competitive Advantage

Our police service does not compete in the traditional business sense. But as a public service we are competing vigorously for trust and confidence that plays out in the trade-offs and decisions made on behalf of taxpayers.

Policing accounts for 8 percent of the city's total budget. Our annual budget of $160 million represents one of the largest single expenditures on any municipal service.

We have an impressive track record in this area. During a time when most other public service expenditures were being cut, the police service expenditures were being increased. This highly valuable asset needs to be protected by ensuring that the police workforce is diverse and able to connect with all the communities it serves.

6. Leadership in Compliance with Policy and Legislative Initiatives

The police service has a statutory duty to provide certain workplace standards concerning harassment, discrimination on the basis of gender, etc. Already, noncompliance with these obligations has cost our police service thousands of dollars in settlements.

We are being directed to become more reflective of the community as a matter of policy. Both the pieces of legislation that cover our organizations are clear in this area. In addition, the police association has made harassment protection a priority for action.

To sum up, Level 3 organizations do the following:

- Understand that certain diversity initiatives can improve the organization's efficiency, recruitment, employee retention, team effectiveness and market opportunities
- Evaluate diversity initiatives qualitatively and quantitatively
- See representation numbers as a means to an end, rather than as the focus of their diversity strategy
- Know initiatives can survive the loss of employee or public interest if the business case remains valid
- Use an inclusive definition of diversity, with a vision of creating an environment that is equitable for all.

Quantitative versus Qualitative Data

Level 3 organizations evaluate progress qualitatively and quantitatively and, unlike those organizations at levels 1 and 2, do not rely on representation as the sole measurement of success. This is because representation has proven to be a slow and lagging metric to determine organizational change. By "lagging" I mean that changes in representation are the result or symptom of something changing in the organization; they are not the cause.

For example, let's say that the senior executive group of an organization consists entirely of white men over the age of 45. Yet, three years later, the executive group has shifted to all middle-aged black women. You would have to look back over those three years to see what in the organization's recruitment and selection practices has changed. The difference in representation numbers signals a change, but rarely does it point to what actually has changed aside from the composition of the workforce.

We can contrast the lagging characteristic of quantitative data with the predictive capacity of qualitative metrics. Qualitative data is primarily related to employee perceptions and attitudes. Qualitative metrics are easily accessible by credible employee attitude and opinion data. For example, if the employee attitude survey shows that 80 percent of women perceive that they are experiencing sexual harassment at work, it is likely that within a short period the retention and representation of women will decrease.

This predictive capacity makes qualitative data twice as important as quantitative data—assuming the organization uses the qualitative data to understand the current quantitative picture. And if you have the option of looking at a credible attitude survey versus only a demographic employee breakdown, you are more likely to learn more about the organization from the employee perceptions of the work environment than from the number of women or minorities that have been hired over the past year.

In Level 3 organizations, as long as they can prove the business case, the organization will be committed to diversity in the workplace. This creates a much higher degree of certainty to the approach than in the Level 2 organizations in that you're no longer relying on the goodwill or interest of a senior executive champion. Still, in light of the recent economic downturn, there are no guarantees. Like any other HR initiative, diversity initiatives are usually seen as overhead, and are likely to be the first thing on the chopping block when an organization looks to cut costs. Even if the organization has articulated a positive bottom-line impact for diversity, the program may not be able to withstand a disastrous fiscal year.

Equity for All: An Inclusive Definition of Diversity

One of the other distinctions of Level 3 organizations is the use of an inclusive definition of diversity. Unlike Level 1 organizations that support only selected target groups, or Level 2 organizations that look to historically disadvantaged groups, Level 3 organizations begin to talk about creating an environment that is equitable for all.

This idea of equity for all was first articulated by Nelson Mandela, who frequently referred to it as "rainbow jurisprudence." Early in his tenure as the first black president of South Africa, he would often remind his countrymen and women that he could not create a South Africa just for black South Africans. His job was to create a nation for all South Africans, regardless of the horrendous history of apartheid.

We try to make this same point to our clients: You can't create a system that's equitable for one, two or four groups. If the system is "more equitable" for me as a black male than it is for you as a white male, it is not equitable. You can't have a little bit of equity. Either you're striving for equity for all or you are not striving for equity for any.

This may sound like a statement worthy of support regardless of the audience. And yet this just may be one of the most contentious items I have fought over the past 15 years. It never ceases to amaze me when people indicate that they are supportive of equity in the workplace but that they want to leave out straight, white, able-bodied males. When asked why they would not be interested in equity for members of this group, the response is always the same: "They had their turn."

This goes back to Problem 5 with diversity today, which I articulated in Chapter 1, that diversity has come to mean equity for some rather than equity for all. To say that straight, white, able-bodied males should be left out of the goal of equity for all because they have dominated the corporate boardrooms over the past 100 years is the start of a slippery slope.

This notion of "You had your turn, now it's my turn" has never worked in the history of humankind. Just look at Kosovo and Rwanda. It certainly didn't work there and will not work in any workplace either. You can't have a little bit of equity. Level 3 organizations believe that you can only structure your diversity program to achieve equity for all versus equity for some.

When I wrote *Diversity at Work*, my primary argument was that business reasons provide an organization's leadership with stronger motivation to implement diversity than do corporate social responsibility, or legislated or litigated equity. I argued that if you could link the diversity model to any kind of business outcome (see sample list above), it was likely that diversity would show up more securely on the leadership agenda. Thus, the "business case" became a rallying cry for many organizations over the past decade or two: as long as the diversity model could be justified in business terms, leadership would embrace it. The problem was that it was difficult to prove a relationship between a more diverse workforce and a better bottom line.

In 2011 an excellent research paper was published called "The Diversity Organization: Finding Gold at the End of the Rainbow." Written by Kristyn A. Scott, Joanna M. Heathcote and Jamie A. Gruman, the paper looked to provide evidence for the business case. The researchers concluded:

> . . . the business case for diversity has been embraced enthusi-astically. Nonetheless, empirical support for the business case is scant. Indeed, although some evidence exists to support the general idea that positive outcomes can result from having a diverse population (e.g., Watson, Kumar & Michaelsen, 1993), research indicates that the impact of diversity is not always positive and may, in fact, be a double-edged sword.[2]

However, the researchers hold out hope for organizations that can move beyond diversity to create an inclusive culture where the commitment

---

2. Kristyn A. Scott, Joanna M. Heathcote and Jamie A. Gruman, "The Diversity Organization: Finding Gold at the End of the Rainbow," *Human Resource Management* 50, no. 6 (November/December 2011): 695–886.

to diversity is embedded into almost everything the organization does and attention to diversity permeates almost every organizational action. In such an organization the commitment to diversity is not based on proving a business case but is linked to the organization's core values, which will not be impacted by market forces. This happens to describe one of the characteristics of a Level 4 organization.

LEVEL 4: INTEGRATED

Organizations at Level 4 have evolved beyond diversity (along with its inclusive definition) into a relatively new area called inclusion. Level 4 organizations do the following:

- Move beyond a group focus to focus on the individual
- Focus on creating a work environment where each person is recognized and developed, and his or her talents are routinely tapped into
- Actively practice talent differentiation strategies
- Value people because of, not in spite of, their differences
- Take steps to move toward an environment that is equitable for all
- Internalize inclusion as a core value, meaning it does not change quickly nor is it affected by economic trends
- See human equity as an essential element of sustainable competitive advantage or organizational effectiveness
- Integrate inclusion into all aspects of the organization.

All employees of Level 4 organizations consider themselves responsible for creating a fair, equitable and inclusive environment, and the organizations are widely perceived as employers and suppliers of choice.

The Concept of Inclusion

I first heard about the concept of inclusion in 1999 from one of the first female deputy ministers in the Canadian federal government, Dr. Janet Smith. She had been appointed to head a task force to explore the question of what it would take to have a representative public service.

Dr. Smith began by looking at the numbers, but soon found that this approach was not getting the task force anywhere. So she decided they needed to examine the concepts of corporate culture and the conversations about equity.

Dr. Smith's familiarity with the management principle of coaching—the idea that each of us is empowered to change our circumstances, but if we view ourselves as helpless victims, we are doomed to failure—led her to consider the designated target groups: women, visible minorities, Aboriginals and people with disabilities—all groups treated as victims in a white male–run system. "The question I asked," said Dr. Smith, "was what if the people in these groups no longer considered themselves as victims. Could I find a way to empower them so that they took their places in a well-functioning system?"

"The corporate culture," continued Dr. Smith, "is defined by those in it as 'how things are around here.' In other words, people's perceptions matter and define the culture. So any effort to empower a group will shift the culture. Culture shows up in conversations."[3] Thus began the shift into the conversation of inclusiveness.

When I first met Dr. Smith, I was intrigued by her concept of inclusion and its focus on empowerment, as opposed to the usual focus on victimized groups and redressing past wrongs. (Noting that she saw lots of *diversity* in the government but not *inclusion*, Dr. Smith would rename her task force the Task Force on an Inclusive Public Service.) Dr. Smith pointed out that there was a relationship between diversity and inclusion insofar as that, in an inclusive environment, diversity is valued. But this is where the relationship ends. In an inclusive environment, *each person* is valued because of the contribution that he or she makes to the workplace. Up until that point, discussion of difference in the workplace was about each *group*, not each person. From civil rights in the United States, human rights in Canada, affirmative action, equal opportunity, employment equity and all the way through to diversity, the focus had been on groups—my group of men, your group of women, his group

---

3. The Report on the Task Force on an Inclusive Public Service, 2000.

of gays, her group of whatever. Smith's point was that inclusion is not about each group; it's about each person being valued because of his or her unique talent.

Smith went on to say that in an inclusive environment, people are valued *because of*, not *in spite of*, the differences. This is significant because up until that time, most of the literature on differences talked about tolerance. But when you think about it, tolerance is simply about putting up with somebody: "Okay, you're gay, I can put up with that"; "You're an American, I can put up with that"; "You don't speak English, I can put up with that." Dr. Smith pointed out that she had seen many work environments where people were tolerated but not respected. She also pointed out that while you can have tolerance without respect, no work environment can have respect without tolerance. Tolerance is a floor you can build on to get to respect. Tolerance was necessary but not sufficient for a work environment where people are valued because of, not in spite of, their differences.

One of the distinct characteristics of Level 4 organizations is that they practice talent differentiation strategies. There is nothing new about talent differentiation. I first came across it in the 1997 McKinsey & Company study known as "The War for Talent." In the study, talent differentiation is described as the recognition that all employees are not equally talented and therefore should not all be treated the same. In their words, ". . . talent differentiation entails assessing the performance and potential of your people and then giving them the commensurate promotion and development opportunities."[4] Organizations that practice talent differentiation believe we are all good at something and none of us is good at everything.

In a Level 4 organization, talent differentiation is practiced through a diversity lens, recognizing that talent comes in all sorts of packages. As in the Level 3 organization, the Level 4 has realized that representation

---

4. Ed Michaels, Helen Handfield-Jones and Beth Axelrod, *The War for Talent* (Boston: Harvard Business School Publishing, 2001), 126.

is a signal for how talent is being handled in the organization. So if one group of people seems to be dominating any occupational category, that's a signal that talent in other groups is being overlooked. Talent differentiation is discussed in more detail in Chapter 4.

Another distinct characteristic of Level 4 organizations is that their commitment to inclusion is not affected by economic trends. One of the biggest differences between Level 3 and Level 4 comes down to one word: *sustainability*. In Level 3 organizations, diversity is pursued as long as the organization can prove the business case. So in a bad economic year, the talk of diversity goes out the door, along with the other good human resources initiatives. But in a Level 4, you could have a bad fiscal quarter and the work related to inclusiveness continues. This is because it is integrated into the core values of the corporate culture and how it perceives talent in the organization. It is seen from a long-term, sustainable, competitive perspective and thus will not come and go with the short-term variability of the economy. As one executive told me, any of his competition can get his organization's products and technology, but the organization's people are its sustainable competitive advantage.

Yet another important characteristic of Level 4 is that all people consider themselves responsible for creating an inclusive work environment. All employees—not just the human resources department, not just the chief inclusiveness officer, not even just the senior executive group, but all employees—share this responsibility. This may seem impossible, but it really does distinguish Level 4 organizations from those that have put in place department infrastructures in an effort to create inclusive cultures. An inclusive culture will not come about simply by creating departments, policies and processes; it will occur because of a change in culture where the actions and behaviors of leaders and employees are consistent with an inclusive culture because of the organization's core values.

The final distinction of Level 4 organizations from the previous levels is that they are widely perceived as employers and suppliers of choice within their community, and they are clearly on their way to being seen as the employers and suppliers of choice for all from a global perspective. We have yet to find an organization that has managed to reach Level 4.

However, one organization, Ernst & Young, has committed to being the first Level 4 in Canada (as documented in Chapter 8).

The jump today from a Level 3 to a Level 4 on the Equity Continuum requires a shift beyond differences merely being recognized to a position where differences are critical. It requires a move beyond the focus on righting historical wrongs for historically disadvantaged groups to a focus on job/talent fit for all employees. And most importantly, it requires a shift beyond the group conversation to a focus on the individual. It is this shift that sets the stage for human equity.

The Evolution beyond Diversity to Human Equity

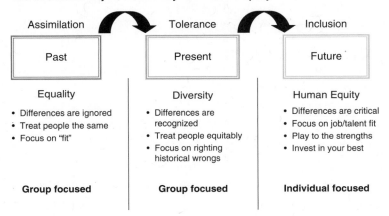

Source: Trevor Wilson, *Diversity at Work: The Business Case for Equity* (Toronto: John Wiley & Sons Canada, Ltd., 1996)

One of the ways organizations can signal the evolution beyond diversity toward inclusion and human equity is how they collect the quantitative representation data. Level 1 to Level 3 organizations generally rely on a selective approach to representative data gathering, focusing on the identification of target or designated groups. In a Level 4 organization, quantitative data is approached from a more inclusive perspective with every employee invited to participate regardless of his or her group.

TWI Inc. first created a workforce census more than a decade ago when organizations facing legislated equity requirements found that certain groups were not participating in the annual self-identification survey. This annual survey was a requirement under the legislation and was designed to allow the organization to get a hard count of its target groups. The lack of participation by members of certain groups meant the organization was unable to file its reports with the government.

The idea of creating a workforce census occurred when someone asked, "Why do we ask only members of target groups to fill out the questionnaire? When the government does a census, they don't count only four groups."

This became the premise of the workforce census. It is based on the way a country approaches census data gathering. Governments seek to collect data from every individual citizen in the country by asking a myriad of questions that can be used for policy design purposes. In the same way, collecting demographic data on all employees, not just selected groups, sends the message that the organization's human capital strategy is relevant to all employees.

A properly designed workforce census can allow an organization to have a better understanding of the needs of its employees by gathering baseline demographic information on the characteristics of the entire workforce population. This information can then be compared to the census metropolitan area data to better understand how inclusive and equitable an environment exists.

The workforce census can also help the organization identify where there may be gaps that could impact on operational effectiveness; for example, knowing how many people speak a certain language internally compared to the surrounding area may help a service provider better serve the community. It will also assist in understanding the needs of the existing workforce in order to develop initiatives that address identified gaps such as child care or dependent care needs. The workforce census can also assist in planning to meet projected needs based on forecasted population changes, such as adjusting succession planning programs.

The following case study about the Mount Sinai Hospital's Workforce Census describes the approach the organization took to move beyond the exclusive group focus of quantitative data gathering toward the more inclusive approach offered by a workforce census. A properly executed workforce census can send the message that the organization is evolving toward inclusion beyond diversity.

CASE STUDY: MOUNT SINAI HOSPITAL'S WORKFORCE CENSUS

By Debbie Fischer, vice president strategy and organizational development, Mount Sinai Hospital

Founded in 1923, Mount Sinai Hospital (MSH) is a large patient care, teaching and research hospital affiliated with the University of Toronto. MSH's mission is to discover and deliver the best patient care, research and education. As part of its commitment to the values of respect and equity, it seeks to be a national leader in all of its inclusion and human rights programs.

In 2007 MSH became the first health care institution in Ontario to collect demographic workforce data including race, ethnicity, disability, sexual orientation, age and gender. There were a number of objectives in collecting this data, among them determining whether diversity in the broader community was reflected in the MSH workforce; identifying gaps in representation in the existing workforce and adjusting employee training, recruitment efforts and hiring practices accordingly; ensuring that MSH is a welcoming environment that reflects the community it serves; and providing a baseline by which to measure the impact of various equity efforts.

Steering Committee

Given the sensitive and confidential nature of the information being collected, MSH sought to address any concerns and maximize buy-in by involving key stakeholders in each stage of the process.

(continued)

The initiative was led by the Human Rights and Health Equity Committee (then known as the Diversity and Human Rights Committee).

A broad-based Workforce Census steering committee was created that was representative of the hospital community nurses, front-line staff, union leaders, members of management and human resources. Working with TWI, the steering committee was involved in every stage of the process. The steering committee identified questions, approved the census questionnaire, developed the communication plan and logistical plan, and oversaw the implementation of the census.

Census Questionnaire

The process of identifying what data needed to be collected was an important educational process for the steering committee and the broader hospital community. The committee had to determine what we wanted to learn about our workforce. How could we ask the questions in a way that would be usable? What would be the most appropriate language for the questions? How could the language both reflect the hospital's values with respect to equity and provide an opportunity to educate the wider hospital community on those values?

It was also important to address the fears and resistance that we were aware would arise. For example, the steering committee decided that questions would not be asked for their own sake. Rather, the census questionnaire would ask only questions that the hospital was committed to take action on. Each question would be accompanied by a brief explanation (no longer than two points) about why it was being asked and the intended use of responses. The questionnaire would use accessible language that was suggestive rather than directive (e.g., "We would like to know" as opposed to "We need to know"; and "We are asking because" as opposed to "Rationale"). The language would also be sensitive to how groups identify themselves and how demographic data has sometimes been used to discriminate against groups rather than advance equity. For questions regarding race or ethnicity, the census would use the categories utilized in the Census of Canada. Finally, the questionnaire's introduction would contain the following statement: "Responses to these questions will be compared with responses from the Census of Canada to help us understand how aligned we are with these skills compared to the community we serve."

After the draft questionnaire was developed, the committee piloted it with several focus groups. The feedback from the focus groups was used to improve and further develop the census questionnaire.

This collaborative and broad-based approach to the development of the census questionnaire ensured that the questions were understandable, reflective of the sensitive nature of the information being sought, placed in a proper context and, perhaps most importantly, producing information that could be used to increase inclusion and equity in the workforce.

One unexpected result of the census design process was that reactions to certain questions dealing with sexual orientation helped to reveal fairly widespread but previously hidden discriminatory feelings toward members of the LGBT community.

Implementation and Communications Strategy

As well as providing input to the questionnaire, the steering committee put much thought into the process of collecting the data. First, the committee understood the importance of ensuring the rights and privacy of the workforce census participants. As such, the committee determined that involvement in the process

(continued)

would be voluntary, confidential and anonymous, and that the data would be stored offsite.

Second, recognizing that the success of the census would depend significantly on leadership buy-in, committee members held several meetings with key stakeholders to outline the census questionnaire's benefits to workforce planning and to an evidence-based organization. This process of consultation earned the trust and support of senior leaders, particularly the president and CEO. Here TWI was instrumental in "normalizing" the asking of demographic questions of the workforce, especially to front-line managers who needed to hear that workforce censuses had been successfully conducted in other industries and organizations.

Third, in order to maximize rates of participation, the committee worked with a communication team and developed a promotional campaign called "Include Me!" The promotional materials included testimonials and frequently asked questions. The extensive communication strategy included posters, lobby displays, pay stub inserts, newsletter ads and staff letters from the president and CEO and from other hospital leaders.

Execution and Results

The census, which consisted of 50 questions, ran from May 14 to 27, 2007. To ensure confidentiality, the questionnaire was administered by TWI, which collected, stored, analyzed and reported the data. Stations with laptops and paper copies of the census questionnaire, and staffed by committee members, were set up in the MSH lobbies, as well as in each unit and department of the hospital. To encourage participation, employees were provided with refreshments, and those who chose to complete a ballot along with filling in the survey became eligible to win prizes. A large lottery drum in the lobby was a helpful reminder to staff to complete their survey and enter the draw. During this time, members of the Diversity and Human Rights Office were always available to assure staff of the anonymous and confidential nature of the survey, to answer questions and to address any concerns.

MSH's workforce census had a good response rate. At the time the census was conducted, there were more than 6,000 hospital staff, including full-time and part-time staff, medical and dental staff, research institute staff, medical students and volunteers. More than 3,300 employees responded to the census and the census sample was representative of the MSH population and its departmental breakdowns; 76 percent of the sample participants were regular, full-time staff, and participants included staff, staff physicians, principal investigators, volunteers and researchers.

Organizational Impact

MSH's workforce census has led to a number of exciting initiatives and developments to increase equity and promote human rights in the hospital. The census highlighted that although MSH did have a diverse workforce, this diversity was not consistent throughout hospital ranks; racialized persons were underrepresented in upper management jobs, while persons with visible disabilities were underrepresented throughout the entire workforce. As a result, MSH developed a new Fair Employment Opportunity Policy. Information gathered from the workforce census also led to better support for volunteers, increased education on human rights and equity, the identification and training of internal interpreters, support for the workforce to pursue educational opportunities, changes in benefit plans, and advanced wellness programming to address the health and fitness of all staff. A rigorous campaign to promote the rights of LGBT staff and patients was implemented to address the homophobia and transphobia that had become evident through the census.

(continued)

The workforce census also had broader organizational impact. The information that it quantified about staffing patterns, employee skills and preferences resulted in several changes in hospital policies, procedures and programs. All staff members are evaluated on equity and cultural competencies, including compliance with human rights and equity policies and procedures. Hiring and promotion for all staff includes consideration of the candidates' commitment to human rights and equity along with other job-related qualifications. Staff satisfaction surveys include questions on the workplace environment and manager fairness.

In terms of increased workplace equity, all hiring follows the principles outlined in the Fair Employment Opportunities Policy and training sessions. All managers and others who participate in hiring attend Fair Employment Opportunities training. Human resources takes a more active role in promoting fair hiring practices.

Finally, to ensure continued progress, the Human Rights and Health Equity Office now has additional resources to support clinical programs in the development and evaluation of health equity initiatives. All centers of excellence within the hospital and hospital departments must measure and meet a key performance indicator related to health equity to ensure their services are accessible and relevant to marginalized populations. An equity communication campaign has been implemented, with posters and brochures challenging attitudinal barriers and encouraging the "Made in Sinai" equity competencies.

Next Steps: Collecting Patient Demographic Data

The results from the workforce census demonstrated that a clear understanding of the demographic makeup of MSH staff is essential to ensuring the best quality of service to patients.

Stemming from the success of this census, the Human Rights and Health Equity Office began to think about the possible benefits of implementing a patient demographic collection tool. After a successful pilot project wherein staff and researchers collected patient demographic data from MSH, Toronto's St. Michael's Hospital, the Centre for Addiction and Mental Health (also in Toronto), and Toronto Public Health, the Toronto Central Local Health Integration Network have begun implementing this patient data collection program across all hospitals in the downtown Toronto area. MSH is leading this initiative.

Lessons Learned for Successful Implementation of Staff Demographic Census

The MSH experience identified the following critical components of successful implementation:

- Building awareness of equity in the organization
- Identifying the benefit for each group in conducting an audit of your workforce
- Anticipating concerns and questions
- Communicate, communicate, communicate
- Making it easy for staff to complete the census
- Asking questions you will act on
- Communicating results
- Considering indicators of a fair workplace: rates of illness, terminations, retention and how fairness is rated in the organization.

The MSH Workforce Census was precedent setting for the hospital industry. It has provided essential information for the

(*continued*)

hospital to understand more about its people than ever before. It is an initiative that will move MSH further along the path toward its vision of becoming a supplier and employer of choice for all. A properly designed workforce census can also be used as a tangible communication vehicle to signal a move beyond an exclusive approach to data gathering, which is used in legislated equity, toward the more inclusive approach to gathering information on all employees. It is a tangible demonstration of what it means to move beyond diversity toward inclusion.

LEVEL 5: INCLUSIVE AND EQUITABLE ORGANIZATIONS

If I don't spend too much space here documenting Level 5 organizations, it's because we have yet to find one. At this point they sit as a bit of a utopian dream, although I am convinced this is a worthy ambition. These are organizations that exemplify Dr. Martin Luther King, Jr.'s dream of creating an environment where people are judged solely on their character. They are not judged by their gender, race or age or by any other superficial demographic criteria. They are judged solely by their ability and talent. Level 5 organizations practice human equity and seek to optimize on all the intangible assets that are available to them—that is, they maximize on total human capital.

Level 5 organizations focus on the gifts and unique abilities of each individual. These organizations work toward the possibility of self-actualization for their entire workforce, a very lofty goal now made possible through the work of positive psychology. These organizations also practice talent differentiation through a diversity lens with the intention to identify best job/talent fit. These organizations believe the old maxim that we are all good at something and none of us is good at everything. They use new management tools and approaches that focus on using individual strengths rather than trying to fix weaknesses.

A Level 5 organization is indisputably perceived as the employer of choice for all. In sum, Level 5 organizations:

- Have achieved the vision of treating people based solely on the content of their character
- Practice human equity by maximizing on all the intangible assets that people bring to the world of work
- Capitalize on individual differences to unleash maximum human potential and self-actualization
- Focus on rigorous talent differentiation to create a job/talent fit
- Have achieved a work environment that is equitable and inclusive for all
- Seek to introduce human equity beyond their own boundaries
- Recognize that human equity contributes to a strong economy
- Are indisputably perceived as the employers and suppliers of choice for all.

WHERE ARE WE NOW?

We've learned a lot about the Equity Continuum over the past few years, and we can now use it to understand the evolution from diversity to human equity over the last 30 years in North America. We can see that legislated and litigated equity was the vehicle that moved many organizations from Level 0 to 1. Then corporate social responsibility practices became the vehicles to move organizations out of Level 1 and into Level 2. When the diversity discussion began more than 20 years ago, it was used to move organizations from Level 2 to Level 3. This was the focus of *Diversity at Work* in 1996: to articulate the so-called business case. I believe that Dr. Janet Smith's work in 1999, documented in the Task Force on an Inclusive Public Service report, showed us a new path to move organizations beyond Level 3 to Level 4. This is the focus of our work today and the prime reason for writing this book. Once an organization moves beyond the group focus of levels 1 to 3, it can firmly link this conversation to talent optimization and human equity. Once there, an organization can use human equity to move to Level 5, becoming the employer of choice for all.

One of the things we now know is how many organizations have moved along the Equity Continuum over the past decade and a half. In 1997 my estimate was that approximately 50 percent of organizations fell between Level 0 and Level 1, 30 percent between Level 1 and Level 2, and about 18 percent between Level 2 and Level 3. Since I had not seen any organizations between Level 4 and Level 5, the remaining 2 percent, I reasoned, fell between a Level 3 and Level 4. In 1998 a group led by Dr. Julie Rowney at the University of Calgary struck a group called the Leadership Diversity Advisory Committee. The group conducted research in the Calgary area and confirmed approximately 50 percent of organizations they studied were between a Level 0 and Level 1, with 20 percent between a Level 1 and Level 2, 17.5 percent between a Level 2 and Level 3, 12.5 percent between a Level 3 and Level 4, and none at Level 5.

Today I would put only 16 percent between Level 0 and Level 1, attesting to the impact of legislated equity. I estimate 40 percent of organizations are between levels 1 and 2, 30 percent between levels 2 and 3, and 12.5 percent between levels 3 and 4. This leaves about 1.5 percent between levels 4 and 5. Thus, most organizations have evolved their discussion of equity in the workplace beyond the legislated approach, but few have yet managed to move beyond diversity into areas such as inclusion and human equity. In the next chapter we will point to the essential role leadership behavior plays in making the transition beyond diversity to human equity.

Chapter 3

THE ESSENTIAL ROLE OF LEADERS AND MANAGERS

Five years ago, TWI Inc. was approached to participate in a new award designed to identify the best employers in terms of diversity. Since the competition focuses on diversity (i.e., organizations aspiring to be a Level 3), the participants are organizations pursuing initiatives related to women, minorities, people with disabilities, Aboriginal people and LGBT groups. We partnered with a company called Mediacorp, which over a decade ago had created an award acknowledging the Top 100 employers. Mediacorp had been approached by several of the Top 100 applicants to create an award to highlight diversity initiatives. At the time, Mediacorp had little understanding of how diversity differed from inclusion or human equity and more importantly had no idea how to measure it. It did, however, know about the Equity Continuum and sought to use it as the measuring stick for this new diversity award.

This partnership has been a rewarding and enlightening experience. It has allowed us to gain an understanding of some of the best practices in the area of diversity and to better understand what it will take to move along the continuum level beyond diversity to reach human equity. We have had an unprecedented inside look at hundreds of organizations in almost every industry and almost every jurisdiction to see what they have managed to do in terms of diversity in the workplace. Perhaps my biggest learning in the past five years is the critical importance of leadership in getting to equitable and inclusive work environments.

For years organizational change experts have said that it all starts at the top—"If your top leaders don't get it, there is absolutely no way anyone else will" and "What's of interest to my boss fascinates the hell out of me" are phrases that come to mind. But frankly up until now we had no real way of proving this. Furthermore, such beliefs had been used before for safety, quality or [insert your favorite paradigm shift here]. But I now realize that when it comes to moving toward a Level 5, there is nothing as important as shifting leadership behavior. If the actions and behavior of the organization's leadership are inconsistent with the espoused corporate values of diversity, inclusion or human equity, people will ignore the internal propaganda, the fancy Intranet sites and glossy reports and take their cues instead from how they get treated by leadership and management.

THE BOSS-HOLE

A few years ago, I was invited to speak at the partnership meeting of a major international law firm. During the meeting, the master of ceremonies asked all the new partners to stand up and be recognized, adding that they had all signed the "no-asshole clause." I turned to a senior partner sitting beside me and asked if I had heard properly. The seasoned partner explained that every new partner had pledged that he or she would not be an asshole while with the firm. "And you've written this down?" I asked. He proceeded to show me the clause, which had been included in the meeting's background material. I was more than impressed and left thinking this was one of the most progressive initiatives I had ever seen. It was not too long afterward that I learned about Stanford professor Robert Sutton and his book *The No Asshole Rule* (which I refer to in Chapter 1, in the discussion of the fourth problem with diversity). Sutton first presented his ideas at a conference that included a large population of representatives from the legal industry. Apparently he felt this was the industry where he had met the highest number of assholes (sometimes called boss-holes).

In his book, Sutton describes working in a high-functioning department at Stanford. When the department director decided to retire, he and the other five employees in the department were approached by human resources to help choose the director's replacement. They were told that if all six of them could agree on the attributes they wanted in their new boss, the school would hire according to their criteria, regardless of the formal job description. The six of them agreed that the chance to choose their own boss was a great opportunity.

These six academics locked themselves in a room for two days to see if they could agree on what they wanted in a new director. Unfortunately, they also took their big Ivy League egos with them. Long story short: they couldn't agree on the attributes they wanted in a new boss. However, they could agree on what they *didn't* want. What they all didn't want was an "asshole." When they informed HR that they could not agree on what they wanted but only on what they didn't want, the HR administrator lobbed the ball back into their court. "Okay," she said, "can you describe an asshole?" The six academics looked at each other and said they thought they could. They went back into the room and after two hours came out with an elegant definition of what they referred to as a "certified asshole": "One who persistently leaves others demeaned, disrespected and de-motivated and has a persistent pattern of contempt for those with less status and power."

The six even identified the common behaviors of a certified asshole, distinguishing a certified asshole (someone who demonstrates this behavior 24 hours a day, seven days a week) from a temporary asshole (someone just having a bad day, which leads to a temporary demonstration of this behavior). The so-called dirty dozen are 12 specific behaviors that a certified boss-hole exhibits on a regular basis:[1]

1. Makes personal insults
2. Invades one's personal territory
3. Initiates uninvited physical contact

---

1. Robert Sutton, *The No Asshole Rule* (New York: Hachette Book Group, 2007), 55.

4. Makes sarcastic jokes and teases
5. Sends withering claims by e-mail
6. Makes status slaps intended to humiliate
7. Rudely interrupts
8. Makes two-faced attacks
9. Gives dirty looks
10. Treats people as if they are invisible
11. Makes threats and intimidations (both verbal and nonverbal)
12. Shames publicly.

If any of these behaviors are familiar to you or if you suspect you may be a boss-hole, take the Personal Leadership Behavior Assessment (below), a brief questionnaire used to measure workplace behaviors related to business outcomes, then check the answer key in the appendix of this book to see if you are a certified boss-hole, a temporary boss-hole or the opposite of a boss-hole, a truly equitable leader. Answer every question as honestly and accurately as possible, thinking about your behavior as it relates to the way you interact with colleagues in your workplace.

Personal Leadership Behavior Assessment

Answer true or false in response to each statement.

1. I rarely encourage people who work with me to view their mistakes as learning opportunities. _____
2. I have little regard for the feelings of the people who report to me. _____
3. I let my nonverbal behavior express the negative thoughts that I cannot say. _____
4. I can be harsh when letting someone know their work is not up to standard. _____
5. When I lead a team meeting, I rarely ensure that everyone has an opportunity to provide input and express their opinions. _____
6. People rarely get my full and undivided attention when they interact with me. _____

7. I have made an example of a person in front of others, instead of handling the matter in private. _____

8. I don't worry about my language or tone when I speak; it doesn't matter to me if I embarrass or hurt others by the way I say things. _____

9. When I am angry, I want people to be very aware of it. _____

10. I have subordinates who are not comfortable (i.e., nervous, uneasy or afraid) providing me with negative information. _____

11. I have raised my voice at a subordinate to express my displeasure. _____

12. I take steps to make it very clear that I am the person in charge and my authority is strictly enforced. _____

13. When I am displeased with someone, I make joking comments that are actually criticisms in disguise. _____

14. When I feel myself getting annoyed or frustrated with someone, I rarely take steps to keep these feelings from escalating. _____

15. I have used intimidation tactics on a team member to get what I want. _____

16. I rarely seek out opportunities to interact with people on my team because relationships are not that important. _____

17. I can be sarcastic toward others when I feel annoyed or displeased. _____

18. If I am in a bad mood, I rarely take steps to avoid taking it out on others. _____

19. I have said negative things about people behind their back. _____

20. Within my team I foster an atmosphere of competition rather than collegial cooperation. _____

The Personal Leadership Behavior Assessment will help signal a truly equitable leader or a possible boss-hole, but the only way to confirm one for sure is to conduct a 360-degree assessment, which involves both a self-assessment and assessment by one's colleagues. This type of assessment, called the Equitable Leader Assessment (ELA), is described in Chapter 10. It is used to identify leadership behavior that is conducive to creating an equitable and inclusive work environment. It is among the top 10 percent performers on the ELA that you are likely to find your most equitable leaders. Accordingly, it is among the bottom 10 percent performers on the ELA that you will find an organization's boss-holes. Our experience is that the top 10 percent practice equitable leadership naturally in a state called unconscious competence. The lowest 10 percent are frequently unaware of their offensive behavior in the workplace, a state we call unconsciously incompetent. As mentioned in Chapter 1, frequently the individuals in the lowest 10 percent group are at such a high level of power in the organization that it could be a very career-limiting move to tell them about their unconsciously incompetent, unacceptable behavior. Consequently their damaging behavior continues, and people either quit their job and leave, or quit their job—and stay. More about this phenomenon known as *psychic absenteeism* in Chapter 7.

The top 10 percent leaders naturally exhibit behavior that leads to an equitable and inclusive work environment. These are the equitable leaders who drive the human equity agenda in the organization by exhibiting behavior that maximizes on total human potential. They are the internal best practice leaders who can be relied on to move the organization further along the continuum. These top 10 percent practice positive psychology management techniques by playing to the strengths of their employees. They practice the talent differentiation strategies described in Chapter 5 and highlighted in the description of a Level 4 organization in Chapter 2. We will come to see that using a tool such as the Equitable Leader Assessment to identify and utilize the highest 10 percent is far more important than simply neutralizing the impact of the lowest 10 percent boss-holes.

Sometimes I am asked why leadership behavior is so critical to moving an organization along the Equity Continuum. I generally respond with a quote from Ralph Waldo Emerson: "What you do speaks so loud I can't hear what you say." When it comes to equitable leadership, people pay less attention to words than actions. One of the Equitable Leader Competencies is ethics and integrity, i.e., leaders who consistently demonstrate honesty, reliability and constancy. Ken Lay, the former CEO of Enron, provides us with a classic demonstration of the Emerson quote. Lay conducted an all-employees meeting on August 16, 2001, in which he gave a convincing recitation of what ethics and integrity in the corporate world should be about. He would later be charged with one of the largest corporate acts of fraud in the history of the United States. Lay's actions, rather than his words, would demonstrate his true belief. The same can be said for the highest and the lowest 10 percent leaders. It is their actions, not their words, that determine how equitable they truly are.

In Chapter 1 I pointed out that one of the problems with legislated equity and diversity is that it has virtually ignored the importance of leadership behavior due to a lopsided focus on representation as the sole measure of progress. In our annual review of the best diversity employers, we consider leadership, as well as three other factors, to determine an organization's final score on the continuum. All of these factors are contained in a model known as the Equity Index.

THE EQUITY INDEX

The Equity Index is a measurement template that provides a context for the importance of leadership behavior. We use it for the annual Best Diversity Employers competition and also when advising our clients on how to assess the impact of various interventions to move their organization along the Equity Continuum toward human equity.

The index looks at four categories of possible interventions:

1. Internal quantitative
2. Internal qualitative
3. External qualitative
4. Leadership behavior.

The percentage cited in each quadrant of the index is the weighting given to the attribute based on the impact each has on moving the organization toward human equity and a Level 5 on the Equity Continuum.

The Equity Index

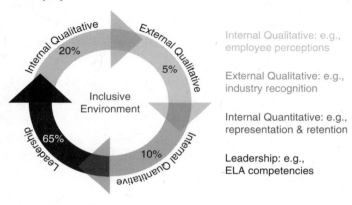

Internal Qualitative: e.g., employee perceptions

External Qualitative: e.g., industry recognition

Internal Quantitative: e.g., representation & retention

Leadership: e.g., ELA competencies

Copyright TWI Inc.©

Internal Quantitative

Quantitative metrics generally fall in the area of representation and retention. Representation looks at the demographic picture of the workforce while retention looks at how these demographics change over time. As mentioned in Chapter 1 this has been the focus of the Level 1 to Level 3 organizations for the past two decades. These organizations have defined their success primarily based on how many of certain selected groups they can attract and retain. Retention is added because representation alone is simply a snapshot in time and a static metric. By adding retention to the quantitative assessment, you have a broader, more dynamic picture of what is happening in the work environment.

For example, one Level 2 organization I worked with had made a commitment to substantially improve the representation of women in senior management and executive positions. They had set an aggressive goal of doubling the number of women in leadership positions within five years. They did the standard self-identification questionnaire to identify the number of women they had at the beginning of the project, and five years later did another self-identification to measure their progress.

It turned out that the before and after numbers of senior women were the same. Simply looking at the representation numbers, one would have assumed that the organization had done little or nothing to improve representation of women in the workforce. Upon closer examination, however, they realized that the 150 women counted five years earlier were almost completely different from the 150 women presently in the organization. In other words, more than half the senior women had left the organization, replaced by a whole new group within the five-year period. More importantly, no one seemed to notice this until the organization moved beyond representation to also look at retention and attrition by demographic group. This allowed them to realize they had a much more significant gender equity problem than simply attracting more women to improve representation. In light of the high rate of attrition, attracting more women was not likely to be an effective solution to meeting their representation goals.

From a quantitative perspective, looking at the ratio of retention to representation rather than representation alone gives a clearer and more nuanced picture of what is actually happening, regardless of the group being monitored.

This does not mean we should ignore representation in the journey to become a Level 5 organization. The value of representation and retention is that they can be used as signals to potential issues in the workplace. But they are only a small part of the picture. As you can see in the figure above, internal quantitative metrics related to representation and retention receive a 10 percent weighting on the Equity Index. That is twice as important as external qualitative metrics such as industry recognition, but only half as important as internal qualitative metrics such as employee attitudes and opinions. Ironically, quantitative evidence is the area that most government departments responsible for legislated equity monitor the most closely. We will see how the collection of internal quantitative data is necessary but not sufficient to understand how far an organization is from a Level 5.

Internal Qualitative

Internal qualitative metrics represent employee perceptions about the working environment. In particular an organization needs to be measuring the perception of employees from various perspectives using different data-gathering techniques, the most common of which is an employee engagement or employee opinion survey. Measuring employee engagement has become the Holy Grail of human capital management. Most large organizations are convinced there is value in monitoring employee engagement because it has direct impact on workplace productivity. But it is our experience that most organizations are content to measure overall employee engagement but not employee engagement among groups.

Like talent differentiation (see Chapter 5), employee engagement must be measured through a diversity lens. For example, let's say that an organization is reporting 80 percent overall employee engagement, as in the diagram below. This is significantly above the external norm. Yet look at what happens when the data is seen through a diversity lens: there is an evident difference in perception by age and race. What must be determined is what is causing one group to perceive the organization differently from other groups—not just the overall employee engagement.

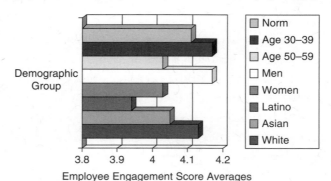

Employee Engagement Score Averages

When dealing with qualitative data it is also important to look at specific employee perceptions in three key areas: perceptions of discrimination, perceptions of harassment and perceptions of abuse of authority. These three areas are typically not measured properly on the average employee attitude or engagement survey, or are not measured at all. This is because most organizations do not know how to properly measure perceptions of harassment and discrimination.

Most employees have had some experience with what they think is discrimination or harassment or abuse of authority in the work environment. If you asked the average employee if he or she has ever witnessed any of these things, the response will be based either on a personal definition of harassment or discrimination, which can be very broad, or a legal definition of harassment and discrimination, which is prescribed and specific. For example, some employees may confuse harassment or abuse of authority with their manager's continued demand for on-time delivery of quality work. A proper reading of any legal definition of harassment would allow you to recognize these demands as a regular expectation of the manager's job even if the employee considers it harassment.

The trick in properly measuring employee perceptions in these prickly areas is to identify questions that describe the act of harassment and discrimination without actually using those words. At the end of this chapter you'll find a series of such questions, which can be added to your existing employee surveys to begin properly measuring these key areas. Over the past decade, we have used these questions to accurately measure the perception of discrimination and harassment in the workplace. These perception numbers, once aggregated and compared with normative data, give a fairly clear picture of how much unacceptable workplace behavior is happening within an organization and to whom. This is much more important information than simply the number of women and minorities, say, that exist within a particular company.

Qualitative data is twice as important as quantitative data primarily because qualitative data can be predictive. For example, if an organization has moved the representation of women in senior executive positions up 50 percent in five years, we would have to go back five years to analyze what the organization did to effect this change. This is why representation is considered a *lagging* metric. However, if the employee opinion data shows that more than 50 percent of women in the organization perceive that they are facing sexual harassment, it is safe to predict that the retention of women will decrease in the not too distant future. From the perspective of a practitioner, this is far more important information than knowing current representation.

External Qualitative

External qualitative metrics are those that allow the organization to measure how it stands up against others in their industry or other best practice employers. There are several cross-industry surveys that provide such a comparison. Some assessments, such as the Catalyst census mentioned earlier, focus on quantitative comparisons of various organizations. Others, such as the Canada's Best Diversity Employers competition, utilizes all four quadrants of the Equity Index to determine a score on the Equity Continuum.

External qualitative metrics have only a 5 percent weighting from a measurement perspective. An organization's ability to win an industry-wide award or receive external recognition for its initiatives may not reflect the reality of its workforce culture. Having said that, external qualitative results should not be totally ignored, especially if the competition is based on a rigorous measurement template.

In Chapter 8 we describe the work of the Trinity Group, a consortium of organizations that have come together in Canada to work on standards for the measurement of diversity, inclusion and human equity. Trinity's mission is to create a robust measurement assessment to objectively assess an organization's progress (that is, its movement along the Equity Continuum) in diversity, inclusion and human equity. Members of the Trinity Group believe that such a tool would allow for the development of standards that could be used to benchmark internally and externally, as well as within and among various industries. The group believes that the creation of standards can inspire continued innovation toward totally inclusive and equitable environments for all.

The Trinity Group's measurement tool is called the Human Equity Assessment Tool (HEAT). This tool measures the five levels of the continuum through the lens of six organizational processes and eight practices, based on the original ISO framework for measuring quality. In the summer of 2012 the Trinity Group updated the original Diversity Assessment Tool, which had been created more than a decade ago, before the concepts of inclusion and human equity became widely known and understood. The enhanced HEAT is a unique and systematic method to identify the discrepancy between desired and actual performance of a diversity, inclusion or human equity strategy. The evaluation identifies the optimal (what is desired), actuals (what is the current state), causes (why a discrepancy exists) and solutions (what should be done to eliminate the gap between optimal and actuals). Information is systematically gathered from all relevant sources within the organization to provide an objective, well-supported case for making appropriate interventions and realignments. We feel that this work has the potential to offer a more systematic approach to the measurement of progress toward a Level 5 organization.

Leadership Behavior

Leadership behavior is the fourth category of the Equity Index. Not surprisingly, it has a weighting of 65 percent. As I said earlier, everything else the organization does in relation to representation, retention, employee opinions or being best of class pales by comparison to the impact that leadership behavior has on moving toward a Level 5 on the continuum.

Some time ago a senior executive asked me, "If there was one thing we could do to make the best employer list, what would it be?" I told the CEO that talking about dignity and respect, work and life balance, and inclusion was probably better than not talking about it, but that ideally the leader would not just talk about these concepts but actually live them.

This conversation happened shortly after my father passed away. My father had a wonderful habit of using old-time Jamaican allegories, metaphors and colloquialisms, most of which I never really understood. One of his favorite sayings was, "The fish stinks from the head." I guess my father was with me when the CEO asked his question because I heard myself responding, "The fish stinks from the head." He asked what I meant.

"If the leadership isn't practicing behavior that leads to an equitable and inclusive environment, then you can bet no one else will. You can bet that if inclusion is not on your agenda as the most influential leader in the organization, it's not on anyone else's agenda either," I explained.

In response, the organization did a leadership intervention that was unprecedented at that time in North America. The CEO mandated that all his direct reports be assessed on key behavioral competencies related to diversity, inclusion and human equity. The CEO chose eight people to assess his direct reports. This prevented the leaders from skewing the assessment by choosing friendly colleagues to provide the feedback.

The next step was to conduct a mandatory executive workshop on the results of the assessment to interpret the aggregate results of this senior leadership team. Perhaps the most important part of this leadership intervention was mandatory coaching for the lowest-performing leaders. Supporting the lowest 10 percent leaders is one of the most significant things an organization can do to move toward a Level 5 on the Equity Continuum.

It was at this point that something totally unexpected occurred. The organization's chairman of the board inquired into what they were up to. The CEO explained the intervention and within a month the chairman mandated the same intervention for the board. This meant that within a short period, the top 50 most influential leaders of this multinational professional services firm had measured themselves on some of the most important behaviors related to inclusion and human equity.

The next step was the CEO and the chairman sitting down with the data for all 50 leaders and setting annual goals for the competencies they measured, including minimum threshold goals to which they will hold each other accountable over the next year. They then added this issue as a standing item to the quarterly executive and board agenda. The chairman has reported that having inclusion and human equity on the quarterly agenda has had more impact on organizational change within the firm than anything else they have ever done.

This story illustrates the old adage, "A value in action is a virtue." Every organization I have visited in the past 20 years has some great and aspirational values, such as integrity, creativity, diversity, inclusion and respect. However, it is only when the key opinion leaders begin to live these values that they become real and employees start to believe them. The question is, how do you get powerful leaders to walk the talk on the organization's values? Chapter 7 describes the eight core competencies of the equitable leader; the role of the Equitable Leader Assessment is explored in Chapter 10. But let us first take a closer look at a leadership intervention by one organization that was designed to improve the sensitivity and responsiveness of its leaders.

CASE STUDY: ONTARIO PUBLIC SERVICE DIVERSITY MENTORING PARTNERSHIP PROGRAM

The Ontario Public Service (OPS) is the second largest employer in the Canadian province of Ontario. It is a large and complex organization comprising approximately 65,000 employees, represented by eight different unions and 23 ministries or departments, which collectively manage and deliver services with a $126 billion annual budget (2012–13). Employees are in a wide variety of professions—from social workers to engineers, forestry workers to customer service representatives, teachers to policy analysts—and they deliver programs and services to 13 million Ontarians across the province. Each member of the OPS brings a unique perspective based on his or her personal and professional experience.

The OPS is committed to leveraging the strength of its diversity, which is recognized as a competitive advantage that Ontario possesses over most other parts of the world.

As a public sector organization, the OPS needed to reach a deeper understanding of the differences inherent in its makeup. From a customer service perspective, that means being responsive to the needs of a very diverse population who often have no choice

(continued)

as to where they acquire certain services (e.g., health care, birth certificates, licenses for driving, fishing or hunting) other than from a public institution. From an internal perspective, it means ensuring that employees feel that everyone is welcome, safe and respected, and are encouraged to contribute to their full potential.

Diversity Mentoring in the OPS

It had been observed that the OPS leadership was not as representative as it could be of the OPS population or the population of the province that it serves, in terms of visible diversity; the results of the 2009 OPS Employee Survey, which provided a detailed demographic profile of the organization, confirmed this observation. This data, along with a strong desire by the OPS leadership to set inclusion as an organizational priority, led to the OPS launching the Diversity Mentoring Partnership Program (DMPP). In 2008–09, the program was launched as a pilot involving all of the most senior public servants (every deputy minister and the secretary of the cabinet), who were committed to lead by example.

Research indicates that behavioral change often results from personal, rather than group, experience. The OPS Diversity Office determined a need to facilitate personal diversity experiences for both its executives and employees. In the program, executive partners have an opportunity to become more culturally aware by understanding the organization from the perspective of employees who are from groups underrepresented in senior management, and understanding the experiences, challenges and barriers that those employees may have or may be facing. These include issues such as group or personal disadvantage, experiences or familiarity with perceived or real discrimination and unfair workplace practices, and cultural differences.

Although the formal mentorship program was launched in 2008 as a 12-month pilot, it was embedded as a key initiative of the OPS Diversity Office 2009 Three-Year Strategic Plan, "Driving Change from a Solid Foundation." In the pilot, 85 employees from five groups underrepresented in senior management participated with 29 deputy ministers and the secretary of the cabinet. The program is based on a reciprocal mentorship model in which learning is deliberately two-way and in which there are no clear mentor/mentee roles. Both executive and employee partners assume the role of mentor or mentee at different times in the relationship. Senior executives learn about the diversity and experiences of staff who may be quite different from them and, in turn, they share their insights and strategies to assist staff to better understand organizational culture and how to succeed in the organization. It is the only program of its kind in the public sector in Canada.

The DMPP supports the OPS strategic priority of achieving behavioral and cultural transformation throughout the organization by providing an inclusive and non-hierarchical environment for reciprocal learning in which executive and employee partners engage in honest, open and meaningful dialogue about diversity, inclusion and accessibility.

Employee partners have an opportunity to increase their understanding of how to navigate a large public sector organization and gain insights into areas to which they may not otherwise have been exposed. This is accomplished through regular interactions (a minimum of six formal meetings over a 12-month period) with a more senior individual with whom they may not have otherwise connected.

Nenita Simmonds has worked in the OPS, on and off, for 20 years. She is originally from the Philippines and is no stranger to the stereotypes and barriers that people from a variety of cultures experience. "There has always been a barrier socially," she says. "As

(*continued*)

a Filipina, people expect me to be a domestic. That's the lens I am viewed through." Simmonds notes that stereotyping is something she has experienced less in the Ontario Public Service than in many other environments, but she says it does exist, for her and for others. For that reason she is a huge fan of the OPS Diversity Mentoring Partnership Program.

Participants in the program took it upon themselves to be the change they wanted to see in the organization. Simmonds was one of the first to sign up. "I decided that if the organization was willing to open the door in this way, then you know what, I want to be a part of that," she says.

Simmonds met several times in 2009 with her executive partner, the then-deputy minister of municipal affairs and housing, John Burke. She says they talked about everything from their families to their jobs.

Simmonds says Deputy Minister Burke taught her to think strategically. She believes she taught him, in turn, an important lesson about what people from underrepresented groups face on a daily basis. For her the biggest legacy of the experience is that she is now a mentor to others—and she plans to be one for as long as she works in the OPS.

"I learned to be a diverse leader. To be diverse is one thing, but to be a diverse leader is to turn that diversity into a strength. To be able to make a conscious effort to say, 'Hey, this is good.' To be able to say, 'We're different, we're comfortable with it and our differences help make the organization stronger.'"

Goals of the DMPP

Through the DMPP, the Diversity Office aims to effect behavioral change in the OPS via increased awareness and understanding of the experiences of employees from groups underrepresented in senior leadership positions, while at the same time providing those employees access to informal networks and mentors who can provide them with advice and encouragement.

The DMPP goals include:

- Contribute to a more diverse and inclusive workplace by facilitating organizational and behavioral change
- Give senior OPS executives an opportunity to better understand the experiences, challenges and barriers that may be faced by employees from groups that are underrepresented in senior management
- Improve access to training, career counseling and learning and development opportunities for underrepresented group members
- Recognize talented employees and make the senior management cadre more representative of the Ontario workforce at a faster pace.

Program Requirements and Selection Criteria

The DMPP pairs senior executives and managers with employees from groups that are currently underrepresented in the senior management cadre: Aboriginals, francophones, LGBTQ (lesbian, gay, bisexual, transgender, queer) employees, persons with disabilities and visible minorities. Employees from these backgrounds (and certain job classification levels for the deputy minister stream) must formally apply to enter the program by completing a simple online application form. They must voluntarily self-identify as belonging to one or more of the target groups and provide a statement as to what they hope to contribute to and get out of the program. Applicants are randomly selected and randomly matched with an

(*continued*)

executive partner either from a different ministry or from another division within their ministry.

Since the pilot in 2008–09, all 23 ministries now administer programs of their own, based on the corporate model. Several ministries have identified other representation gaps in their program areas and have extended the eligibility criteria to include young professionals and/or women in correctional service.

Program Streams and the Partnership Meetings

The DMPP consists of two streams:

- The Deputy Minister and Associate Deputy Minister Stream, which is open to employees from the identified underrepresented groups in the feeder groups into management and are not members of a bargaining unit. Employee partners are randomly matched with a deputy minister or associate deputy minister from a ministry other than their own.
- The Assistant Deputy Minister, Director, Manager Stream, which in most ministries is open to any staff member from the identified underrepresented groups in the ministry. Employee partners are randomly matched with executive partners from another ministry or are matched within their home ministry but across divisions to avoid a potential conflict of interest.

Executive and employee partners receive a dedicated program orientation training session. They are provided with a program guide that structures the relationship over the required six meetings of the program and guides both partners through discussions on different dimensions of diversity. Resources are also provided to facilitate an effective mentoring relationship. A midterm evaluation provides mentoring partners with an update on their progress and an opportunity to share their accomplishments and/or challenges.

Executive and employee partners spend a minimum of six hours together over the course of the 12-month program cycle. This is a key deliverable of the OPS Diversity Strategy, and links to the government's Talent Management initiative and human resources strategies. Partners work together to:

- Develop a plan that includes six or more partnership meetings of approximately one-hour duration over the course of the program cycle;
- Determine the goals and objectives they would like to achieve;
- Submit final evaluation of the process; and
- Agree on actual achievements.

David Lindsay, former deputy minister of energy and infrastructure, had three employee partners during the pilot year in 2009. The highlight of this experience was a canoe trip in which his mentoring partners accompanied him, as well as their visits to various ministry offices around the province to meet with stakeholders. Lindsay says he is a proud supporter of the Diversity Mentoring Partnership Program.

For him, the best part of the program was what he learned from his partners. "I can now speak with passion about something I previously only vaguely understood," he says. "You go through this program and you go from being sympathetic to empathetic. Knowing on an intellectual level what people from diverse backgrounds go through is a good start, but feeling it in your gut is different. It makes you realize this is not some abstract magazine article you're reading, it is a real person having a real experience. That's what this program has taught me and I'll never forget it."

(*continued*)

Performance Measurement

In the 2008–09 pilot, 100 percent of deputy ministers led by example and partnered with 85 OPS employees in reciprocal mentoring partnerships. Deputies tied their participation in the pilot program to diversity commitments in their performance contracts. By 2012, the OPS Diversity Mentoring Partnership Program had taken root deeper in the organization and was available to many more employees. There is success in numbers. Since 2008, there have been more than 1,500 diversity mentoring partnerships across the OPS.

In the deputy minister and associate deputy minister stream, there have been 303 employee partners since 2008.

In the ministry-delivered programs below the deputy ministers, there have been nearly 1,300.

Former program participants who are interested in giving back to the organization and continuing the mentoring journey are now part of an alumni association that is available for ministries to tap into for support (as coaches, panel members or public speakers) to their ongoing programs.

Mentoring: Making a Difference

The DMPP formally recognizes diversity mentoring participation in performance, learning, and development plans, and develops corporate diversity champions (executive and employee partners) who are able to share their personal knowledge and commitment to inclusion and accessibility throughout the organization.

The vast majority of program participants surveyed in 2011–12 said that their participation in the program had an impact on how they think, act, and make decisions, and that they believed that diversity mentorship would have an impact on the organizational culture of the OPS.

The program's success includes executive partners who report gaining a better understanding of their employee partners' experiences in the workplace and the systemic organizational barriers they may be facing.

For example, according to Cynthia Morton, deputy minister in the Ministry of Labour, "Conversations with my mentees allowed me to hear about and see aspects of the OPS that I was not aware of . . . my mentees were dedicated to public service despite the challenges they faced."

Employee partners also report an increase in their understanding of organizational culture and how to better navigate a large public sector organization with greater confidence. According to Jennifer Wong, a staff member who participated in the program and is now a member of the executive board of the alumni association, "I found the Mentoring Partnership Program to be rewarding . . . the program provided me with the opportunity to meet a diverse group of people striving to succeed within the OPS. I believe the program has created an environment of belonging and inclusiveness within the OPS community."

Given the feedback from program participants, it is clear that the OPS has made significant progress toward behavioral and cultural transformation, and has the commitment to do much more.

PART TWO

IMPLEMENTING HUMAN EQUITY

Chapter 4

HUMAN CAPITAL AND THE DIFFERENTIATION OF TALENT

In this chapter we seek to describe the importance of human capital and how it serves as the basis for human equity. We will show that the differentiation of talent allows for the practice of human equity by optimizing on all available human capital. Just as there is a relationship between capital and equity in the financial world, there is a similar relationship between human capital and human equity in the world of human resources.

HUMAN CAPITAL: FROM HUMAN RESOURCES TO HUMAN EQUITY

From Human Resources to Human Equity

Human Resources	Human Capital	Human Equity
☐ Programs	☐ People	☐ Optimize human capital through a diversity lens
☐ Policies	☐ Skills	☐ Positive psychology approach to people management
☐ Leadership	☐ Intangibles	☐ Talent differentiation through a diversity lens
	☐ Knowledge	

The first time I heard the term human equity was in 2001 when my firm started work in South Africa for Coca-Cola. At that time the South

African government had instituted its version of legislated equity to combat the effects of apartheid. The employment equity legislation was designed to right the wrongs of apartheid and impacted every employer, including Coca-Cola. But Coke decided it wanted to go beyond the requirements of the legislation and move toward linking its equity initiatives to a business case.

The Coke South Africa business unit eventually won an internal award for its overall business results. In fact, it won this award two years in a row, which was unprecedented in the history of the Coca-Cola Company. As the Coke South Africa president, Doug Jackson, received the award, he remarked that half the company's progress was due to what it was doing in the area of human equity. When Jackson first spoke the words "human equity" I think he actually meant "employment equity"; nevertheless, the phrase struck me. As soon as he said it I knew intuitively that there was something called human equity, even though I didn't know what it was. I knew human equity was not human resources but it was not until I came to understand human capital that I could explain it.

To understand human equity, it is important to first distinguish between human resources and human capital. These terms are frequently used interchangeably but they are not the same. In brief, human resources can be seen as the programs, policies and leadership of the employees in an organization. By and large, in most organizations, human resources is the organization's biggest cost. The primary activities of human resources are designed to manage and control this cost.

Human capital is different in that people are not seen as a cost but rather as an investment or asset. Human capital seeks to look at the skills, knowledge and intangibles inherent in the human resources. Human equity builds on this idea of seeing people as assets, and focuses on optimizing human capital. Just as there is a relationship between capital and equity in the financial world there is a relationship between human equity and human capital.

I remember my first introduction to human capital. I met a man by the name of Joe who gave me his business card. His title was director of human capital. He asked me if I knew what human capital was. I admitted that I didn't but my guess was it was the latest euphemism for human resources. He smiled and said that if I had 30 minutes he would explain the differences between human resources and human capital. I figured 30 minutes to learn something new was well worth the time. When I walked out of his office half an hour later I understood that human capital was so much more than just looking at the cost management of people. Human capital looked at the skills, experience and intangibles that people brought to the world of work.

One of the early leading human capital thinkers is a Nobel Prize–winning economist by the name of Theodore Schultz. Schultz wrote a persuasive essay in the *American Economic Review* in 1961 called "Investment in Human Capital." In this essay he postulated that "human capital comprises all the intangible assets that people bring to their jobs that they trade for financial and other rewards."

What did he mean by "intangible assets"? Not too long after reading this essay, I heard a story about the New York Life insurance company. Apparently it had been looking for a new CEO. One candidate promised the board that if he were chosen as the new CEO he would double the company's insurance premiums in less than five years. The board asked how he planned to do that, as that would be a feat unprecedented in the insurance industry. His answer was, "Hire me and I will show you."

They did hire him and his first executive act was to set up a meeting with the human resources department. He asked the HR reps to provide him with the files of the best insurance salespeople in the company—the ones who had sold more than $1 million worth of insurance every year for at least the past five years. He told them to do whatever they needed to do to find this group of outstanding salespeople.

The group scoured the sales files and found some 100 individuals who met the criteria.

"What do you want us to do now?" they asked the CEO.

"I want you to dissect them," he replied. "This group has something that our other salespeople don't have. There is a golden thread that runs through all of them, an intangible that is common among all of them. Use your human resources tools to find it."

The HR group went to work. They took the hallowed group through every psychological and competency test they could find, tests like the Myers-Briggs, FIRO-B, Kolbe A, B and C, the Flow State Scale, the Personal Growth Initiative Scale, the Seligman Optimism Test, the StrengthsFinder, the DISC, the Schwartz Value Survey and the NEO Personality Inventory. After months of testing they set up another meeting with the CEO to share the results.

"We have good news and bad news," they announced. "The good news is we think we have found your golden thread. You were absolutely right: all of these 100 high-performance salespeople have this trait, regardless of whether they have been here two months or 22 years."

"Okay, so what is the bad news?" the CEO asked.

"The bad news is you are unlikely to find it in potential hirings, and for two very good reasons. Reason one, it is hidden. It is not something that we have ever thought of, so we have never put it on a job description or succession plan. Reason two is that it is transparent—these people don't even notice that they have it. It's so natural to them that they don't put it on their resume or cover letter. They just assume everybody has it." But, the HR group concluded, if you look hard enough, you can find it.

The trait they were referring to is optimism. Apparently, in the insurance world, a salesperson can face up to 50 hang-ups before they land one confirmed meeting. These 100 salespeople faced this type of rejection every day and still woke up each morning believing they would sell that day. These were individuals whose outlook on failure was that what happened was an unlucky situation (not personal) and really just a setback (not permanent) for this particular situation, but not for all their goals (not pervasive). One of the tests the HR group had administered was the Seligman Optimism test. These folks had rated way above the norm on optimism. The company incorporated optimism as a core competency in its job description for insurance salespeople and doubled its premiums in less than three years.

It is unlikely that any of these salespeople ever took a college course on optimism. It is also unlikely that they learned it on the job. Optimism is one example of the intangibles that Schultz was referring to. It may be innate or come from social conditioning, but every one of this high-performance group brought it to work every day.

The new CEO understood that the complete definition of talent goes beyond the "tangible" information that shows up in most resumes, i.e., credentials and technical experience. He was pushing the HR department to go and find the intangibles, which requires a bit more work. The work they did to identify this trait is an example of human capital. The ability to optimize on this trait and use it to contribute to the success of the organization is an example of human equity. If human capital consists of all the intangible assets people bring to the workplace, human equity is about optimizing on all the intangible assets that people bring to the workplace.

Some leaders have an innate ability to spot intangible assets. They recognize that what is truly special and unique about an individual is probably not related to the school they went to, the degree they acquired or the technical skills they have built by way of experience. What makes them different is related to their innate strengths, their passions, their attitude toward work, their personality, their unique life experience and their virtues.

We call these intangible traits SHAPE V, which is an acronym that stands for strengths, heart, attitude, personality, experience and virtue. In Chapter 6 details the SHAPE V Talent Model and describe effective tools that can be used to identify the intangibles. The SHAPE V Talent Model is an important element of human equity and how to optimize on available human capital. As with the example above with the insurance company, it takes a bit more work to identify these intangibles, but it is well worth the effort, especially in today's business environment.

What is driving the need to move beyond human resources to human capital and human equity can be broken into three areas:

1. The need to attract high potential talent in an increasingly competitive labor market.
2. The need to retain top talent in an increasingly competitive labor market.

3. The need to engage top talent at a time when more than 40 percent of employees are somewhat or completely disengaged.

Now we can see that this is really what the focus of human equity is about—discovering the multitude of variations that make everyone unique. When compared to the old paradigm of diversity we see how trite and superficial it is to reduce human conversations to differences based merely on skin color, gender, sexual orientation, etc. As discussed earlier, these characteristics may inform but they do not define an individual.

As discussed in Chapter 2, it's time to advance the conversation to the next level. It is time to move beyond the group conversation inherent in diversity toward the talent differentiation conversations of human equity—a concept that focuses on maximizing the diverse talents of your total workforce. Here talents encompass the combination of intangibles such as innate abilities, personality, unique life experiences, virtues and values. These are the things that truly differentiate one person from another, not just skin color, gender, sexual orientation, etc. We will see that because of the relatively new field of positive psychology (discussed below) we now have specific tools to help identify the intangible traits within employees and apply them in the world of work. These tools are used in the SHAPE V Talent Model and ground the human equity discussion.

We are now at a critical juncture in the human management journey. Leaders and managers alike are asking the same question: What do we do next? The answer is to move the dialogue beyond the group to the individual. Maximize on the intangible and unique talents of each member of your workforce. Move toward human equity—where the unique differences of each individual can contribute to a sustainable competitive advantage.

HUMAN EQUITY AND POSITIVE PSYCHOLOGY

Another piece of the puzzle in the journey to discovering human equity was realizing the link between human equity and positive psychology. In the nineties the Gallup organization sought out the answer to the question: "What do the world's greatest managers do differently?" Their extensive research surveyed more than one million employees and 80,000 managers in more than 400 organizations globally. This research, the largest study of its kind ever conducted, identified great managers as those with the best sales, profit and customer satisfaction scores, the lowest turnover and the best employee engagement scores. It went on to identify what the secrets of these managers were. As the study reported:

> Great managers present no sweeping new theories, no prefabri-cated formulae. All they can offer you are insights into the nature of talent and into their secrets for turning talent into lasting performance . . . Their path demands discipline, focus, trust and perhaps the most important a willingness to individualize because everyone is different.[1]

One of the key findings of the Gallup study was that great managers played to an employee's strengths while managing around his or her weaknesses. I remember first hearing this finding and thinking about my 30 years in the corporate world. I thought about the various managers I worked for in several different organizations. How many operated this way? I could think of only one. I'll call him Jim, even though I will never forget his real name.

Jim was an unlikely candidate as a manager within the buttoned-down world of banking. He wore an earring, which was out of the box in the 1980s. He would exclaim enthusiastically, "You're a wonderful person!" whenever you did something he appreciated. He had a bit of a dual personality, taking on a very anti-establishment identity by night as a rock-and-roll singer for a passable garage band. In many ways his stage persona reminded me of Mick Jagger. Having said that, when he came to the world of work he was pleasant, level-headed and responsible.

---

1. Marcus Buckingham and Curt Coffman, *First, Break All the Rules: What the World's Greatest Managers Do Differently* (New York: Simon & Schuster, 1999), 12.

In my years in the corporate world I had come to hate the annual performance evaluation. For me it was an hour in which the manager would spend 55 minutes pointing out my weaknesses (or, using the corporate speak, "identifying my challenges") and using the last five minutes to acknowledge something positive, which would justify an average merit increase in salary. I found the process a real pain for both the person being evaluated and the manager providing the feedback. Except with Jim.

I remember walking into one annual performance evaluation where Jim spent a full 50 minutes waxing eloquent on all the things I had done well. He pointed to every success and accomplishment over the past year. Every few minutes I would glance at my watch waiting for the real performance evaluation to start. After about 50 minutes, I was truly feeling like a king. I got up, put on my jacket and prepared to leave. I was so exhilarated but also confused by the unorthodox evaluation. As I got ready to leave, Jim added, "Oh, by the way, you really suck at math."

Now I had gone through four years of university trying to avoid a statistics course, even though it was a requirement for my degree. Why? Because I suck at math. I had barely passed tenth-grade math and had committed to never taking another math course. Why? Because I suck at math. I had taken math courses that the bank offered and had failed most of them. Why? Because I suck at math. In other words, Jim was not telling me anything I did not know. But he pointed out that every year I had to make a presentation to the department that included a lot of math. "You are pretty good at the presentation," he said, "you are just lousy at the math. Now your workmate Judy is great at math. How about we team you with Judy for this presentation. We will make you accountable for the final presentation but Judy is responsible for the math." I thought this guy was a genius. And I danced out of the performance evaluation knowing I would never have to do math again in that job.

It was more than a decade later that I read Marcus Buckingham's book based on his research for Gallup, *First, Break All the Rules*. I realized that Jim is one of those rare managers who plays to his employees' strengths and manages around their weaknesses. Jim could easily have recommended or even mandated that I take another math course, expecting a different result (demonstrating Einstein's definition of insanity). Instead, he chose to team me with someone who was great in the area where I was weak. His individualized approach to management led to the creation of superior results using the combined power of a team. Instead of attempting to fix my weaknesses and change me, he worked around my weakness, played to my strength and changed the job.

The experience with Jim hints at an interesting design flaw of our current management model: it is deficit-based. Since the Second World War, the traditional model of management has been based on the premise that there is something missing in the employee, something that needs to be fixed. In a deficit model of management, the job of the manager is to figure out what is wrong and provide guidance, counsel and support to fix this deficit. There should be little surprise that the prevailing model of management is deficit-based because it is based on the prevailing approach to human psychology.

Recall the discussion in Chapter I about the results of an academic literature review done by Dr. Martin Seligman in the late 1990s. Seligman found many thousands of psychology articles that focused on anger, anxiety and depression, but comparatively few articles on joy, life satisfaction or happiness. The psychological establishment, he demonstrated, reflected a deficit-based orientation.

This is not to say that deficit-based psychology has been without benefits. Over the past 50 years deficit-based psychology has influenced our understanding of hundreds of human pathologies. As Seligman points out:

> . . . unprecedented strides have been made in understanding, treating and preventing psychological disorders . . . there now exist effective treatments, psychological and pharmacological, for more than a dozen disorders that in the recent past were frighteningly intractable. But there has been a cost to this emphasis. Scientific psychology has neglected the study of what can go right with people, i.e., we have a disease model of human nature which is imbalanced and based on the assumption that human

beings are inherently fragile and flawed . . . Positive psychology proposes that it is time to correct this imbalance and to challenge the pervasive assumptions of the disease model. Positive psychology calls for as much focus on strength as on weakness, as much interest in building the best things in life as in repairing the worst and as much attention to fulfilling the lives of healthy people as to healing the wounds of the distressed.[2]

In short, Seligman's challenge was to ask his psychological colleagues what would it take to move people from zero to plus 200. His question was, "What if we could use psychology to bring people to Maslow's highest order of needs, that is, self-actualization?"

Thousands of psychologists responded with an overwhelming yes, and the science of positive psychology was born. Positive psychology is not to be confused with positive thinking, which is the pursuit of happiness without the science. Positive psychology seeks to study basic human values such as happiness, engagement, motivation, joy, laughter, mindfulness and other esoteric human values previously thought to be unmeasurable.

To attest to its fast-growing popularity we need only look to Harvard. The first positive psychology course at Harvard was taught by Dr. Tal Ben-Shahar in 2002. Eight students registered and two dropped out before the course was complete. Within five years the course had grown to the largest class at Harvard with almost 1,000 students enrolled. Positive Psychology had replaced Economics 101 as the number one course at the prestigious school.

I took my first positive psychology course online in 2008, with more than 5,000 people around the world; it was taught by Dr. Ben-Shahar. Like many others, I sincerely feel it is something needed and wanted in the world of management and in the Western way of life.

---

2. Christopher M. Peterson and Martin E. P. Seligman, "Positive Organizational Studies: Lessons from Positive Psychology," in Kim S. Cameron, Jane E. Dutton and Robert E. Quinn, eds., *Positive Organizational Scholarship: Foundations of a New Discipline* (San Francisco: Berrett-Koehler Publishers Inc., 2003), 14.

Why is positive psychology so needed today? In the United States today, rates of depression are 10 times higher than they were in the sixties. The average age for the onset of depression is half of what it was in 1960 (14 versus 29). And this is not just the case for the United States. Over half the British population said they were very happy in 1957 compared to just 36 percent in 2005, and this is despite the fact that wealth had tripled in the UK over the past 50 years. As Mihaly Csikszentmihalyi, another pioneer of positive psychology, asks, "If we are so rich, why aren't we happy?"[3]

Things are not much better in the world of work. According to Aon's global survey, employee engagement, the Holy Grail of the corporate world, has been virtually flat for the past three years, with a whopping 42 percent of employees somewhat or completely disengaged. This has led to higher rates of job stress, lower productivity and, as we see in recent headlines, increased anger and workplace violence.

The next piece of the journey is to understand the link between positive psychology and how the most effective leaders deal with talent. The Gallup research summarized in *First, Break All the Rules* found a common theme among great managers regarding how they view people. The insight is: "People don't change that much. Don't waste time trying to put in what was left out. Try to draw out what was left in."[4] This insight runs counter to a management mindset that is built on the belief that people can learn to be competent at anything and each person's greatest room for growth is in his or her area of greatest weakness. The greatest managers believe that each person's talents and unique and enduring and opportunity for growth is not in fixing the weakness but in developing or refining the unique strength. In other words, we are all great at something but no one is great at everything. Focus on what someone is good at.

If we take human equity's focus on optimizing talent, and put that together with positive psychology's focus on what is working, along with the research finding that great managers believe that talent is developed

---

3. Mihaly Csikszentmihalyi, "If we are so rich, why aren't we happy?" *American Psychologist* 54, no. 10 (1999): 821–827.
4. Buckingham and Coffman, *First, Break All the Rules*, 67.

by focusing on existing strengths, you then come to better understand the logic of an area called talent differentiation.

HUMAN EQUITY AND TALENT DIFFERENTIATION

> I am convinced that along with being the most efficient and effective way to run your company, talent differentiation also happens to be the fairest and kindest. Ultimately it makes winners out of everyone.
>
> —*Jack Welch* [5]

If we believe that human capital is about all the intangible assets that people bring to the world of work, and that there are 10 to the power of 2.5 billion possible combinations of human DNA available in 7 billion packages, then it follows that we are all created to do something different. Talent differentiation is the vehicle that great people leaders use to optimize on the intangible assets that each employee brings to the world of work. In other words, talent differentiation is how to move human capital to human equity. As the Jack Welch quotation above suggests, when talent differentiation is practiced properly, it can also be one of the most compassionate and effective forms of human resource management. Done properly, it is a key element of moving an organization toward optimizing on total human capital.

I remember the first time I had to fire someone. Helen had been my administrative assistant for as long as the company had been in business. She was loyal, hard working and always eager to please. As our company grew we knew that we needed to elevate the role of administrative assistant to the more senior role of executive assistant. This was much more than a title change; it meant an incredible shift in responsibility and autonomous work. In light of Helen's loyalty and positive attitude toward the company, we decided to give her the right of first refusal on the job. We

---

5. Jack Welch, *Winning: The Ultimate Business How-To Book* (London: HarperCollins, 2009), 38.

explained that she would have a three-month probation period to prove she could do it. After about two months it was clear to us that this was not the job for Helen and that the jump in responsibility was too much for her. Since we didn't have the budget to carry both positions, it meant that we would have to let Helen go.

Up until that point, I had never fired anyone. I dreaded the thought of firing someone I cared about as much as Helen. I called her into my office and told her I was going to give her an idea of what the new job would involve every day within five years. I went through the job description line by line and translated that into regular activities expected of the person who held the job. I wanted her to be clear on what each new responsibility would require of her going forward. After a 45-minute detailed description I said, "Now, Helen, based on what I have just told you, do you really want this job?"

She answered so quickly that I was a bit startled. "No!" she said emphatically.

"Okay," I said, "now we can work on finding the job that you do want." Members of our team worked with her to identify the things she was looking for in a job, reached out through our network and found her a job, one she still holds today.

It is not often that you hear the words "kind" and "fair" in the same sentence as the legendary, tough-minded neutron Jack Welch. But I do believe that what Welch, the former CEO of General Electric, was pointing to in the quotation above relates to Helen's story. I truly felt that every moment Helen was spending in the job of executive assistant was preventing her from getting to her real job, a job that was waiting for her elsewhere. As her manager, my role was to get her to see this and then let her go to find what it was she really wanted to do and could do better than most people.

The equitable leader knows that focusing on talent is one of the most important elements of moving an organization toward human equity. Optimizing the unique difference of each employee in the workforce requires an enhanced approach to talent differentiation. Talent differentiation was first advocated in the influential 1997 McKinsey & Company report, "The War for Talent." This groundbreaking report described the challenges faced by companies at that time, such as global political and economic risk, and increased competition to attract and retain talented people when the economy is growing and the natural workforce supply is on the decline. The report predicted an unprecedented war for talent that would force organizations to work harder at identifying and retaining their best performers. The only thing the report did not predict was the greatest economic crisis since the Depression. This economic downturn certainly slowed the war for talent, but there is no doubt that the demographic changes to the workforce continue to be relevant and will be more so as the economy improves. Progressive organizations look to get ahead of this inevitability by paying more strategic attention to their talent optimization strategies using talent differentiation.

HOW TO PRACTICE TALENT DIFFERENTIATION

Properly implemented, talent differentiation becomes a key element of an effective strategy to maximize on the potential of everyone in the workforce. It was practiced by Jack Welch at General Electric, and has been experimented with in many organizations. The difference in what we are advocating is talent differentiation *through a diversity lens*.

The Four Categories of Talent Differentiation

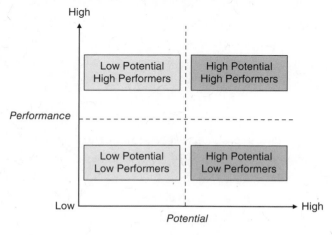

The talent differentiation chart provides an overview of how talent differentiation works. It starts by dividing the workforce into four distinct groups.

High Potential/High Performers

High potential/high performers represent approximately 10 percent of the workforce and contribute approximately 80 percent of the output. This relatively small group of employees are the ones who are extremely valued in the labor market when a recession ends. We sometimes refer to members in this group as the "clonables," i.e., if we were to ask leadership to name the people in their organization that they would clone if they could due to their impact on productivity, these would be the people they would name. They are clearly the cream of the crop as it relates to productivity and output, and they clearly have found the place to apply their unique abilities and strengths. Our experience shows that most managers spend the least amount of time with this group, seeing them as self-sufficient and requiring little management attention. This is a mistake (more on this in Chapter 5).

High Potential/Low Performers

High potential/low performers represent about 40 percent of the workforce. It is a very important group because it's the feeder group for the high potential/high performers. This is a group with the "right stuff" to lead the organization, but they are struggling with some issue, an issue that likely can be corrected through proper performance management, coaching or mentoring and a good accountability framework—for instance, they may need to improve in their budgeting or managing staff or meeting deadlines. The strategy for members of this group is to do whatever it takes to improve their performance so that they too can become high potential/high performers. If performance management is handled well, this group has the potential to become the next stars of the organization.

Low Potential/High Performers

Low potential/high performers are sometimes called the "Steady Eddies." They represent approximately 40 percent of the workforce. The individuals in this group are solid performers in their current positions but may lack the potential to grow beyond their existing level. For example, I may be a great salesperson, but I don't have what it takes to be a good sales manager. The contribution of this group to the organization is critical to the company's success because they are such important and impressive performers in their current positions. The challenge here is to find creative ways to reward their contribution in order to keep them engaged and motivated even though they are unlikely to receive future promotions. How do you continue to motivate when money serves as a relatively short-term incentive only? We will come to see that this can be done by turning to other levers, such as autonomy, mastery and purpose.

Low Potential/Low Performers

Low potential/low performers represent only about 10 percent of the workforce yet are a very significant group because they drain productive output, frequently requiring management attention for the wrong reasons. In our experience, management spends too much time with these individuals by responding to the problems caused by their underperformance. This group requires the most attention from supervisors, human resources and, in extreme cases, legal counsel. This group should be acted on quickly because they poison the environment for the other, more productive, employees. Keep in mind, however, that when people are honestly trying to do a job with all the knowledge, skills and ability they have and still failing, it may simply be because they are in the wrong job. Your challenge is to help determine where they best fit. This is where human equity comes in. This best fit may be across the hall in another department, or across the country in another organization. Using the principle of optimizing talent, every low potential/low performer in one job has a job waiting for him or her where he or she will be a high potential/high performer. Using the SHAPE V Talent Model in Chapter 6 can help determine where that fit is.

For talent differentiation to work, managers must understand how to best utilize the natural strengths and talents of their employees. However, talent differentiation starts with a thorough assessment of which group each employee falls into, followed by the crafting of the appropriate management strategy. In the next chapter we introduce a detailed talent management tool that outlines the types of discussions to have around each group to create a better fit in the workplace to maximize on each employee's potential. Each box in the talent management tool offers a different management strategy. For example those high potential/low performers require a focused performance management plan over a set period of time. A different management strategy is required for low potential/high performers, who will be developed into training others on the area where they excel.

The next chapter explores a case study of talent differentiation in action. We will look more closely at implementing how to practice talent differentiation through a diversity lens. It is meant to demonstrate how to practice talent differentiation by conducting a talent differentiation analysis of each employee using the SHAPE V Talent Model, explored in Chapter 6.

Chapter 5
TALENT DIFFERENTIATION IN ACTION

Human equity adds another component to talent differentiation in that it is practiced through a diversity lens. When talent differentiation was first introduced, this distinction about the diversity of talent was not considered. Let me explain.

As we described in Chapter 3, internal quantitative representation numbers can reflect an organization's ability to attract and retain the best talent. Typically, however, in an effectively designed diversity program, they serve as signals. For example, if your recruiters continually bring in talent from only one demographic group, or only one demographic group continues to be promoted in the organization, this should be a signal to you. Likewise, if all your high potential/high performers always show up as white males over the age of 45, this should be a signal that something is wrong with your talent differentiation strategy. And if all your low potential/low performers are Chinese women in wheelchairs then that should be a signal that your talent differentiation strategy is broken.

Talent is distributed throughout the workforce population regardless of gender, race, culture, sexual orientation, etc. If you are doing a good job of attracting and developing the best talent, you should see some diversity in the workforce population and some diversity in the boxes of the talent management tool. If you are recruiting in an area that is, say, 40 percent people of color and 30 percent Muslim, and all your high potential/high performers are white, Christian males, it is likely there is some form of bias in your recruitment and talent management process. This doesn't mean all your recruiters and managers are racists; it simply means there is some form of attitudinal or systemic bias in the recruitment and development process.

A few years ago, I was struck by the huge security team at Denver International Airport. There must have been more than 200 people doing security at some 20 inspection stations. As I waited in line, I noticed that almost everybody doing security was African–American, whether man or woman. I asked myself, in light of the demographic composition of Denver and in light of the knowledge, skills and abilities needed to do an airport security job, what is the likelihood that the talent to do this job will always show up in an African–American skin bag? The airport authority must be missing talent.

Looking at talent through a diversity lens is what human equity brings to the discussion of talent differentiation. It allows an organization to check to see if it is reaching all the available talent internally and externally by checking the demographic diversity of the boxes in the talent management tool.

The following case study examines an organization that practiced talent differentiation from a human equity perspective.

CASE STUDY: DYNAMIC INDUSTRIAL COMPANY PRACTICES TALENT DIFFERENTIATION

Dynamic Industrial Company operates cleaning programs for large automotive manufacturers. The company operates in more than 150 different locations throughout Canada, the United States and Mexico, with several thousand employees and 400 managers.

In 2005 Dynamic found itself in a crisis and its operating model had to change. Before that time each of the company's 150-plus sites could operate autonomously. However, their customers were starting to integrate their sites and centralize their processes. Dynamic needed to adapt quickly and follow suit by systematizing their operations.

Dynamic faced a huge cultural shift. Its 15 years of success had been built upon a culture where each site operated in competition with each other, in silos. Its future would rely upon its ability to have each of the sites work in concert with each other and in a more uniform way.

This also required shifting the way the company had dealt with people. While the organization had a formal human resources department with human resources managers in each location, its approach to people could hardly be called strategic. The VPHR was not even invited to the regular executive meetings unless there was a human resources crisis. In most of the business units the HR department was a glorified personnel department that handled payroll, picnics and pensions. Most of the HR managers were not trained professionals and in many cases were the wives of the business unit manager. (I say wives rather than spouses because all the business unit managers were males and almost 90 percent were white and over the age of 45. They could have all come from the same family. To say diversity was not Dynamic's strong suit would be an understatement.)

The CEO's idea was to shift their strategy around people. He started to call it a talent differentiation strategy. He wanted to get a better idea of the talent they already had and what the existing talent could contribute to the coming change within Dynamic. He reached out to his VPHR to help him design this talent strategy. He was a bit taken aback by the enthusiastic response of the VP, who had been trying to explain concepts such as human capital, talent differentiation and talent reviews to the CEO and the executive for years. However, without the burning need for change these ideas had previously fallen on deaf ears. The CEO asked the VPHR to draw up a talent differentiation strategy.

(continued)

The Talent Differentiation Strategy

The Talent Differentiation Strategy started with a comprehensive assessment of each business unit from a business and talent perspective. The idea was to dedicate a full day per business unit to have a rigorous debate about the people in each group. This was unprecedented in the company and an incredible investment of time for the CEO. The plan was for the CEO and the VPHR to go to each unit and spend a day talking about the overall strengths of their talent pool in the various areas. The CEO would lead each meeting and the conclusions for each business unit would be rolled up to a division level to get an overall perspective of the organization. The idea was for these reviews to identify both current as well as future leaders, i.e., those who may have been overlooked in the haphazard talent process up until then. The initial focus was on the 400 manager positions within Dynamic and their feeder positions.

The next piece of the strategy was to have a rigorous debate about each person, which required the CEO to acknowledge that all of his employees were not equal. Even though he held it that most of his employees were committed hard workers, he had to accept that some contributed more than others to the impact and results within the organization. The strategy called for the creation of four groups.

Group 1: Those who consistently delivered superior results and whose performance served to inspire and motivate others. The VPHR referred to these as the "clonables," i.e., if it were possible, this would be the group to clone throughout the organization to maximize on overall business results. Although this group represented a relatively small population within Dynamic, they would be key to the upcoming business transformation.

Group 2: Those who were solid performers who may have been meeting expectations but were still underperforming in some way. This group had the right stuff to make it to Group 1, but might be stymied by limited upward mobility or a lack of direction from a development perspective.

Group 3: Those who could be relied on to deliver acceptable and maybe superior results in a particular area but could not be relied on to create something bold or innovative. These were some of the most reliable workers in the organization who were well suited to their existing positions but were not the ones who would lead the change to come.

Group 4: These were the underperforming managers in the company and everyone knew it. Dynamic had a paternalistic corporate culture, a culture that protected this group. The CEO was proud of the fact that Dynamic had not downsized during the most recent economic recession and had treated its people as "family." This had protected a group of managers who had worked exceptionally hard during their time with the company, and some who had been strong performers in the past but who had not kept up with the pace of change and certainly did not have the skills for the upcoming change.

This idea of differentiating people by groups was the toughest piece for the CEO, who felt it was not his place to judge any person. However, the VPHR invited the CEO to see this in the same way they embraced annual performance reviews, which had become a mainstay of the Dynamic culture. Although the talent differentiation process would be more public, it really was about being transparent about performance within the organization.

In order to accomplish the talent differentiation strategy properly, other people would need to be invited into the debate. In some cases the review of talent would include the business unit managers and the promising Group 1 from lower levels in the organization. The executive would spend a full day on each business unit and segment the talent using a tool the VPHR called the Talent Management Tool (see diagram).

(*continued*)

Talent Management Tool

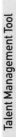

Potential	Performance: 1 – Best of Class	2 – Good Overall Performance	3 – Needs Improvement	4 – Unsatisfactory
1	**Top Talent** ★ — Exceeds performance expectations. Has great deal of potential for the future. Should be developed and challenged in a bigger role **1**	**Talent** ● — Demonstrates high potential and consistently good performance. Should be able to increase performance level **2**	Demonstrates high potential but is underperforming. Is role right? Do they need mentoring or other development? **3**	◆ Demonstrates high potential but is seriously underperforming. Immediate 60 – 90 day action plan to improve performance **4**
	Talent Producers ▢ — Exceeds performance expectations. Demonstrates potential to develop into a limited number of roles. Strong contributor. Retain and motivate **5**	**Contributors** △ — Consistently good performer with potential to develop into limited number of larger roles. Keep motivated to perform even better **6**	Some limited potential but underperforming. Needs to improve performance before considering development. Needs to improve performance in order for potential to be confirmed **7**	◆ Some potential for progression, but is significantly underperforming. Immediate 60 – 90 day action plan to improve performance **8**
6	**Talent Experts** ● — Exceeds performance expectations. Has reached full potential in current business context. Use to develop and train others **9**	**Experts/Specialists** ✚ — Consistently good performer with low potential to develop in current business context. Should be kept motivated to perform even better **10**	◆ Reached full potential and is underperforming. Immediate performance management plan. If no improvement, manage out of current position **11**	◆ No leadership behaviors exhibited and seriously underperforming. Manage out of current position **12**

Performance

4 – Unsatisfactory   3 – Needs Improvement   2 – Good Overall Performance   1 – Best of Class

Potential Rating Legend

- ★ Top Talent
- ▢ Talent Producers
- ● Talent
- ● Talent Experts
- △ Contributors
- ✚ Experts/Specialists
- ◆ Placement Issue
- ✹ Too New

Group I candidates were identified as top talent. The strategy was to invest highly in this group. In order for someone to be considered part of this group there had to be no doubt about their impact on company performance. The decision to invest in this group meant doing whatever it took to keep them engaged and inspired to stay with the organization. This would mean spending more time with these individuals to help them shape their careers by providing customized developmental opportunities that built on their strengths. There was also a discussion about who could mentor these individuals, not only to help them develop but also to help resolve any problems that might cause these individuals to leave the organization. The idea was to help Group I candidates find assignments that would stretch their abilities and make them feel appreciated, recognized and valued for their unique contributions.

One of the biggest changes for Dynamic was the suggestion that, besides giving the top talent group better and faster development opportunities, they should also get paid more. Dynamic had a traditional philosophy of paying every person doing the same job the same salary. The VPHR was proposing that Group I candidates be paid relative to the value they brought to the organization. There was some fear in shifting to this new model, but it was recognized that differentiating developmental opportunities for top talent would not be enough to keep these high performers as external demand for talent increased. The truth was that, until this talent differentiation exercise, Dynamic had taken this group for granted, and if more attention was not paid to them they would eventually leave. In fact, the VPHR conjectured that many high performers in the past had left without knowing how highly regarded they were by the company's leadership.

(continued)

Group 2 candidates were identified as talent. These individuals certainly had the potential to move to Group 1 but had room for improvement with their performance. The overall strategy was to grow and develop this group by increasing their capabilities and consistently affirming their accomplishments. The idea was to encourage them and, by using a more frequent performance management assessment process, see if their performance was improving. This group included those who had exhibited high potential but were seriously underperforming in their present position. The plan for this group would consider the possibility of moving them to another role better suited to their skills and abilities.

One of the innovative suggestions for the talent differentiation strategy was to utilize a positive psychology approach to improve performance by identifying those areas that could be delegated to others on their team. This meant that for both Group 1 and Group 2 the areas where they did not show excellent performance could be removed from their jobs and delegated to others who had shown capability in this area. This added to the overall intention to motivate and inspire the solid contributors and demonstrated that the organization was being attentive to their individual needs. It also played to the distinctive strengths of the individuals who were clearly high potential but working at lower levels of performance.

Group 3 candidates fell into four categories: the talent producers who were the strongest contributors in the role they were currently in, but who did not quite demonstrate the potential to move beyond; the contributors who had consistently provided good overall performance in their existing role, but who were unlikely to move into more influential leadership positions; the talent experts who had exhibited excellent performance but had reached their potential as it related to leadership, and yet who could be an excellent resource for mentoring and training; and finally the experts (a subset of this group) who had also reached their full potential, but who were providing consistently good performance and could be used to specialize in their areas.

The challenge for the Group 3 candidates would be to keep them motivated even though they were unlikely to see the career progression opportunities or lucrative salary increases of Group 1 and Group 2. The VPHR turned to some research in the area of human motivation for the answer. He came to realize that there are other "levers" of motivation beyond the so-called hygienic factors of salary and promotion.

In his excellent book *Drive: The Surprising Truth About What Motivates Us*, Daniel Pink advocates a more effective way to motivate employees than the typical carrot-and-stick approach of management. According to Pink, whose book summarizes the work of occupational psychologists over a number of years, understanding and utilizing the human need for autonomy, mastery and purpose is a better way to motivate a workforce.

Steve Jobs once spoke in an interview about autonomy at Apple. He proudly explained that there are zero committees at Apple, and that one person is responsible for each major task in the organization. People rely on that person to deliver on that task. He believed that this created a collaborative atmosphere and "a system based on trust and responsibility." As long as the employee is cognizant of the results expected, he or she can be left to figure out how to produce them. As Pink says, "Perhaps it's time to toss the very word 'management' into the linguistic ash heap alongside 'icebox' and 'horseless carriage.' This era doesn't call for better management. It calls for a renaissance of self-direction."[1]

(continued)

---

1. Daniel Pink, *Drive: The Surprising Truth About What Motivates Us* (New York: Penguin Group, 2009), 92.

Dynamic realized that increased autonomy could be a very effective tool for Group 3 individuals. These were individuals who had proven they were more than capable of doing their existing job, and one of the psychic rewards that could be used to retain them was increased autonomy. This can be shown by giving them more room to make decisions and openly sharing more information about the business so that their decisions are more fully informed. It was believed that as long as they were paid well for their contribution, the increased autonomy would impact advantageously on their future motivation.

According to Pink, mastery is the second effective motivator for this group. He cites Harvard professor Teresa Amabile's description of mastery as "the desire to do something because you find it deeply satisfying and personally challenging and[it] inspires the highest levels of creativity, whether it's in the arts, sciences or business."[2]

Over a decade ago I was introduced to the concept of "unique ability," which originated with entrepreneurial coach Dan Sullivan. Sullivan took us through an exercise where we systemically identified our level of ability for a variety of activities, using one of four descriptors: incompetent, competent, excellent and unique ability. I quickly identified that I was incompetent at any activity related to numbers. No real surprise, given that I am a bit dyslexic. On the other hand, I found I loved anything related to speaking and was frequently told it was one of my unique abilities.

Sullivan explained that unique ability refers to a set of talents that we have been developing all our lives. According to Sullivan, when you identify people's unique ability and allow them to work with that ability, they exhibit superior skill, energy, never-ending improvement and, most important, passion. When we practice

2. Pink, *Drive*, 116.

our unique ability we enter the psychological state that positive psychology pioneer Mihaly Csikszentmihalyi calls "flow," or "optimal experience." Some people never find their unique ability; in fact, most people never even find something they feel they are very good at—which may be why almost 75 percent of workers feel disengaged at work.

The VPHR at Dynamic believed that many of the Group 3 individuals were spending some of their time on activities where they were practicing their unique abilities. One of the ways to increase the psychic income and motivation was to help them identify their unique abilities and rearrange their jobs so they could spend even more of their time doing those things they are great at and love to do. This is similar to the situation I described in Chapter 4, in which my manager rearranged my job to reduce the amount of time I spent doing math and increase the amount of time I spent on public speaking. This meant reassigning tasks at which these high performers were less competent and in which they found less enjoyment, and teaming them with others who had complementary areas of competence.

The last group was Group 4. This group included individuals who were underperforming or seriously underperforming and did not show the potential for future growth. In light of Dynamic's past paternalistic culture, it was hard to accept the VPHR's recommendation that they act decisively on this group to move them out of their existing positions. Once again the VPHR recommended that these discussions be approached from a positive psychology perspective, where the belief is that every moment people spend in a low potential/low performance role is keeping them from the high potential/high performance job waiting for them somewhere else, either within or outside the company.

(continued)

The VPHR argued that when members of Group 4 were kept in leadership positions, there were direct and indirect costs to the organization. The VPHR cited research from people who had worked for underperforming bosses where people reported that the situation prevented them from developing, learning and making a bigger contribution to the bottom line of the organization. It also increased their likelihood of wanting to leave the organization, something referred to in the research literature as "intention to turnover." The research also found that bosses who fall into Group 4 are less likely to develop their subordinates, are unlikely to serve as good role models or coaches and are not likely to boost the morale of their staff. These are critical factors to making the talent differentiation strategy work.

The CEO agreed with much of the VPHR's analysis but still struggled with the idea of taking decisive action on Group 4. He wondered if it was fair and humane, especially in light of the unstable economic climate. He thought about his employees' families and how moving the employees out of their current positions could impact on their longer term careers.

The VPHR helped the CEO overcome these ethical issues by showing him that if he did not make the tough decisions on this group of people, who may be preventing Dynamic from becoming successful, then he could be putting the thousands of other employees at risk by not making this change.

The CEO pushed back on the VPHR to have the most rigorous discussions about Group 4. He wanted to ensure that the Group 4 people could not be developed for future roles. He began to wonder why they had not moved on low performers in the past. He decided to ask his leadership team. In these discussions he came to realize that almost everyone in Dynamic's leadership wanted the company to do something about low performers but they never had. There were plenty of excuses.

Some said they weren't sure enough to provide an informed judgment about the Group 4 individuals. Some admitted to being fearful about criticizing others, which would expose them to the same level of assessment. Many thought that any person could be developed, which flew in the face of the opinion of some of the most successful managers in the organization. Others felt the lack of action was simply due to the fear of litigation or fear of not being able to find a better replacement. However, one of the most frequent reasons for inaction on the low performers was an entitlement mentality. In other words, Dynamic had been unwilling to fire or demote people who had contributed to the company and met expectations in the past. Thus the Group 4 individuals had been in their positions for many years and had demonstrated loyalty to the company.

The VPHR suggested two ways to deal with the Group 4 individuals. The first was to allow the underperformers ample time to improve their performance after providing candid feedback and targeted coaching support. If the Group 4 individuals did not adequately respond, then the organization would develop a transition plan for a compassionate exit. Dynamic needed to avoid a mistake frequently seen in organizations, i.e., shunting the low performers to other jobs within the company. It is much easier to simply "dump" a low performer in another department, even if he or she is likely to struggle there as well. The most effective approach to performance issues is to deal with them when they arise.

The other option suggested was to move an underperformer (especially one who was once a high performer) back a level or to a lateral position. The hope was that these underperformers could become successful again if they found a job more appropriate to their skill and talent level. It is conceivable that if low performers

(*continued*)

are working hard at their position and still underperforming, they are simply in the wrong role. These are lose–lose situations, for the organization and the individual. The individual loses because his or her life is probably unhappy, and the organization loses because it has an unproductive worker.

Once the talent segmentation was completed the next phase of the Talent Differentiation Strategy was to create action plans for each individual reviewed. The objective of the action plan was to ensure that there were actual consequences coming out of the talent differentiation discussions. This did not mean a lengthy development plan for each individual, but the action plan would capture three to five agreed-upon actions that would be immediate next steps. Some examples of typical action plan items could include recognizing the contribution of a Group 1 individual and providing a 20 percent salary increase, assigning a mentor/coach to a Group 2 individual, providing a job-shadowing mentee to a Group 3 individual, and creating a three-month exit strategy for a Group 4 member.

The next step in the Talent Differentiation Strategy was to write action plans for the business units based on the assessment of the unit's overall talent strength. This would include a discussion about each function within the business unit, including an assessment of what talent issues could be holding the unit back. It would also include an assessment of how well or poorly the unit was doing regarding recruiting, developing and retaining top performers, and how well the unit was doing in acting on underperformers. This was also where the issue of diversity would be tackled.

As stated, diversity within Dynamic had not previously been a topic of discussion. Now, the VPHR began to look at talent differentiation through a diversity lens. This allowed Dynamic to use representation and retention numbers as a signal to see if its business units were reaching all available talent internally and externally by checking the demographic diversity of the boxes in the talent management tool.

Each business unit plan included an agreed-upon set of actions the business unit would take to strengthen its talent pool over the coming year. These actions included a summary of actions that resulted from the individual assessments, e.g., replace five Group 4 employees. The business unit plans also included actions to be taken on broader issues such as developing new recruiting strategies to improve diversity. The business unit plans were meant to be no more than five pages, which included a list of specific actions the business unit would take to improve on identified weaknesses.

Accountability and Follow-Up

The final step in the Talent Differentiation Strategy was a framework to hold leaders accountable for delivering on the business unit action plans. Each leader would be asked to assess his or her performance against the plan on a quarterly basis and at the end of the year. Each business unit would annually determine if its talent pool was significantly stronger, how well it had moved on underperformers and whether unwanted attrition had improved.

In the VPHR's strategy, accountability also meant having consequences for those who did not deliver on the action plans. This required some form of mechanism for follow-up, including formal follow-up meetings as part of the company's quarterly operating review. Dynamic created a Performance Map Process through which each leader was assessed to ensure consistency of performance.

Performance Map Process

THE RESULT

The result of all this intervention was that Dynamic was able to make the huge cultural shift it needed: after 15 years of working as separate entities, its sites began to work in concert and talent was strategically positioned in the organization. By breaking down the silos among its sites, Dynamic began to look at the full human capital it had available and worked to optimize on all available talent. Managers were encouraged to spend most of their time with their Group 1 employees and act decisively on their Group 4 employees. They spent their development time for Group 2 using development tools that maximized on the employees' strengths, unique abilities and even personalities. (These tools will be discussed in more detail in the next chapter.)

The Dynamic case demonstrates talent differentiation at work. In the next chapter we will examine some of the tools that are required to bring talent differentiation to life.

Chapter 6
THE SHAPE OF TALENT

We need someone who is genetically programmed to recognize and avoid serious risks, including those never before encountered. Temperament, independent thinking, emotional stability and a keen understanding of both human and institutional behavior are also important. I've seen a lot of very educated people who have lacked these virtues.

—Warren Buffett[1]

Earlier in this book I wrote that if diversity is to evolve to human equity—that is, optimizing on all the tangible and intangible assets people bring to the world of work—we need to move beyond a group focus to the individual. Among those "intangibles," we could list a person's attitude, his or her life experiences, and virtues such as optimism (remember the story of the New York Life insurance salespeople?). In this chapter we take a deeper look at these intangibles and how to measure them.

For many years the corporate world has relied on two proxies to measure individual talent. The first is credentials, which provide a convenient estimate of the facts a person has mastered or the knowledge an individual possesses. The second is a person's technical skills, which are usually assessed by previous work experience. For example, if a person

---

1. "Warren Buffett tackles the tricky question of succession," *Telegraph*, May 5, 2012.

has prepared a budget in one organization, it is a pretty safe bet he or she can do it in another. The overlap between the "right" credentials and the "right" skills has become the standard way to identify the best candidates for recruitment or promotion. But could there be more?

In his groundbreaking book, *Good to Great*, Jim Collins notes:

> In a good-to-great transformation, people are not your most important asset. The right people are. In determining "the right people," the good-to-great companies place greater weight on character attributes than on specific educational background, practical skills, specialized knowledge or work experience ... One good-to-great executive said that his best hiring decisions often came from people with no industry or business experience.[2]

There truly is nothing new about this perspective. In fact, to some, it is just common sense. But while it may be common sense, it is far from common practice. There are, however, a few legendary leaders who did not just talk about the importance of recognizing great talent but actually practiced it. One such leader is Jack Welch, the former CEO of General Electric.

Apparently Welch was obsessed with finding the best talent, and he would look long and hard to find it, sometimes even conducting reference checks himself on people applying for relatively junior management positions. The surprised HR people receiving his calls would ask why he was doing a reference check on someone this junior. "Don't you have an HR department that does this?" they would ask. "Yes," he would reply, "but I am looking for something." "What are you looking for?" "I can't tell you," he would respond.

What he meant was that he was looking for something intangible. It was not something he could put into words, it was a *je ne sais quoi*. He knew it when he saw it and knew it when he heard it. He would ask the referral source to simply describe what the candidate was like at work—how they acted, their work ethic, their attitude. He was interested in

---

2. Jim Collins, *Good to Great: Why Some Companies Make the Leap ... and Others Don't* (New York: HarperCollins Publishers, 2001), 64.

things that were not covered in the candidate's resume. If his personal reference check unearthed some information about the candidate that was of interest to him, he would interview the candidate himself. After this interview, if he still thought the candidate had the indefinable "it" factor, he would hire the person and immediately put him or her on a developmental path to an executive position.

The epigraph that opens this chapter reflects what Warren Buffett believes would be the most important traits of his eventual successor. He was looking beyond educational qualifications and technical skills; the traits he was searching for could not be learned in school or acquired through years of experience. As he says, they are "genetically programmed" into some people.

THE SHAPE V TALENT MODEL

What was it that Buffett, Welch and other legendary people leaders know and see about talent that the rest of us may miss? The SHAPE V Talent Model can help us answer this.

The SHAPE V Talent Model®

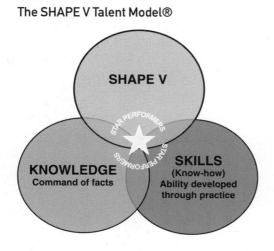

The model consists of three elements: required knowledge and/ or credentials, required practical and/or technical skills and the various intangibles of SHAPE V (discussed below). In the past we have relied on the overlap between knowledge and skills to identify the best candidate for the job. The SHAPE V Talent Model adds another element, what we have been calling the intangibles, that is, those things that are so unique to each person that it would be impossible to replicate them anywhere else. Finding and using these intangible traits is one of the prime objectives of human equity. This model seeks to put into words what great people leaders intuitively perceive about high potential talent. It puts a label on the intangible attributes so that other people leaders can also begin looking for these traits.

What Shape Does Talent Take?

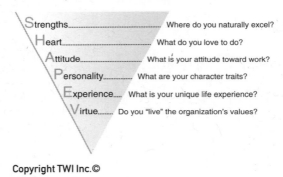

Strengths................................... Where do you naturally excel?

Heart.. What do you love to do?

Attitude.................................... What is your attitude toward work?

Personality................ What are your character traits?

Experience..... What is your unique life experience?

Virtue........ Do you "live" the organization's values?

Copyright TWI Inc.©

"S" for Strengths

"S" stands for strengths. Marcus Buckingham and Donald O. Clifton describe strengths in their 2001 book *Now, Discover Your Strengths,* which came out of the 1999 Gallup StrengthsFinder research. According to this work, strengths are described as "consistent near-perfect perform-ance in an activity."[3] Strengths-based work has come into vogue since the advent of positive psychology. It is based on the importance of lever-aging personal and individual strengths. Gallup identified 34 qualities in employees that make them successful in a Western workplace. As such,

---

3. Marcus Buckingham and Donald O. Clifton, *Now, Discover Your Strengths* (New York: Free Press, 2001), 25.

Gallup's strengths are not technical skills that show up in the bottom right circle on the SHAPE V diagram. Strengths can be innate and, unlike skills, are not learned. For example, one of my strengths according to the StrengthsFinder assessment is connectedness. It is the ability to see connections between things and bring together previously unassociated ideas. I have never done a course or program to learn how to do it, and even though I rely on this strength I have no idea where it came from.

The primary question to ask when looking at a person's strengths is: "Where do you naturally excel?" Strengths are things that seem to come naturally, not requiring a great deal of effort. They are the various qualities about you that make you successful in the workplace. For example, according to the StrengthsFinder assessment I have a strength called communication. The definition in my StrengthsFinder report states, "You like to explain, to describe, to speak in public and to write." How I describe this strength is that I am a storyteller. Somewhere I heard that the best communicators are storytellers and it allows them to get their point across and leave a lasting impression on people. Once again I did not learn this in a course; I have learned it by way of practice and using it continuously in the world of work.

There are several tools available to help someone identify his or her strengths. Some of the best known are the Clifton StrengthsFinder 2.0, Realize 2, Strengthscope and StrengthsQuest. These tools help to focus in on a person's strengths, which is the first step in the SHAPE V Talent Model. It begins to shed some light on who a person really is, beyond the knowledge and skills that show up on a resume. Allowing people to identify and explore their strengths can help them apply those strengths more in their work, helping them be more effective and fulfilled in their day-to-day activities.

"H" for Heart

The "H" in "SHAPE" stands for heart—the passion people have for certain activities. This area is well described in the book *Unique Ability* by Catherine Nomura, based on an idea espoused by entrepreneurial coach

Dan Sullivan. Sullivan describes unique ability as "a set of habits and talents that you have been developing all your life. Over time, you have had the opportunity to apply these talents to many different situations. When you feel most successful, you are combining these special talents with your intelligence and applying them to what you really care about."[4] In short, the "H" area represents an activity that you so love to do (i.e., have a passion for) that you would do it even if you were not paid to and that you are so good at that you are in the top 5 percent of people who can do it as well as you. In fact, you are probably not good, but great.

This area is also related to the concept of flow, which originated with Mihaly Csikszentmihalyi. Flow is described as "optimal experience" or the psychological state that people enter when they are doing an activity they so love that time seems to pass without noticing. In 1996 the Flow State Scale was created to measure this state of optimal experience. Since its creation, flow has been extensively studied in positive psychology.

I first identified my "H" areas using the Unique Ability exercise created by Dan Sullivan and featured in the book *Unique Ability*. The tool allowed me to identify those activities in my life that I love to do and am actually great at. It also allowed me to identify activities I hate to perform and at which I am incompetent. After completing the exercise, I was surprised to see how little time I was spending on those activities that I loved to do and felt I had superior ability in. Identifying these areas allowed me to restructure my work and delegate my incompetent activities to those who could perform them better than me.

I noticed when I was completing the Unique Ability exercise that it was fairly easy for me to identify my incompetent areas, that is, those things I hate to do and am awful at, but not as easy to identify those areas I love and am great at. I think this is because we are sometimes reluctant to say we are great at anything. One way to identify your unique ability is to ask others who may know you. They may be able to spot the activities that you excel at more objectively. Keep in mind, however, that only you will be able to tell if you truly love these activities.

---

4. Cited in Catherine Nomura, *Unique Ability* (Toronto: The Strategic Coach, Inc., 2009), 28.

I remember explaining the concept of unique ability to my mother and asked her what she thought her unique ability was. "Cooking," she responded quickly. I was stunned. I knew my mother was one of the best cooks I had ever met but never realized that she actually loved it. When I realized that was her unique ability it allowed me to better understand the thousands of hours she spent in the kitchen preparing meals with a level of vigor and care rarely witnessed.

Understanding a person's unique ability provides a much more accurate picture of who a person is, beyond his or her credentials and technical skills.

"A" for Attitude

In the positive psychology literature there is a whole branch of research dedicated to what is called "flourishing at work." The focus is on how to boost motivation and performance in individuals to generate improved overall employee engagement. Much of the research suggests that an employee's attitude toward his or her work impacts on his or her ability to flourish. The hypothesis is that there are three attitudes toward work. First, there are individuals who approach their work as a job. As such, they are generally working for the financial rewards of their regular paycheck. The second attitude relates to individuals who approach their work from a career perspective. They take a bigger picture than the biweekly paycheck and may view advancement as their most important reward. Finally, there are those who view their work as a calling. These are individuals who have an even wider perspective on their work and link it to some kind of meaning or legacy. For example, I know a lawyer who clearly does not work just for the money. He is a litigator and when you watch him work it is evident that he is driven to correct a past wrong. He demonstrates more than a technical competency for the law; he makes the practice of law into an art form. It is a pleasure to watch him at work.

Uncovering a person's real attitude toward work can be a bit tricky. There are many politically correct ways to have a conversation about attitude. In the past I have tested a person's attitude toward work by asking and testing some specific questions such as the following. (I'll use only the male pronoun to keep things simple, but of course the same questions could also be asked of a woman.)

- Does he take personal responsibility for adapting to change or blame external conditions?
- Is he fully committed to his work?
- Is he a drag or an enabler for change?
- Does he take personal responsibility for the direction he takes?
- Does he behave as though he is the owner of this business?
- Does he take personal responsibility to continuing education and building his career?
- Does he hold himself accountable for outcomes?
- Does he seek to add value and contribute more than he costs?
- Does he seek to deliver the highest quality service possible?
- Does he manage his own morale?
- Does he practice continuous improvement?
- Is he a fixer or a finger-pointer?

Once again, understanding a prospective employee's attitude toward his work will be far more instructive than knowing the tangible assets of his education and technical skills.

"P" for Personality

In 2009, almost $500 million was spent on personality testing in North America. There are well over 2,500 personality questionnaires on the market, and each year dozens of new companies appear with their own "new" products. Some of these products are broad-spectrum tests designed to classify basic personality types, some are designed to test candidates for suitability for a particular job and some are designed to test for particular traits—for example, honesty and integrity.

One of the most popular personality tests is the Myers-Briggs Type Indicator (MBTI). The MBTI was originally developed in the 1940s by Katharine Cook Briggs and her daughter, Isabel Briggs Myers, who thought that an understanding of personality preferences would help women who were entering the workforce for the first time identify the sort of wartime jobs that would suit them best. By the early 1960s, the initial questionnaire had become refined into the MBTI.

While the MBTI is one of the more popular tests, it turns out not to be one of the most reliable or a good predictor of job/talent fit. One of the more reliable personality tests is the Kolbe, which divides people into four basic personality types: fact finders, follow throughs, quick starts and implementers. When I took this test I learned I was a 9 out of 10 in the quick start category. This meant I had an innate need to generate ideas and would look at things at the 100,000-foot level. My project manager turned out to be a 9 out of 10 in the fact finder category, which meant she had an innate need for detail and analysis. While I always knew the two of us were different, this added piece of information about our personalities enabled me to understand *where* we were different. It also allowed me to quantify how different we really were. It allowed me to make space for her obsession with detail and her desire to analyze everything, thus reducing the number of conflicts we had. I came to understand that while I was wired to approach life from a ready-go-set paradigm, she approached it from a ready, ready, ready, set, set, set and then go perspective. After I read her Kolbe profile it gave me space to better understand how she approached her work.

I truly believe that understanding an individual's personality can provide more profound information about that person than the usual tangible talent metrics of education and technical skills.

"E" for Experience

The "E" in the SHAPE V model stands for (life) experience. It is the area that incorporates elements of the old group focus of diversity. It can include, for instance, how my life experience as part of a racial minority could influence my life, or my experience as an immigrant, or as a spiritual person, a parent, a Canadian, a baby boomer or whatever other group I may belong to. We all have unique life experiences that we bring to our work. Generally they are ignored, yet they can provide some amazing insight into the unique perspectives of an individual.

I think of my friend Gerry, who teaches positive psychology in two colleges. Gerry was born with less than 20 percent sight, making him legally blind. But his parents never treated him as someone who had a disability or "handicap." When he turned 15 years old, he wanted to get a part-time job just like his older brothers and sisters had done before him. His parents encouraged him to go ahead, even though they had some anxiety about the type of job he could get because of his sight. Eventually Gerry landed a job delivering newspapers overnight in one of the most dangerous neighborhoods in Detroit. He figured out a way to map out his route, got a bit of support occasionally from his brother (such as working the other side of the street) and successfully delivered the newspapers for more than two years.

Looking back, Gerry is sure that his parents sat up worrying most nights about his safety and probably waited until he returned home before they fell asleep. But because he didn't know he wasn't supposed to be able to do this job, he just figured it out (necessity being the mother of invention). When I hear Gerry relate this story, it tells me much more about what kind of worker he is than does the degree he has or his past jobs. It points to something about his courage, his persistence and his work ethic.

Life experience in SHAPE V is the trait that leads to the quality that is frequently referred to as "diversity of thought." Most fully sighted people have little idea what it is like to live as Gerry does (missing 80 percent of his sight) or as my mother (who is missing 98 percent of her sight) does. As such, they may not be able to understand what both of these people call the advantages of not being able to see. I remember being amazed by their belief that choosing what they see versus being informed by their eyes gives them a huge advantage when dealing with people. Talk about diversity of thought!

It is also important to remember that life experiences may inform who a person is, but none of them necessarily define a person. For example, the fact that I was brought up in a very poor household may not mean I am frugal with money; likewise, the fact that my son Alex is a millennial may not mean he is not loyal.[5]

In his book *Geeks and Geezers*, Warren Bennis observes that the majority of the most impressive leaders he has met have passed through a crucible that tested them to the depths of their being and empowered the successes they realized later in life.

> At some time in our respective journeys, we find ourselves in a crucible that really tests who we are. In this crucible you learn who you are and what you want to become. Without it, you cannot be certain how you will respond under extreme pressure and whether you will be true to your values. Having survived the crucible, you will know that indeed you can take on any challenge and come out of it a better person for the experience.[6]

We all have unique life experiences. We all have a story. Understanding this story can give insight to who a person really is. It can reveal the essence of who a person is, rather than what he or she has done. Many times the unique life experience comes from a defining moment in a person's life such as a critical illness, the loss of a job, a divorce or something else high on the trauma scale. The old adage that you may have no control over your life but you have total control of how you react to life is part of understanding this area. Gerry could have hidden behind his so-called disability and had a reasonable excuse not to work, or at least not to work hard. But when you listen to him tell his story, you realize fairly quickly that this is not a man who embraces a victim mindset.

A person's life experience can also give access to the final piece of the talent model represented by the final letter "V."

---

5. For more on the traits of different generational groups, see Ron Zemke, Claire Raines and Bob Filipczak, *Generations at Work: Managing the Clash of Veterans, Boomers, Xers, and Nexters in Your Workplace* (New York: AMACOM Books, 2000).

6. Warren Bennis, *Geeks and Geezers: How Eras, Values, and Defining Moments Shape Leaders* (Boston: Harvard Business Press, 2002), 95.

"V" for Virtue

> What do we need to flourish as human beings? We need to learn certain character traits like loyalty, self-control, courage and truthfulness. Aristotle called these traits "excellence," often translated as virtues.
>
> —*Barry Schwartz and Kenneth Sharpe*, Practical Wisdom[7]

"V" stands for virtue, not to be confused with a value. A value in action is a virtue. One of the best-known illustrations of this in the business world is the 1982 Tylenol crisis. Then-CEO of Johnson & Johnson James Burke enabled his company to respond quickly and responsibly to the deaths of several people from Tylenol caplets laced with cyanide. Although Johnson & Johnson bore no responsibility for the incidents, Burke's very open public response to pull all its product off the market until new packaging could be designed not only saved the brand, it wound up enhancing Johnson & Johnson's reputation as a responsible company.

Compare Burke's response with the virtues exhibited by Ken Lay, Bernie Ebbers and Dennis Kozlowski of Enron, WorldCom and Tyco respectively. These three executives alone destroyed more than $300 billion in shareholder value, yet they had been public proponents of business ethics and values.

A more recent example is the BP disaster in the Gulf of Mexico in 2010. The oil spill, called the largest accidental marine oil spill in the history of the petroleum industry, directly led to the death of 11 men and an estimated almost 5 million barrels of oil discharged into the Gulf over a period of three months virtually unabated. Two years after the disaster, BP and the U.S. Department of Justice reached a settlement of $4.5 billion in fines and other payments and BP pled guilty to 11 felony counts related to the deaths of the 11 workers. The Justice Department also filed criminal charges against three BP employees. On November 28, 2012, the

---

7. Barry Schwartz and Kenneth Sharpe, *Practical Wisdom: The Right Way to Do the Right Thing* (New York: Penguin, 2010), 7.

EPA announced that BP will be temporarily banned from seeking new contracts with the U.S. government because of the oil company's "lack of business integrity" during the Gulf of Mexico oil disaster.

Like many others who had gone before them, BP had always espoused the corporate values of ethics and integrity. The problem is they simply didn't practice what they preached. It turns out that values and virtues matter when it comes to predicting how an individual or organization will respond, especially when crisis hits.

In 1999 a major piece of research was conducted on leadership values and virtues with a group of psychologists led by Martin Seligman and Chris Peterson. This team of psychologists looked at the virtues valued in civilizations as long ago as 2,500 years, examining societies such as ancient Greece, but also tracing civilizations up to today and even researching organizations such as the Boy Scouts. The idea was to identify the enduring virtues that were valued by these various societies and organizations.

Then the researchers went around the world to identify the virtues that continue to be valued today. This research took a total of three years and is the most comprehensive research ever done in the area of human values and virtues.[8] The research identified six "buckets" of human values that, from a historical and global perspective, stand the test of time:

1. Wisdom and knowledge
2. Courage
3. Humanity
4. Justice
5. Temperance
6. Transcendence.

The six buckets of virtues show up in the world through various actions. It's one thing to talk about dignity and respect; it's another to

---

8. The work is documented in Seligman and Peterson's *Character Strengths and Virtues: A Handbook and Classification* (New York: Oxford University Press, 2004).

actually practice it. So the question is, what do wisdom and knowledge, courage and justice, etc., actually look like? How would we know when someone is practicing these values?

Seligman and Peterson's *Character Strengths and Virtues* categorizes these six overarching values into 24 character traits. Here are the formal definitions of the six values and their associated character traits, according to the handbook.

Wisdom and Knowledge

According to the research, the value of wisdom is not the same as intelligence, which means it cannot be measured by way of IQ. Wisdom is knowledge that has been hard fought and then used for good. Some call it noble intelligence. Aristotle referred to it as "practical wisdom." Wisdom is associated with the following character traits:

- Creativity: originality/ingenuity
- Curiosity: interest, openness to experience
- Judgment: critical thinking, open-minded
- Love of learning: mastering new skills and topics
- Perspective: wisdom, providing wise counsel.

Courage

According to the research, courage is defined as the capacity to overcome fear. There are three types of courage: physical, moral and psychological. Courage need not be a single act such as running into a burning building to rescue someone. It can be far more subtle, such as the willingness to intervene when someone is being mistreated. Think of Rosa Parks quietly refusing to give up her seat on the bus.

Courage shows up in the world through the following character traits:

- Bravery: not shrinking from fear, speaking up
- Perseverance: persistence, finishing what one starts
- Honesty: authenticity, integrity
- Zest: vitality, enthusiasm, energy.

Humanity
The value of humanity is defined as "improving another's welfare through interpersonal strengths, altruistic and pro-social behavior." Humanity includes a willingness to engage in acts of generosity, kindness and benevolence that elevate those who witness these acts.

Humanity is demonstrated through the character traits of:

- Kindness: generosity, compassion, nurturance
- Social intelligence: being aware of the motives/feelings of self and others
- Love: valuing close relations with others.

Justice
The value of justice relates to that which makes life fair. Justice translates to the notion of equity, including rewards being apportioned according to the contribution one makes. This virtue includes considerations of equality or perceived need within individuals. Justice is impersonal in nature, implies impartiality and is done for the sake of what is fair.

Justice can be found in someone who demonstrates the character strengths of:

- Teamwork: citizenship, loyalty, social responsibility
- Fairness: being just, not letting feelings bias decisions
- Leadership: organizing group activities, encouraging a group to get things done.

Temperance
The value of temperance can be summarized in the phrase "everything in moderation." Those who exhibit temperance demonstrate control over excess and self-restraint. Temperance is the practiced ability to monitor and manage one's emotions, motivation and behavior in the absence of outside help. The failure to demonstrate temperance can lead to personal and social problems such as alcoholism or problem gambling. From a business perspective, temperance (or lack of it) was certainly a relevant

factor in the examples of WorldCom, Enron and BP cited above. Temperance can be thought of as a form of self-denial.

Temperance can be demonstrated through the following character strengths:

- Forgiveness: mercy, accepting others' shortcomings
- Humility: modesty, letting one's accomplishments speak for themselves
- Prudence: careful, cautious, not taking undue risk
- Self-regulation: self-control, discipline.

Transcendence

The final value is transcendence, which is defined as "an overall connection to something higher in meaning and purpose beyond ourselves." It is that which is beyond human knowledge and sometimes understanding. This virtue reminds us that we are small in the grand scheme of things but not insignificant.

The character strengths associated with transcendence are:

- Appreciation of beauty and excellence: awe, wonder
- Gratitude: thankful for the good, feeling blessed
- Hope: optimism, future mindedness, future orientation
- Humor: playfulness, lightheartedness
- Spirituality: faith, purpose, a sense of meaning.

● ● ●

I first came across the classification of character strengths research a few years ago. It was featured in a course introducing an online measurement tool called the Values in Action survey (now called the VIA Inventory of Strengths). This survey was designed to allow participants to identify their top five character strengths. I had done other strengths-based surveys, but I was intrigued by the "Values in Action" moniker. When our firm had created the SHAPE V Talent Model years ago, it was used to help our clients better understand the intangibles referred to in the human capital definition. I identified the "V" as virtue, as opposed to value, after I had heard somewhere that a value in action was a virtue. However, at the time of creating SHAPE V we had no idea how to measure virtue. Needless to say, years later when I heard about a tool that could measure values in action, I immediately wanted to know more. It completed the SHAPE V Talent Model and has allowed us to measure an intangible trait that is difficult to perceive in an individual.

Over the years I ended up taking the VIA assessment at least three times. It turned out that one of my strongest character strengths, the one that repeatedly showed up in my results, was spirituality. Those who are closest to me know that my spiritual journey, which started more than 25 years ago, has been, up to now, a very private affair. It is something that I rarely mentioned in public presentations and certainly did not write about.

It occurred to me that if spirituality is one of my strongest character strengths, then not using it, usually for fear of people's reactions, was like going into a boxing match with my strongest arm tied behind my back. Since realizing this, I have slowly started to "come out of the closet" on this particular character strength. I can say without hesitation that understanding my spirituality will give you a much better understanding of who I am as a person, and is far more important than knowing my education and career path. Yet it would be difficult for someone to guess at my spirituality externally because I rarely exhibit any of the traits of a religious person. In fact, I often say that on most days I am anti-religious, even though I am deeply spiritual. The difference for me is that religion is about a relationship with some institution, with its accompanying rules and regulations, while spirituality is about a source beyond myself.

I shared this epiphany with Karen Milner, my prime contact for more than 15 years at John Wiley & Sons, and indicated that I didn't think I could write this book the way that I had written my first book, *Diversity at Work*. I explained that the first book was written with no reference to my spirituality, that it was pretty well a buttoned-down corporate treatise. There was no indication of my private spirituality or belief in a power beyond myself. I indicated that I didn't think I would be able to write the second book separated from my spiritual voice. I was shocked and pleasantly surprised when Karen supported this direction.

Perhaps the most important aspect of these 24 character strengths is that they can now be measured. In 2000, Martin Seligman, in partnership with Dr. Neal Mayerson, created the VIA Institute on Character. This institute oversees the research on the VIA Survey, which is the scientific tool that measures the 24 virtues. At this point the VIA Survey has been taken by almost one and a half million people globally. It can be used to help organizations put people in positions where they can best make use of their character strengths.

Research has shown that deploying one's character strengths at work is linked with greater work satisfaction, greater well-being and higher meaning in life. In fact, the two most important predictors of employee retention and satisfaction are reporting that you use your top strengths at work and reporting that your immediate supervisor recognizes your top strengths.

As we evolve our work in human equity and look to move beyond the group to the individual, the SHAPE V Talent Model will be a key practical tool in showing leaders and managers how to maximize on the unique differences of their entire workforce. The model can provide leaders with a template to position performance management, career development and succession planning. By adding the intangibles to the talent discussion, we may be very surprised about the shape talent actually takes.

One of the most interesting ways we have applied the measurement of virtues available through the VIA is with something called the Golden Thread analysis. It is based on the premise that just like education and technical experience, character also matters. Some would say that it matters more than a person's credentials or skill, but few would say it is irrelevant to finding and keeping "the best" candidate for a job. Allow me to explain how it works.

THE GOLDEN THREAD ANALYSIS

The Golden Thread analysis is based on the SHAPE V Talent Model. When applying the model, more than one SHAPE V tool could be used to identify an individual's intangible assets. Our firm has used it to identify core attributes of high potential/high performers in an organization in order to better align the organization's recruitment and selection process with identified best leader attributes. It also is key to improving the organization's processes, practices and competencies so that its leaders may effectively coach and mentor high potentials, providing the opportunities and experiences necessary to be successful to make it to the top.

This idea of a golden thread came to me about a decade ago when one of our clients decided they wanted to pursue a diversity outreach strategy. They had decided that instead of recruiting only those students at the Ivy League schools with the highest GPA, they would begin to include some graduates of the historically black colleges (HBC) in their employee search. They arrived at one of the colleges and attracted a large audience of curious soon-to-be graduates. Since both the school and the recruiters had no real history with each other, there were lots of questions raised about the fundamental way the organization operated.

One young man asked about getting to the top of the organization—what did it take?

"You mean to become a partner?" the recruiter asked, to clarify.

"Yes, if that is the top," the student responded.

"Well, you have to be a chartered accountant and have at least 10 years' experience on a major audit."

"Do you have anyone in your organization who is a chartered accountant, has more than 10 years' experience on a major audit but is not a partner?" the student asked.

"Of course," the recruiter answered. "Most people who work in our firm never become partner."

"Then it can't be that; there must be some other golden thread," the student countered.

A friend of mine who had been trying to make partner at this firm was watching the exchange. On recounting the story to me, she realized that the question the student had asked was also her question. She had no idea what it took to make it to the top of her organization. Was there a special course she needed to take, was there a secret handshake or someone special you needed to know? After more than seven years of working with the organization, she still did not know.

Fast-forward 10 years and the new vice president of HR in another professional service firm was concerned that their recruitment strategy was out of step with what they needed for future executive talent, especially in light of the new focus on revenue growth and business development. This firm's recruitment strategy was based on visiting the best schools and hiring those graduates with the highest GPA. The vice president wondered if the type of recruits that this process would produce was what the organization would need down the road to substantially increase its revenue.

We proposed a project designed to find out if the VPHR was right. We called the project the Golden Thread analysis, and designed it around the "V" in the SHAPE V Talent Model. The objective of the project was to identify core attributes of high potential/high performers within the organization in order to better align the recruitment and selection process with identified best-leader attributes from a knowledge, skills and character perspective.

The process started with a group of HR leaders, including the VP of HR, identifying those leaders in the organization referred to as the "clonables"—those individuals who were seen as superstars in the organization. They were called clonables because they were the ones the organization would clone if it could because they exhibited all the desirable traits one would want in a leader and had achieved exceptional business results. In short, these were the most successful leaders in the organization based on the metrics that were most important to the business at the time and for the foreseeable future. Each leader was provided with a pre-interview questionnaire based on the 24 VIA categories. The intention was to get these leaders thinking about what virtues really mattered in their journey to the top.

The next step was to interview these exceptional leaders. The interviews were designed to look at all three elements of the SHAPE V model—that is, required knowledge or credentials, required technical skills and virtues. Questions were asked about the comparative importance of GPA, technical skills, entrepreneurial mindset as well as character traits. Each leader was also asked who they thought were the most effective leaders within the organization and these were added to the interview list. After each interview, each leader was asked to complete the online VIA assessment. The assumption was that these leaders would exhibit the character traits they had identified in the pre-interview questionnaire and the interview itself.

Not surprisingly most of the leaders felt that the intangible areas represented by SHAPE V were far more important than knowledge and skills. One common response was that although you could add knowledge and skills if they were missing, it was unlikely you could add things like attitude or values. The other observation was that, when the interviews finally took place, most of the clonables spent much of the time talking about the character traits they felt were essential to being a good leader—traits such as confidence, hopefulness, optimism, resilience, transparency, ethics, future orientation and willingness to mentor others to become good leaders.

The final step in the process was to revisit the recruitment process to see how well it was working to identify these traits in potential job prospects. As noted in Chapter 10 in the discussion of the Equitable Leader Assessment, asking people to rate themselves in these areas may not result in accurate responses because of the level of hopefulness these people may have—that is, they rate themselves as they want others to see them. This is why the 360-degree component of the assessment—that is, a self-assessment along with assessment by one's colleagues at all levels of the company—is essential.

The information we gathered from this analysis was used to improve the organization's processes, practices and competencies, first, in the realignment of the selection criteria for campus and experienced hires. It was then also used to identify developmental gaps to enable high potential/high performers to be successful in their current and future roles by equipping people leaders and counselors with effective tools and resources to coach and mentor these individuals to reach their full potential.

Chapter 7

THE EIGHT CORE COMPETENCIES OF THE EQUITABLE LEADER

In 2002 one of our clients asked about the role of leadership in moving toward a Level 5 on the Equity Continuum. The core question was, "What are the characteristics and behaviors of an equitable leader?"

We turned to the Research Unit for Work and Productivity (RUWP), part of the Ivey School of Business at the University of Western Ontario, which had helped us "quantify" the Equity Continuum at the organizational level (see Chapter 9). The RUWP was a consulting group comprising graduate students and overseen by faculty in the Industrial/Organizational Psychology Department. The group was led by Dr. Julie Carswell. We went on to hire members of the Western team, including Dr. Carswell, who would continue to work on measuring the impact of leadership on moving toward a Level 5 on the continuum.

The research team started with the hypothesis that individuals, specifically leaders, play an important role in creating, supporting and sustaining an equitable and inclusive work environment. The group set out to develop a measure of equitable leadership, with the objective of identifying a series of leadership competencies that did just that.

Approaches to measuring equity and inclusion at the organizational level and linking it to leadership behavior were still in the infancy stages at the time. The team started with a thorough review of the literature and organizational best practices both locally and globally in order to identify leadership qualities that were linked to effective "diversity management," inclusion and "talent optimization."

One of the areas the researchers came across was the relatively new (1998) discipline of positive psychology, which sat in opposition to the traditional clinical psychology focus of what is wrong with people—that is, deficit-based psychology. The RUWP team argued that the existing management and leadership models taught for decades in business school were typically based on deficit-based psychology, including the commonly accepted models of Herzberg's Motivator/Hygiene concept, Skinner's Behavioral Modification, Management by Objectives and Frederick Winslow Taylor's classic Scientific Management. As such, the competencies and behaviors of leaders would have evolved from the prevailing belief about people postulated by deficit-focused organizational psychology.

The RUWP team reviewed hundreds of leadership competencies from private sector and public sector organizations to identify the prevailing traditional leadership competencies. The results of the review, shown in the figure below, identified characteristics of intelligence, interpersonal skills, charisma, ambition, energy, business knowledge and integrity. Having leaders who consistently demonstrated these competencies would lead to productive work environments that valued productivity, flexibility, tolerance, equality and learning.

Traditional Model of Leadership

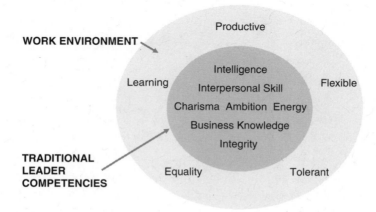

WORK ENVIRONMENT

Productive

Learning   Intelligence   Flexible
Interpersonal Skill
Charisma Ambition Energy
Business Knowledge
Integrity

TRADITIONAL
LEADER   Equality   Tolerant
COMPETENCIES

The RUWP team then turned its attention to the competencies that came out of a positive psychology paradigm. These characteristics would be used to create work environments that capitalize on individual strengths and the valuing of difference, and that are supportive and encouraging of equity and inclusion.

This process led to the identification of seven Equitable Leader Competencies: openness to difference, equitable opportunity, accommodation, dignity and respect, commitment to diversity and inclusion, knowledge of diversity and inclusion, and change management. Five years later, spurred on by huge, unprecedented corporate frauds, among them Enron, WorldCom and Tyco, an eighth competency was added: ethics and integrity. The eight competencies have come to be labeled the Equitable Leader Competencies. It should be noted that the research team was advocating that the Equitable Leader Competencies *build* on the traditional leader competencies, rather than simply replacing them.

The eight competencies are:

1. **Openness to Difference:** Demonstrating a positive attitude toward others who are different; actively seeking out opportunities to learn about cultures and lifestyles that are different from one's own.

2. **Equitable Opportunity:** Making employment decisions regarding team members (such as promotion, project staffing, development) on the basis of merit and skill.

3. **Accommodation:** Demonstrating creativity when solving problems and adaptability when responding to the needs of different employees.

4. **Dignity and Respect:** Creating a work environment that encourages open, transparent communication, and where the opinions and contributions of all team members are valued.

5. **Commitment to Diversity and Inclusion:** Enthusiastically endorsing and participating in programs to create and support diversity and inclusion in the workplace.

6. **Knowledge of Diversity and Inclusion:** Engaging in behaviors that reflect a general understanding of the meaning of "diversity

and inclusion" and demonstrating knowledge of best practices and relevant legislation related to diversity and inclusion.

7. **Change Management:** Contributing to the development of an organization that values diversity through the implementation of effective change management practices.

8. **Ethics and Integrity:** Embodying the principles of fair and ethical conduct and demonstrating honesty, reliability, responsibility and constancy in one's daily work life.

The RUWP team proposed an enhanced model of leadership that would move an organization along the Equity Continuum, as seen in the following figure.

Enhanced Model of Leadership

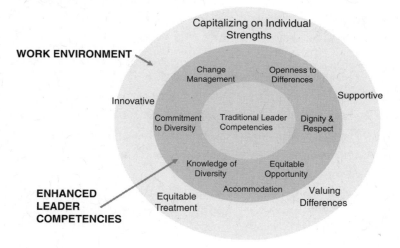

NOT ALL WHOPPERS ARE THE SAME: WEIGHTING THE CORE COMPETENCIES

Over the years we have come to understand that these eight competencies of the equitable leader are not equally weighted. I'll illustrate by borrowing from the fast-food menu of Burger King. Competencies such as openness to difference, accommodation and change management would qualify as "Whoppers." These are very important competencies for leaders to demonstrate if an organization looks to move toward a truly equitable and inclusive work environment for all. However, while these three competencies are necessary, they are not sufficient to really create long-term, sustainable change.

To guarantee real movement on the continuum, you need to upsize to the Double Whoppers with cheese and bacon—to the competencies that are the essence of equitable leadership. Our research shows that there are three such competencies.

The Three "Upsized" Competencies

1. Dignity and respect
2. Ethics and integrity
3. Equitable opportunity

Over the past decade our research has found that if leaders do not consistently demonstrate these three competencies, it is virtually impossible for an organization to move toward a Level 5 and human equity, where the skills and abilities of the total workforce can be optimized.

This leaves two other competencies, which I label the "Junior Whoppers": knowledge of diversity and inclusion, and commitment to diversity and inclusion. As I've said, when it comes to equitable leadership, actions speak louder than words. Leaders may speak eloquently of knowledge and commitment to diversity and inclusion but practice the previously mentioned dirty dozen boss-hole behaviors. Treating people as if they are invisible, using one's authority to threaten and intimidate, and frequently humiliating and shaming one's subordinates will cause far more damage to the workplace environment than any flawed policy or procedure. Over the past decade we have measured the impact of leadership behavior within organizations. This has led me to the conclusion that everything else you do to create more equitable and inclusive work environments can be nullified if leadership behavior is inconsistent with the vision of a Level 5.

The Three Groups of Leaders

While all organizations differ, we have found that there are three common groups of leaders within organizations. The highest 10 percent are represented in the first figure of this section, the lowest 10 percent are represented in the second figure and the average 80 percent are represented in the third figure.

The Highest 10 Percent of Leaders

The highest 10 percent are those leaders who continuously, sometimes naturally, exhibit behavior that will lead to an inclusive and equitable work environment. They typically mark themselves slightly higher than the average leader (bar 1 (self rating) compared with bar 3 (self norm)) in almost all eight areas. However, their colleagues typically rate them significantly higher than they score themselves (bar 2 compared with bar 1). But the most noteworthy finding is that this group's colleagues and direct reports typically rate them much higher than the norm (bar 2 compared with bar 4).

One interpretation of these results is that the top 10 percent think they are above average in the eight core competencies but know there is always room for growth. One leader asked, "Do you think anyone would ever be scored a 5 out of 5 on ethics and integrity or dignity and respect? Aren't these characteristics where continuous improvement applies, i.e., you never stop trying to improve?" It's a good point.

The fact that their colleagues have rated them so much higher than the norm could mean that there are things these individuals are doing naturally. We call this *unconscious competence.* This sometimes makes it difficult for them to explain to others what they are doing because they do it so naturally and make the assumption everyone operates like they do. I remember one man who was rated almost a perfect score by his colleagues on accommodation. While he had rated himself slightly above the norm, this was nowhere close to the score his colleagues gave him. He had no answers to the gap until I asked him about work and life balance. He admitted that a few years earlier he had had a major health scare because he was working exceptionally long hours without any kind of a break. His doctor had warned him that his demanding and relentless schedule

ELA Highest 20 Percent versus TWI Norm[1]

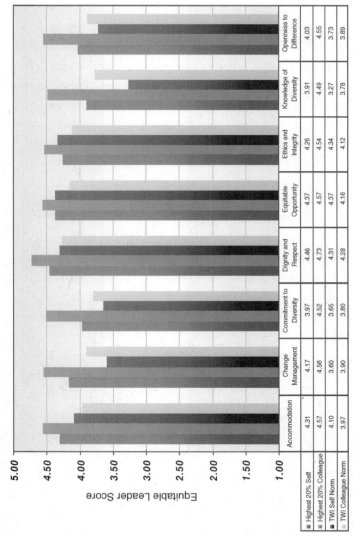

	Accommodation	Change Management	Commitment to Diversity	Dignity and Respect	Equitable Opportunity	Ethics and Integrity	Knowledge of Diversity	Openness to Difference
■ Highest 20% Self	4.31	4.17	3.97	4.46	4.37	4.26	3.91	4.03
■ Highest 20% Colleague	4.57	4.56	4.52	4.73	4.57	4.54	4.49	4.55
■ TWI Self Norm	4.10	3.60	3.65	4.31	4.37	4.34	3.27	3.73
■ TWI Colleague Norm	3.97	3.90	3.80	4.28	4.16	4.12	3.78	3.89

Equitable Leader Score (vertical axis, scale 1.00 to 5.00)

1. The 1 to 5 scale is both how the person rates themself as well as how they get rated by their colleagues. The self rating is Bar 1, the colleagues' rating is Bar 2, and Bar 3 is the TWI self norm, which includes over 1,500 leaders who have rated themselves on the ELA. A comparison between Bar 1 and Bar 3 allows us to gauge the leader's perception of their own behavior (i.e., above, below or around the normal perception). Bar 4 is the colleagues' norm, which represents over 7,000 colleagues who have rated their leader. A comparison between Bar 2 and Bar 4 allows for an assessment if the leader's behavior is above, below or at the norm. When a leader's colleagues score him or her significantly higher (i.e., 3 or more) than the colleagues' norm, this competency is identified as a high performing area.

was not sustainable and if he did not slow down, his body would do it for him. One day on an overseas business trip he had a heart attack and was taken to a foreign hospital where he spent several days. This short but impactful interruption to his busy life led to an epiphany that caused him to quit his workaholic lifestyle. A classic life-changing event.

He explained that when he sees members of his staff going down that workaholic road, he will step in and have a conversation with them about what really matters in life. Sometimes he will go as far as sending them home without their laptops or smartphones. He knows that in this age of technology a person can easily end up working 24 hours a day, seven days a week, unless they make a point of choosing not to. It was then that we both recognized the reason his staff had given him exceptionally high scores on accommodation.

The Lowest 10 Percent of Leaders

Whereas the highest 10 percent are sometimes known as unconsciously competent, the lowest 10 percent are sometimes known as *unconsciously incompetent*. This group includes the boss-holes introduced in Chapter 3, i.e., those who persistently leave others demeaned, disrespected and demotivated and who have a persistent pattern of contempt for those with less status and power.

One noteworthy observation of the lowest 10 percent is that they frequently give themselves perfect or near-perfect scores on the eight competencies, which is much higher than the way leaders typically rate themselves (bar 1 (self score) compared with bar 3 (self norm)). Another interesting observation is that their colleagues rate them much lower than they rate themselves (bar 2 compared with bar 1) and significantly lower than the average leader is rated by his or her respective colleagues (bar 2 (colleague score) compared with bar 4 (colleague norm)).

When asked why they rated themselves as high as they did, it's clear that leaders from this group sincerely feel that they continuously demonstrate these competencies. It is only after you share the behavior of the top 10 percent that they realize they may be overestimating their competency and may also have room for growth.

ELA Bottom 20 Percent versus TWI Norm[2]

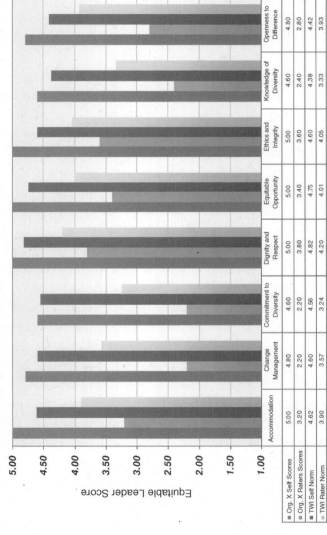

	Accommodation	Change Management	Commitment to Diversity	Dignity and Respect	Equitable Opportunity	Ethics and Integrity	Knowledge of Diversity	Openness to Difference
Org. X Self Scores	5.00	4.80	4.60	5.00	5.00	5.00	4.60	4.80
Org. X Raters Scores	3.20	2.20	2.20	3.80	3.40	3.60	2.40	2.80
TWI Self Norm	4.62	4.60	4.56	4.82	4.75	4.60	4.38	4.42
TWI Rater Norm	3.90	3.57	3.24	4.20	4.01	4.05	3.33	3.93

Equitable Leader Score

Copyright TWI Inc.©

2. When a leader's colleagues score him or her significantly lower than the colleague norm this competency is an area of opportunity.

Perhaps the most surprising observation we have about the bottom 10 percent is that their inequitable behavior is totally transparent to them: they have huge blind spots about how they treat people. As pointed out earlier, however, their behavior is very apparent to everyone who works for them. Our interpretation is that their high self-ratings are not caused by any level of dishonesty but rather by hopefulness. In other words, their rating of themselves is how they want people to rate them.

As also mentioned earlier, this leads to an interesting pattern, especially for those leaders in the organization with substantial institutional power. By the time a leader reaches an executive position in an organization, few people have the "permission" (and the courage) to tell them about their day-to-day behavior. Since they think their behavior is perfect, they don't perceive a problem, so their behavior continues unabated. Eventually people "vote with their feet" and leave the organization. Or in some cases, especially in current economic conditions, people "quit" but stay in their job.

One of the major benefits of identifying this lowest 10 percent is that an organization can begin to quantify how much this behavior is costing via soft costs such as psychic absenteeism, as well as hard costs such as replacement and outreach, time spent on complaints by supervisors, HR, legal counsel, overtime and lost or damaged client/customer/stakeholder relationships.

The Average 80 Percent of Leaders

Perhaps the best news after a decade of measuring the Equitable Leader Competencies is that between 60 and 80 percent of leaders are slightly above or below the average on these eight competencies. They also seem to have a fairly realistic grasp of how they are perceived by their coworkers, compared with the bottom 10 percent who are wearing rose-colored glasses. The "ELA Average Example" figure that follows shows a typical example of the average 80 percent in most organizations. We can see that the average leader in a typical organization marks themselves slightly higher than the norm (bar 1 (self score) compared with bar 3 (self norm)). And in most cases their colleagues rate these leaders at the norm (bar 2

ELA Average Example[3]

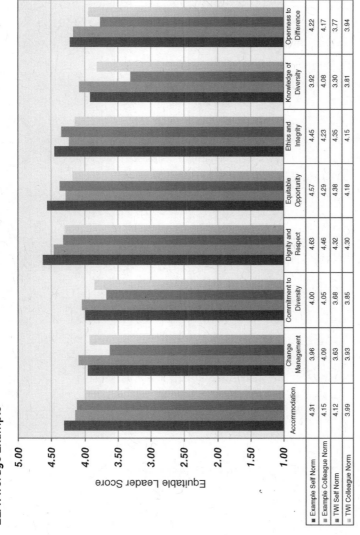

	Accommodation	Change Management	Commitment to Diversity	Dignity and Respect	Equitable Opportunity	Ethics and Integrity	Knowledge of Diversity	Openness to Difference
■ Example Self Norm	4.31	3.96	4.00	4.63	4.57	4.45	3.92	4.22
■ Example Colleague Norm	4.15	4.09	4.05	4.46	4.29	4.23	4.08	4.17
■ TWI Self Norm	4.12	3.63	3.68	4.32	4.38	4.35	3.30	3.77
■ TWI Colleague Norm	3.99	3.93	3.85	4.30	4.18	4.15	3.81	3.94

Copyright TWI Inc.©

---

3. When the leader's colleague norm is comparable to the external colleague norm, the competency is identified as an area for growth.

(colleague score) versus bar 4 (colleague norm)). In most cases their people also rate them a bit lower than the norm and in two cases higher than the norm (bar 2 versus bar 1). But even when there is a difference, it is not the type of gap witnessed with the lowest 10 percent, which would indicate some form of self-awareness blindness. In fact, in the case of openness to difference and commitment to diversity and inclusion, the average leader in this organization appears to have a very accurate self-assessment compared with the way they are seen in the world.

At the end of the chapter is a case study of an organization that has used the Equitable Leader Assessment for its top leaders. It will provide a description of how the instrument can be used to hold its leaders accountable for behavior that is consistent with the creation of an equitable and inclusive work environment.

Let us now take a closer look at the eight competencies, in order of importance, with the most important appearing first.

RANKING THE EIGHT CORE COMPETENCIES

1. Dignity and Respect

Dignity and respect together make up the most important of the Equitable Leader Competencies. Leaders who exhibit this competency are likely to create work environments that encourage open and transparent communication where the opinions and contributions of all team members are valued.

Our research indicates that the highest 10 percent leaders of this competency consistently:

- Foster open communication avenues, including forums for information sharing and for discussion of ideas and concerns.
- Acknowledge and recognize the efforts and accomplishments of coworkers.
- Address coworkers in an attentive and respectful manner.
- Provide constructive criticism along with problem solving, feedback and coaching to help employees hone their talent.

- Intervene or help employees facing difficulty or challenges arising from disrespectful workplace behavior.
- Recognize fellow employees as individuals and make an active effort to understand personal norms.
- Support individual goals and endeavors.
- Actively confront stereotyping, prejudice and discriminatory behavior.

In our years of measuring the Equitable Leader Competencies, it is apparent that, in general, leaders have a relatively good perspective on where they are on this competency. The current normative scores are made up of more than 1,000 leaders who have assessed themselves using the ELA Self-assessment tool and more than 5,000 colleagues who have assessed their leaders using the ELA Colleagues Assessment tool. This is the same assessment available by accessing the following website: www.equitableleader.com. You will receive a report that will allow you to assess your scores compared to the normative scores. (Turn to page 301 to see how you can save $100 on ELA Assessment Tools.)

In the area of dignity and respect, the current TWI self norm is 4.28 (bar 3), and the current TWI colleague norm is 4.28 (bar 4). This means that the average leader views herself in much the same way that her colleagues view her. This is good news because it is very difficult to instill this competency in a leader who is lacking it. As in the case with a couple of "Double Whoppers with cheese and bacon" competencies, teaching courses on dignity and respect, writing policies on dignity and behavior or adding this to a leadership competency list is unlikely to shift a person who does not already practice dignity and respect. Shifting behavior in this competency requires a structured coaching support program with a time-framed action plan for improvement. This coaching can also be approached from a positive psychology approach using tools such as the VIA Assessment mentioned in the previous chapter.

We will come to see that dignity and respect, like the other Double Whoppers with cheese and bacon, are based on character and moral skills, rather than technical skills and knowledge. We will also come to see that exhibiting this competency comes with practical wisdom, which is explored in Chapter 10.

Core competencies such as dignity and respect might be called "motherhood" competencies. This means they are such desirable traits that all leaders want to have them. As such, leaders tend to mark themselves quite high in the area and in at least 80 percent of cases they are correct in their ratings.

This is the case for all but the lowest 10 percent. In most cases, members of this group rate themselves significantly higher than their colleagues in dignity and respect. The lowest 10 percent rate themselves a 4.63, which is higher than the rating of 4.46 that the highest 10 percent of leaders gave themselves. However, colleagues rated the lowest 10 percent leaders 4.13 (lower than the norm). In contrast the colleagues rated the highest 10 percent an impressive 4.73, significantly above the norm of 4.28.

Lowest 10 Percent Behavior

The day-to-day behavior of the lowest 10 percent in the area of dignity and respect is predictable. These leaders frequently demonstrate behavior that is inconsistent with this core competency, such as rude interruptions, personal insults and distracted listening (e.g., checking a smartphone in the middle of a conversation). The lowest 10 percent also practice exclusive behavior, which can include incidents of discrimination, harassment and abuse of authority. More importantly these leaders ignore such behavior in the workplace and neglect to take action when they witness disrespectful workplace behavior, even though as directing minds of the organization they have a higher responsibility to act.

2. Ethics and Integrity

Ethics and integrity is the second most important equitable leader core competency. Leaders who exhibit this competency embody the principles of fair and ethical conduct and demonstrate honesty, reliability, responsibility and constancy in their daily work life.

The current self norm for ethics and integrity is 4.26, whereas the current colleague norm is 4.14. Using 0.3 as a statistically significant difference, this means that, as with the core competency of dignity and respect, the average leader views himself in much the same way his colleagues view him. Ethics and integrity is another "motherhood"-type competency that all leaders think they should have, so the self norms are some of the highest of the eight.

Our research indicates that the highest 10 percent leaders of this competency consistently:

- Take responsibility for their behaviors.
- Exhibit transparency in their actions, and communicate pertinent and important information to others.
- Are knowledgeable about their organization's ethical values and codes.
- Place a high value on the importance of principled and honorable conduct.
- Ensure consistency between their actions, behaviors and words.
- Act as a role model for standards of ethical behavior.
- Follow through on commitments made to others.
- Comport themselves according to the rules and guidelines for conduct set out for all persons.

Lowest 10 Percent Behavior
The lowest 10 percent behavior reflects leaders who are not open in their dealings with others and who do not provide people with relevant, accurate and reliable information. These are leaders who frequently do not honor their commitments to coworkers, clients or other business associates. They are also leaders who rarely consider the impact their actions will have on others.

Just think of the Enron, WorldCom and BP examples I mentioned in earlier chapters. The leaders of these organizations clearly did not take into account the consequences of their fraudulent behavior. Nevertheless, it is likely they would hold themselves champions of ethics and integrity. (Witness Ken Lay's August 2001 all-employees briefing on ethics and integrity.)

3. Equitable Opportunity

The third most important core competency (and the last of the "Double Whopper with cheese and bacon" competencies) is equitable opportunity. As stated, this competency is the ability to make employment decisions (e.g., promotion, placement on projects, development) on the basis of true merit and a comprehensive understanding of talent. The heart of this competency is the ability to practice rigorous talent differentiation (explained in chapters 4 to 6).

The current self norm for equitable opportunity, like the other two high priority competencies, is quite high at 4.36—higher, in fact, than any of the other eight self norms. The good news is that the colleague norm is also very high at 4.21, indicating that the average leader has a fairly good grasp of his or her behavior in this area.

Our research indicates that the highest 10 percent leaders of this competency consistently:

- Base employment decisions on objective criteria and a comprehensive definition of merit that moves beyond knowledge and technical skills.
- Ensure that training opportunities are designed to develop employee strengths rather than fix weakness.
- Ensure that team members have the opportunity to contribute by utilizing their SHAPE V talents.
- Use the SHAPE V Talent tools for recruitment, development and succession planning.
- Use a positive psychology approach to professional development and identification of career opportunities for employees.
- Provide team members with opportunities to work on assignments that will further develop their unique abilities.
- Practice rigorous talent differentiation strategies for the good of the organization and the employee.

Lowest 10 Percent Behavior

The lowest 10 percent in this category rate themselves much higher than average managers rate themselves (4.58), but their people rate them lower than the average manager is rated (3.78). The lowest performers in this category lack a comprehensive understanding of talent and what merit really looks like. They rarely practice talent differentiation, which means they could be ignoring some of their most valuable employees and spending their time on individuals who have already proven they are not right for a particular job. The lowest 10 percent are also likely to base employment decisions on subjective or biased criteria, such as favoritism, which may also lead to an inequitable distribution of assignments. Finally, the lowest 10 percent rarely provide high-potential employees with opportunities to work on assignments that challenge and develop their skills.

We now turn to the second most important set of Equitable Leader Competencies—the ones I refer to as "Whoppers." These are the competencies that are necessary but not sufficient to move an organization to the next level on the continuum.

4. Accommodation

Accommodation is the ability to balance the needs of the organization with the needs of the individual employee, and involves managing work and life balance issues. Leaders with high competency in this area exhibit creativity when solving problems and adaptability when responding to the needs of various employees. They are also much more likely to use technology to the fullest.

The highest 10 percent in accommodation consistently:

- Apply a problem-solving approach to create a win-win situation for employees and the organization.
- Exercise negotiation techniques to generate the best possible outcome.
- Adopt an open attitude toward testing new perspectives and approaches.
- Adapt their interaction style to be appropriate to the situation and/ or the individual.
- Actively seek out information and methods for the best way to accommodate the needs of employees.

- Possess a motivated and positive attitude—even when facing difficult challenges or delicate situations.
- Solicit information and inputs from other persons to derive solutions.

In the book *The Way We're Working Isn't Working*, author Tony Schwartz states:

> The all too common dynamic in today's workplace is parent-child. Most employers tell employees when to come to work, when to leave and how they're expected to work when they're in the office. Treated like children, many employees unconsciously adopt the role to which they've been consigned. Feeling disempowered and vulnerable, they lose the will and confidence to take real initiative or to think independently . . . The real measure of people's effectiveness in an organization ought to be based on the value they create, not the number of hours they work. That requires a relationship between consenting adults, grounded in trust, fueled by mutual responsibility and regulated by periodic accountability.[1]

I think of my two youngest children: Briana, 14, and James, 9. Neither has ever known a time when the Internet did not exist. For both of these young people the concept of time and space is vastly different from mine as a baby boomer. A friend recently told me about getting her 16 year old a summer job at her company. The job required her daughter to spend all day on the telephone making calls. After she had been briefed on the job she asked her new supervisor if she would be meeting any of the people on the floor in the office. Her supervisor answered no, she would be on the phone all day. The daughter then asked if she had to come into the office every day. When the supervisor answered yes, the girl asked why. The supervisor told her somewhat testily that it was her job.

---

1. Tony Schwartz, Jean Gomes and Catherine McCarthy, *The Way We're Working Isn't Working* (New York: Free Press, 2010), 228–229.

The daughter tried to explain to the supervisor that she was just making phone calls, which she could do from anywhere, including her family room at home. She further pointed out that it took her over two hours to commute to and from work every day—valuable phone time if she did the calls from home. As my friend recounted this amusing story, she confessed that she too was somewhat stymied coming up with a logical response to her daughter's questions. Her only answer was, "That's the way we have always done it."

Lowest 10 Percent Behavior

While the average leaders rate themselves almost exactly the way their colleagues rate them (both at approximately 4), the bottom 10 percent rate themselves much higher than the average leader. Needless to say, the lowest 10 percent are rated much lower by their colleagues than the average leader is rated (3.62 versus 4.00).

These lowest 10 percent fail to recognize that different people are motivated by different things. As such, they do not adapt their style of leadership to align with the motivations of their employees. Perhaps the most important failing of this group is that they do not demonstrate healthy work and life balance themselves, even if they advocate it. A classic case of what you do speaks so loudly . . .

While accommodation does not rank among the three most important competencies, it is still a very important area, particularly as technology becomes more and more sophisticated, allowing work to be done virtually from anywhere at any time. Leaders competent in accommodation have come to terms with the outdated notion of "face time," especially when it comes to what is known as knowledge work (as opposed to manual labor).

What leaders who are strong in accommodation seem to understand is that the industrial mindset arising from Taylor-ite factory efficiency designs (Frederick Winslow Taylor was a 19th-century pioneer of efficiency in manufacturing) is based on the belief that employees require hour-by-hour supervision. The assumption is that, without the supervisor, workers will slack off and work will not get done. It's a paradigm based on mistrust and the assumption of childlike irresponsibility. We will come to see that this deficit-based concept of management is inconsistent with the needs and wants of today's worker.

5. Change Management

Leaders who exhibit the core competency of change management use change management practices that are likely to create work environments that encourage open and transparent communication where the opinions and contributions of all team members are valued. Examples of change management include leaders who ensure that the issues of inclusion and human equity stay on the executive and leadership agenda. These are leaders who create systematic plans for change based on the identification of obstacles using an appreciative inquiry template.

Our research indicates that the highest 10 percent leaders of this competency consistently:

- Challenge the status quo and champion new human equity initiatives.
- Take steps to ensure that the organization is flexible and ready to respond to changing conditions.
- Ensure that the required systems, processes and structures are in place to support change initiatives.
- Involve their team in the change process by sharing information and obtaining feedback.
- Create action plans for change based on a positive psychology/ appreciative inquiry approach to organizational change.
- Encourage others to take personal responsibility to ensure that human equity goals are achieved.
- Monitor information about the progress of change efforts and adjust the strategy accordingly.

In terms of change management, the highest 10 percent rate themselves much higher than does the average manager: 4.17 versus 3.60.

Their colleagues rate them higher than they rate themselves and much higher than they rate the average leader: 4.56 versus 3.90.

The lowest 10 percent rate themselves 3.8, which is higher than the average manager, but their colleagues rate them 3.48, much lower than the rating of 3.9 for the average manager.

Lowest 10 Percent Behavior
The lowest 10 percent frequently are a source of resistance to equity and inclusiveness initiatives. They generally stick with so-called tried and true approaches to work, and rarely demonstrate leadership commitment and cooperation with inclusion and human equity change initiatives.

6. Openness to Difference

Openness to difference often falls into the "necessary but not sufficient" category of core competencies. This competency is the ability to demonstrate a positive attitude toward others who are different from oneself, including actively seeking out opportunities to learn about different lifestyles.

The highest 10 percent leaders of this competency consistently:

- Take the initiative to learn about different people and groups.
- Make an active effort to interact and develop relationships with all types of employees.
- Demonstrate empathy toward individual issues and concerns.
- Display openness to differing opinions, approaches and/or perspectives applied to work.
- Actively build inclusive work teams to capitalize on opportunities that may arise from unique abilities and thinking.
- Stay attuned to potential problems between individuals or within teams, and act to solve interpersonal issues before they escalate.
- Avoid early judgment by confirming perceptions with evidence.
- Encourage a cooperative approach to tasks, and display sensitivity/ understanding about what motivates different people.

The highest 10 percent in this competency rate themselves 4.03, which is the norm, versus their colleagues, who rate them a 4.55—much higher than the average leader is rated at 3.92.

On this competency, the lowest 10 percent follow the pattern we have seen with the other competencies, once again rating themselves higher than average leaders rate themselves at 4.42, while their colleagues rate them lower than the average leader.

Lowest 10 Percent Behavior

The lowest 10 percent leaders do not consider situations from multiple perspectives. In fact, they can be negative or hostile when encountering new or opposing opinions or perspectives. As such, they are likely to surround themselves with people who look and think just like them, which leads them to build homogeneous teams.

The last two "Junior Whopper" categories are knowledge of and commitment to diversity and inclusion. The two are related and both are sometimes difficult to judge externally. These categories have the lowest self norms and colleague norms out of the eight competencies.

7. Commitment to Diversity and Inclusion

The competency of commitment to diversity and inclusion is the ability to enthusiastically endorse and participate in programs that create and support equity and inclusion in the workplace, programs that will move the organization to the next level on the continuum.

The highest 10 percent leaders in this competency consistently:

- Seek out, encourage and promote inclusion and human equity.
- Apply human equity thinking/theory to all aspects of work and the workplace.
- Recognize and explain the business case for human equity.
- Share human equity knowledge and thinking with others.
- Create a climate of appreciation and awareness by continually communicating and reinforcing the value of human equity.

- Convey their personal commitment to achieving human equity objectives.
- Promote participation in training opportunities that relate to inclusion and human equity.

The highest 10 percent in this competency rate themselves higher than average leaders rate themselves, but their colleagues rate them much higher than they rate the average leader: 4.52 versus 3.87. The lowest 10 percent rate themselves higher than average leaders rate themselves, but, once again, their colleagues rate them lower than they do the average leader.

Lowest 10 Percent Behavior

The lowest 10 percent do not understand the business case for inclusion or human equity, just as they did not understand the previous business case for diversity. The lowest 10 percent rarely utilize the talents of all employees to achieve superior performance. These leaders are also unaware of the evidence that shows the positive impact that inclusion and human equity initiatives have on organizational effectiveness.

8. Knowledge of Diversity and Inclusion

The core competency of knowledge of diversity and inclusion is the ability to engage in behaviors that reflect a general understanding of the meaning of diversity, inclusion and human equity.

The highest 10 percent leaders of this competency consistently:

- Seek opportunities to broaden and develop knowledge relevant to inclusion and human equity.
- Can articulate the effects and relationships between diversity, inclusion, human equity and improved organizational performance.
- Demonstrate knowledge and understanding of workplace policies that promote inclusion and human equity.
- Apply knowledge and understanding to facilitate initiatives to promote human equity in their own function and department.

- Act as a human equity resource for other leaders.
- Understand how to evolve beyond the group conversation of diversity to the individual focus of inclusion and human equity.
- Understand the distinction of positive psychology and its relevance to human equity.

The highest 10 percent rate themselves higher than average leaders rate themselves: 3.91 versus 3.26. Their colleagues rate them much higher than they rate the average leader: 4.48 versus 3.85. In contrast, the lowest 10 percent rate themselves higher than the average leader, at 4.60, but their colleagues rate them lower than they rate the average leader at 2.40.

Lowest 10 Percent Behavior

The lowest 10 percent rarely seek out relevant resources that can help them become informed about equity and inclusion issues within the organization. These leaders rarely set time on the agenda to bring people "up to speed" on developments in this area and are usually unaware of legislation relevant to equity and inclusion.

WHAT IS THE MEASURE OF AN EQUITABLE LEADER?

Measurement of the eight competencies of an equitable leader are essential to movement on the Equity Continuum. Introducing these competencies to the most influential leaders in the organization (i.e., those who impact on development and retention of best talent) and holding them accountable for their behavior is the most important intervention you can make to create organizational transformation toward a work environment that optimizes on talent.

And you should start with yourself. Take a minute to visit the equitable leader site (www.equitableleader.com) and fill out your own free self-assessment under the ELA. Review your results compared to the norm and begin to determine if you are in the highest 10 percent, the lowest 10 percent or the 80 percent who make up the average.

The following case study shows how the Equitable Leader Assessment can be used in an organization. It follows the theme that unless leaders are held accountable for their behavior, it is unlikely that human equity can be achieved.

CASE STUDY: THE EQUITABLE LEADER ASSESSMENT AT DELOITTE

By Jane Allen

Professional services firm Deloitte has its Canadian roots in Montreal, 1858—nine years before Confederation. As Canada matured into a modern nation, Deloitte also adapted to reflect the changing face of business and society. One advantage has been the global nature of its operations: closely connected to Deloitte organizations all around the world, the firm understands the value of multiple perspectives.

Deloitte is in the business of providing solutions to complex client challenges. "We offer clients the insights of our talented people," says Frank Vettese, managing partner and chief executive.

"And we do our best work when everyone feels valued and is able to contribute to their fullest potential." Frank's words are echoed in the elements of Deloitte's straightforward business case for diversity and inclusion, one that appeals to the firm's results-based professionals:

- The talent pool is shrinking and becoming increasingly diverse.
- Engaging people throughout their career lifecycle is critical to enabling them to perform their best.

(continued)

- Client organizations are becoming increasingly diverse and multinational.
- Well-managed diverse teams are more innovative and produce better results for clients.

With major operations in the multicultural hubs of Toronto, Montreal, Calgary and Vancouver, as well as numerous smaller offices across Canada, creating an environment where people from a wide variety of backgrounds can thrive has always been a business imperative. But the firm-wide, top-down commitment to diversity and inclusion didn't happen overnight.

Creating Momentum

The firm had a long history of initiatives for the retention and advancement of women, including business development events and networking and mentoring programs. Even so, diversity and inclusion had not yet permeated the firm.

An important development was the creation of the executive-level chief diversity officer (CDO) position, a role Jane Allen has filled since 2008. Around that time, Jane sent out a voicemail for a Gay Pride event at work. "A senior partner responded that the simple existence of that voicemail was a sea change," she recalls. "It allowed some people to feel more confident bringing their whole selves to work." The CDO worked with a National Diversity Council as well as 15 regional chapters to implement diversity initiatives.

In 2010, Deloitte took its diversity agenda outside the organization, holding the first in what has become an annual series of cross-country roundtables and public reports called the "Dialogue on Diversity."

Fostering Tone at the Top

With these initiatives, Deloitte was making genuine efforts to build diversity awareness and acceptance. But things weren't changing quickly enough—the presence of women and visible minorities in the leadership ranks was below expectations. In 2010 the firm was ready to take the next step and support the executive team in becoming champions.

To focus its diversity efforts at the executive level, human equity consultant Trevor Wilson was engaged. When asked how to set the tone at the top, Trevor recommended assessing the diversity knowledge and behavior of each of the 25 members of the management team. The point of the exercise was to challenge the person's true nature—did he or she present an inclusive front? The key innovation in the process was the appointment of independent reviewers selected by the CDO and the managing partner. By benchmarking an individual's perception of his or her own inclusiveness and contrasting it with the perceptions of people who knew him or her, a true picture would emerge.

"We had some initial reactions such as denial and discomfort at the management team sessions. This was okay. Some people became more aware. Some became advocates. But the more people told me they had a problem with Trevor, the more we knew we were doing the right thing," said Alan MacGibbon, managing partner and chief executive at the time.

Those whose self-assessment differed significantly from their objective assessment were asked to attend a one-hour meeting with Trevor to discuss the results. All other management team members had the option of having a one-on-one discussion of their score. While the assessments weren't always what they had hoped or expected, the leaders believed wholeheartedly in what they were doing.

(continued)

Later that year, Deloitte board chair Glenn Ives enlisted Trevor to conduct a similar initiative with the board of directors. "The exercise made us realize that we still had a lot of work ahead of us," says Glenn.

But by the end of 2010, 45 of the most senior influencers among the firm's 800 partners had voluntarily participated in a process that allowed them to clearly understand their own challenges—and committed to setting a stronger tone from the top.

Identifying Diverse Leaders

Because Deloitte continually recruits and trains a significant fraction of its workforce from the ground up—and because it serves a cross section of Canadian organizations in virtually every region, size and sector, the diversity imperative is perhaps greater than at other organizations. Thriving in the knowledge economy requires long-term plans for attracting, retaining and developing top talent.

With a partnership structure, the early identification of future partners and the admission of top talent to the partnership is one of Deloitte's most important business decisions. Admission to the partnership in many cases is life-changing for a person, and comes with tremendous responsibilities and accountabilities.

Inclusiveness now plays a noticeably heightened role in discussions among the management team regarding candidates for admission to the partnership. Each of the firm's five services—tax, assurance and advisory, consulting, financial advisory and enterprise risk services—puts forth its partner candidates for discussion. The management team challenges each leader's commitment to being truly inclusive of top talent when selecting candidates. The focus is not on affirmative action, but on ensuring that all candidates, not just an exclusive subset, had been provided with the right level of support and opportunities so they would be ready to be successful as partners.

During one round of partner-admission discussions, the management team found that the strongest candidate in Toronto happened to be on parental leave. As a result of their reinvigorated commitment to diversity, the senior leaders chose to admit her to the partnership while she was at home caring for her newborn.

Helping Talented People Thrive

Today, Deloitte's management remains devoted to continuous improvement. In 2011, the Diversity Council became the Inclusion & Diversity Council, with the added responsibility of advising the CEO and executive team on diversity strategy. Explains Frank Vettese, "No one at the top of the firm challenges the business case for diversity. We've made it clear what's expected: every Deloitte leader is accountable for demonstrating leadership in this area by providing visible support for our vision and strategies, and each leader must make a conscious effort to support diversity—to move from talking about it to taking action." In fact, the requirement to "value the diversity experiences all of our people bring" is a stated, formal performance objective for all firm members. Adds Glenn Ives, "We no longer discuss whether we do it, but how we do it." Over the past few years, the company-sponsored people networks have expanded beyond women to include the LGBT community, Deloitte Dads, Canadian Black Professionals and the Canadian Asian Network. And in 2012, 48 percent of new leadership appointments were women or visible minorities.

Frank Vettese acknowledges that a move toward full inclusion is a journey, and will always be a work in progress. As a professional services firm, Deloitte typically looks at financial quarters, but this requires a long-term perspective as well as patience. However, there are measurable results—not just within Deloitte, but also in

(continued)

the community. The Dialogue on Diversity program has gained significant recognition for bringing focus to the workplace challenges of new Canadians, people with disabilities, and Aboriginal youth. In 2012 Frank became a founding member of the board of Carleton University's Centre for Women in Politics & Public Leadership, which collaborated with Deloitte on a benchmark study of women's leadership. Deloitte's chief counsel, Ken Fredeen, was appointed chair of a federal government panel on increasing opportunities for people with disabilities in the private sector.

At Deloitte, the efforts to advance diversity and inclusion have changed both the culture and the tone at the top. It is a place where people can make the choices that frame their career and life experiences and where being a talent leader means creating a high-performance environment in which the best people thrive. "Each Deloitte individual must have the opportunity to 'own their career'—to realize what they are capable of and what is possible. By making diversity part of the everyday experience, we've set Deloitte on a trajectory that will truly make us distinctive," concludes Frank Vettese.

Chapter 8

ERNST & YOUNG: A JOURNEY TOWARD HUMAN EQUITY LEADERSHIP

By Julie Dossett, Jeannine Pereira and Lynn Wilson

Professional services firm Ernst & Young (EY) has a long history of grappling with the challenge of building a diverse and inclusive organization. Its journey, which began in earnest in the early 1990s and which continues today in renewed form, reflects how deeply its "people first" approach has become embedded in the firm's values.

As a global organization, EY is committed to continually challenging itself in all the countries in which it operates to create a diverse, inclusive and equitable environment for its people. A fundamental element of EY's global strategy relates to inclusive leadership.

> We want to lead the market through high-performing teams. People who act inclusively not only believe that "difference matters," they know how to integrate diverse perspectives to create high-performing teams. We must develop these skills in all of our people to help transform the diversity of our global organization into a competitive advantage.
>
> —*EY Global People Strategy, 2012*

One example of how this global strategy is brought to life is detailed in the following account, which traces the path followed by Ernst & Young in Canada, both as part of a larger global organization committed to diversity and inclusiveness and as an industry leader in Canada.

EY has earned consistent recognition for its workplace culture through annual awards, such as Canada's Best Diversity Employers and Best Workplaces in Canada.[1] Its journey illustrates the evolution of the practical understanding of human potential in a large organization. Tracing the firm's path from early thinking driven largely by gender-equity issues in the accounting field, to national and global cross-sector recognition for diversity and inclusiveness, and now its vigorous focus on the notion of the individual rather than the group, reveals insights into an organization that has embraced both the complexity and promise of moving beyond diversity and inclusiveness toward human equity (i.e., optimizing on total human capital).

1992–1996: LAYING THE FOUNDATION

The roots of EY's current strategies around the potential of its workforce lie in ground that was tilled for the first time in the early 1990s.

As the 20th century drew to a close, Ernst & Young found itself at an important crossroads in its Canadian operations. Its core business streams of accounting, auditing, tax and transaction advisory services were facing rapid change with ever-shifting competitive conditions. In response, the firm's leadership developed a new, wide-ranging strategic plan to navigate the turbulent period ahead. As part of a broader move toward strategic differentiation, the firm explicitly acknowledged its own human resources as an intrinsic component of the organization's success, linking its traditional "clients first" and "professional excellence" values directly to attributes of people and the way they would work—teamwork, recognition and reward, and openness—to become the employer of choice.

The new values represented a significant shift from the conventional thinking in the professional services field. "Teamwork" would require colleagues to collaborate significantly more across traditionally separate business units to provide the best possible client services. "Recognition

---

1. Canada's Best Diversity Employers administered by Mediacorp Canada Inc. and Best Workplaces in Canada administered by Great Places to Work Institute Canada.

and reward" enhanced the organization's commitment to performance-based metrics for promotion and compensation and explicitly acknowledged the importance of its people in the business performance equation. "Openness" signaled an understanding that increased collaboration would require greater trust and transparency in the organization. In retrospect, it also represented a nascent recognition of the importance of becoming open to new ideas, new thinking and new perspectives.

The fresh values were integrated into a strategic business plan that for the first time situated the goal of developing human capital on the same level as more conventional business objectives, such as superior client service, technological innovation and profitability. It was an overt acknowledgment that Ernst & Young's business performance was dependent on a stable, high-performing workforce, and evidence of the firm's growing belief that it had to maximize the impact of its largest investment—its own human capital.

Driven in part by this new business-imperative thinking around people, and in part by emerging diversity issues in the profession—particularly, the advancement of women in the sector—EY's Canadian team spent the next few years building a new body of knowledge on diversity in its ranks, which inspired the early steps that laid the foundation for its subsequent achievements.

Broadly, those early years of 1992 through 1996 can be considered an era of foundation building of a more diverse and inclusive organizational culture. In addition to the new people-focused values, EY conducted its first People Survey in the Canadian organization, which revealed meaningful and often surprising gaps between leadership and employee perceptions of leveraging diversity at all levels of the firm. Plumbing these results further through current-state assessments aided by key metrics and focus groups, EY established a cross-functional national diversity committee and, as a signal of intent and commitment, appointed a director of diversity—albeit initially only as a part-time assignment. The director and committee were charged with the responsibility of developing the business case for diversity, gathering ongoing input and support internally, and implementing programs targeted at driving fair treatment.

Through feedback from randomly selected individuals and committee members, EY plotted its current state on the Equity Continuum. Over time, the firm tracked its progress on this continuum with ongoing input from its people. To refine this measurement process, EY was a member of the Trinity Group during the 1990s. The Trinity Group comprised 12 organizations working together with the Research Unit for Work and Productivity at the University of Western Ontario's Ivey School of Business to develop a robust set of definitions for key processes and practices related to fostering a diverse and inclusive work environment (see Chapter 9). An in-depth online survey tool—the Human Equity Assessment Tool—was developed that remains in place today.

Ernst & Young's Progress on the Equity Continuum©

Source: Trevor Wilson, *Diversity at Work: The Business Case for Equity* (Toronto: John Wiley & Sons Canada, Ltd., 1996).

These early years were focused on a transition from assimilating what differences there might be among colleagues, to tolerance, as well as on target-driven programs designed to address challenges in the organization and its recruiting process. Mandatory training programs were launched to encourage dialogue about diversity in the EY environment, and alternative work arrangements were reinforced, primarily designed to support women. These arrangements were most successful when communicated openly with team members and with clients, to meet everyone's needs.

Along the way, Ernst & Young grappled with the struggles common to any organization making a concerted effort to shift old thinking to new.

Focus groups surfaced the range of reactions that would continue to characterize diversity and inclusiveness dialogue for years to come:

- "Don't these equity programs exist just so we can meet government regulations?"
- "I don't want special treatment; just treat me equally."
- "Why does any of this matter? Let's just focus on client service."
- "Where are the role models for me?"
- "What about me?" (this often from white males)

Essential in countering the inherent resistance to change was the explicit effort made by the firm's leadership to link the value of diversity to the firm's competitive strategy. As EY's Canadian chairman and CEO expressed it, "Recognizing the value of a diverse workforce is key to maintaining our firm's competitive edge. We need the best people to serve our clients. To build long-term relationships with these clients, we need an environment where the best people stay and flourish."

This statement is still true today for the firm; however, we will see that how this type of work environment is achieved has certainly evolved.

Leaders expressed the importance of overcoming "unconscious incompetence" as it related to diversity and differences. Unconscious incompetence referred to stereotypes, thought processes, beliefs and behaviors that were so well established that they operated without awareness or intention. Through awareness programs, mentoring initiatives and structured career development plans, leaders became attuned to potential barriers to career progress and committed to being "consciously competent." Important dialogues occurred that compared perceptions with the reality of people's experiences at EY. Gradually, gaps in the perceptions of fairness between leadership and employees were eliminated.

1997–2000: CULTURE SHIFT

During the next evolutionary stage of the diversity strategy at Ernst & Young, the firm built on the incremental improvements tracked from the early phase of activity. For the first time, there was a purposeful and conscious shift from the firm's traditional "clients first" culture to a "people first" culture. This transformative philosophy explicitly acknowledged the importance of EY's human assets, stating an organizational commitment to:

- Making people paramount in all the firm's decisions
- Providing opportunities for people to build their skills and careers
- Fostering an inclusive, innovative and flexible work environment
- Building lifelong relationships with people.

And, in return, it established a shared responsibility. EY's people would commit to:

- Aiming high and succeeding
- Taking ownership of their own careers
- Living firm values with a particular focus on quality.

This focus was fundamental to EY developing and retaining its people while dramatically shifting its place on the Equity Continuum.

At the global level, EY expanded its People Survey, which assessed individual and team engagement, to cover the entire globe, while the Canadian firm continued more in-depth explorations through focus groups across Canada. Meanwhile, the director of diversity position evolved to a full-time responsibility, and client-serving partners (rather than business support unit leaders) were tapped to lead gender equity, ethnicity and flexibility efforts—two developments that telegraphed the growing strategic importance of diversity.

At the Americas level, the appointment of the Americas market leader as executive sponsor for inclusiveness also signaled that diversity had taken on a new profile in the firm's structure. Also at the Americas level, EY hosted its first Women's Leadership Conference and established the Rosemarie Meschi Award to honor the contributions of EY leaders to the advancement of women in business. Minority Leadership Conferences followed. To encourage authentic conversations, conference tables were equipped with a sign to be held up by participants when discussions were not tackling the real roots of a difficult issue.

2000–2010: SHIFTING DEFINITIONS AND OWNERSHIP

By 2000, Ernst & Young's strategies and efforts across the Americas were aligned and the diversity imperative was active and well entrenched. And it was evolving, too. That year, the inclusiveness committee led a process to evaluate and update the language of diversity in the firm to better accommodate a maturing understanding of its principles. Extending beyond the previous decade's primary framework based on visible differences, the new "Vision of Inclusiveness" committed "to provide an inclusive, open, flexible and supportive workplace, enriched by the different backgrounds of our people. In an environment that values our people and their differences, we intend to be the professional services firm of choice for our people and our clients."

By 2005, on the basis of focus group feedback, an important enhancement was made to the Canadian vision to acknowledge the importance of each person feeling included: "Ernst & Young is committed to providing a work environment that is and feels inclusive for all our people. At Ernst & Young, you are respected for the skills and talents you contribute and the impact you make—and you are expected to demonstrate that respect for others every day."

By now, the connection between people and client service was embedded in the firm's language, and with this new iteration of diversity thinking came renewed efforts to expand the impact and implementation. The firm embarked on efforts to foster alignment and measurement. Tactics included a series of Inclusiveness Awareness Workshops and cross-cultural training, differential development programs and an inclusiveness snapshot measurement tool that tracked progress on key measures related to people's progress and engagement, and client experiences. Comparisons were made across business units. These tactics were reflected in the following one-page framework adopted across the firm.

Ernst & Young's Road to Equity

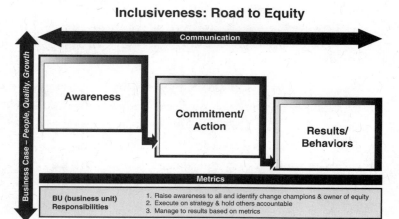

At the same time, an Inclusiveness Steering Committee was established with a broader mandate than its predecessors, along with related task forces focused on issues particular to certain groups. Other tactics implemented during this time included:

- A Diversity Census to deepen the understanding of each person's background
- A flexibility survey to determine how deeply flexibility was embedded in EY's work environment, and whether individuals felt empowered to work flexibly
- A CEO-led webcast for "Beyond," a vehicle for bringing together the firm's LGBT community and its allies
- People resource networks designed to support those EYers with shared interests and needs
- Additions to EY's Global People Survey, in which respondents were asked if statements such as the following described their experience at EY: "feeling free to be myself," "encouraging and respecting varying viewpoints, perspectives and styles," "having the flexibility needed to achieve personal and professional goals" and "being able to succeed with diverse backgrounds and experiences."

Characterizing this phase of diversity action was a concerted effort to draw a direct line between diversity of thought, attracting talent and attracting clients to the firm's market leadership objectives. As well, ownership of inclusiveness thinking was increasingly diffused to business units throughout the organization, with expectations for identifying change champions, increased accountability and a focus on metrics-based results.

By 2010, Ernst & Young had tied diversity and inclusiveness to its global success, created a leadership development process for its partners—including assessments—and established the global Chairman's Values Award to honor EY individuals who embodied the firm's values, described prominently throughout the organization as:

- People who demonstrate integrity, respect and teaming
- People with energy, enthusiasm and the courage to lead
- People who build relationships based on doing the right thing.

Equally significant at this time was the shift to a more external focus to the Canadian firm's diversity and inclusiveness efforts. Early on, Ernst & Young recognized that not only would its own commitment to fostering a diverse and inclusive workplace be a competitive advantage in its own sector, but also that it would become a valuable platform for differentiating its brand to a broader audience. By 2010, a new role of chief inclusiveness officer (CIO) was created in Canada, and a new energy propelled the firm's efforts externally.

"It became apparent that there was a real opportunity here, not just to transform and leverage our internal development, but to contribute to the growth of inclusiveness in our whole sector—and beyond," recalls Fiona Macfarlane, EY's British Columbia managing partner and a member of the firm's executive committee, who was appointed as the firm's first CIO.

Ernst & Young became a vocal and influential advocate in the Canadian business space, actively promoting board diversity through industry organizations, sponsoring supplier diversity and related community initiatives, and advocating the value of diversity at CEO roundtables and other influencer events. EY also published a number of internal articles and external thought leadership pieces, either specific to Canada or leveraging EY's global research and thought leadership content, such as *The New Global Mindset: Driving Innovation through Diverse Perspectives.*

2010: DEFYING THE PLATEAU

Despite its considerable efforts and progress, by late 2010 Ernst & Young's leadership felt the firm's diversity and inclusiveness (D&I) strategy had reached a plateau. While the "people first" culture was now firmly embedded, there was a powerful sense that the program was due for a renewal, not only to meet the fast-evolving economic circumstances that were having profound impact on the global business environment, but also to bust through the lingering limitations that seemed to be holding the firm back from leveraging the rich talent base both inside and outside the firm.

In June 2010, Ernst & Young announced the appointment of its new Canadian chairman and CEO, Trent Henry. A career EYer, yet demonstrably younger than most CEOs of the large professional services firms, Henry brought a fresh energy and broad perspective earned from global experience, which he felt had been paramount in shaping his career, capabilities and thinking. He quickly endorsed the idea of recalibrating the firm's D&I strategy to foster a more nuanced appreciation of individual perspective and experience. It was particularly relevant as he and the executive leadership began to develop the organization's ambitious growth strategy for the coming years. In their plans for market growth amid ongoing economic uncertainties, the firm's leadership could see on the horizon changes in both its clients' needs and the labor market that would rapidly sharpen the need for a sophisticated talent development and retention approach. It was time for a radical change in thinking. And like a perfect storm, a number of factors converged to forge just the right environment to make it possible.

Not long after taking the helm at Ernst & Young, Trent Henry set out a bold goal. He announced that he wanted EY to be the first Canadian organization to achieve a "4" rating on the Equity Continuum spectrum. Henry, along with the People and Inclusiveness leaders in the firm, acknowledged that this would require a profound shift in the organization's understanding and approach. It is embodied in EY's employee value proposition: "Whenever you join, however long you stay, the exceptional Ernst & Young experience lasts a lifetime."

Stephen Shea, newly appointed as the firm's managing partner of people and as a member of the executive committee, expressed frustration with the growing "diversity fatigue" at the organization. "Superior execution of our tactics over the previous several years had left us with a sense of fatigue. Our metrics indicated our improvement had plateaued. We had to ask ourselves whether more energy and effort with the same tactics would enable us to break through. We thought not."

At the same time, people were growing tired of hearing about programs for certain groups to the exclusion of others, frustrated that they were excluded from specific efforts to recognize the less obvious elemental differences each individual might bring. Even after all the training and dialogue, and the impressive achievements Ernst & Young had earned, some in the firm were struggling to leverage the understanding or appreciation of inclusive thinking into business or team goal-setting beyond conventional metrics. Others were expressing concern that all this activity on diversity and inclusiveness was at risk of being seen as a distraction from core business objectives, particularly as the global economic conditions worsened.

2011: THE A-HA! MOMENT

EY leaders, including Henry, Shea, Macfarlane and longstanding inclusiveness champions Jeannine Pereira, Lynn Wilson and Lynn Lapierre, became intrigued by the potential of TWI's human equity concept. It appeared to address the fatigue factor and similar barriers that were impeding the firm's ability to fully leverage its two decades–long investment in a "people first" approach, which had seen important advances in the firm but had stalled around the 3.6 mark on the 5-point scale. What's more, they saw that there was both room and opportunity for EY to pursue a unique leadership role in Canada in this regard—one that would optimize its people's careers, benefit its clients, fuel its reinvigorated brand strategy and propel competitive advantage.

The firm was committed to seeking meaningful and advanced measurement models for this stage in the evolution. Pereira and Wilson helped launch a renewed Trinity Group, called Trinity II, with Trevor Wilson of TWI Inc. and eight leading Canadian organizations to refresh the Equity Continuum.

Lynn Wilson, EY's director of leadership and organizational effectiveness, recalls how challenging and rewarding the Trinity II discussions were. "The high-energy commitment to evolving the continuum was apparent from our first meeting," she says. "Our intense dialogues to update the Equity Continuum statements occurred over several months and were grounded in both our years of experience and our determination to foster an even richer workplace of the future."

Trinity II focused on embedding human equity principles into the Equity Continuum. Trevor Wilson defines human equity as:

- Focusing on the unique and intangible assets each employee brings to the workplace
- Building on the individual perspective of inclusion
- Focusing on talent differentiation strategies, innovation and diversity of thought
- Maximizing strengths to find the right fit between the employee and the job.

"The human equity framework would allow us to shift the lens so we could reveal the intangible, unique assets each individual in our organization could contribute," explains Shea. "But it did not reduce our commitment and the evident need for group opportunities and support like the Beyond program for our LGBT communities, and the professional networks we'd established for women, minorities, parents, flexibility and accessibility."

He continues, "It then dawned on us that if we integrated this holistic thinking in our processes—from recruitment, talent development, promotion and even client service—we ultimately wouldn't need those special group programs. People would be recognized for the unique assets they bring as individuals to our teams. That was the missing piece of the puzzle we'd been struggling with for years. It was our a-ha! moment."

With a genuinely engaged and supportive chief executive who could enthusiastically articulate the link between the firm's human capital philosophy and its key market focus and growth themes of polycentric globalization and entrepreneurship, Shea and his colleagues knew there would be no better time to capitalize on Ernst & Young's strong foundation in innovative diversity and inclusiveness thinking. So they got down to work.

New Model, New Mandate: Inclusiveness Steering Committee

A new Inclusiveness Steering Committee (ISC) was formed. Previous committees had comprised representatives from EY Canadian management who would set priorities and targets for gender, LGBT and ethnic diversity networks. Right from the start, the new ISC was conceived in a radically new fashion. In a rigorous selection process, EY partners were invited to consider volunteering to join the new group of five representatives—a task that would require a commitment of approximately 300 hours each year for a two-year term.

"We weren't certain what kind of response to expect," explains Lapierre, who readily acknowledged the considerable time burden and shift in thinking this commitment would represent to EY partners. She and her colleagues were delighted when they discovered that 25 eminently capable individuals from across the firm had stepped forward. Lapierre recalls, "It was a validation to us that we had tapped into something really big." Pereira echoes this: "People were motivated—hungry to make important and meaningful change happen."

Each volunteer was evaluated against a detailed array of values, strengths and perspectives, and the list was whittled down further in a formal interview process with the inclusiveness leaders and Trevor Wilson from TWI. "Even at this embryonic stage, it was important to us that we apply the principles of human equity," explains Shea. "It was a huge undertaking to not simply talk the talk but walk the talk, considering and evaluating the unique contribution each individual volunteer had to offer to the process."

The evaluation was essential, as the committee's work would be substantially different from previous incarnations of D&I work teams. Beyond meeting quarterly to set direction, the new ISC members were charged with significant responsibilities, each leading a designated area of focus and driving some of the firm's thorniest equity challenges.

It started with a careful review to identify where action could have the most impact. Then the ISC connected these themes with the key processes that would be essential in moving Ernst & Young in Canada to a Level 4 on the Equity Continuum. The team grouped the topics so that they could be structured around a common project plan, landing on five key drivers of success for EY people and clients.

Five Drivers of Success at Ernst & Young

1. Recruitment

Driven by a desire to move selection criteria beyond academic marks, demonstrated leadership skills and entrepreneurial interests, the partner worked with EY leaders to define the "golden thread" for identifying and cultivating the best talent—those skills and characteristics that indicate long-term leadership potential.

CEO Trent Henry is particularly passionate about seeking the golden threads specific to EY leaders. "This is about thinking ahead," he says. "We need to identify those characteristics and experiences common to the best performers at Ernst & Young, to find the leaders who best embody the kind of full-circle thinking that will guide the firm, its people and its clients in the years ahead. Our future is in their hands, so we need to be attracting not just the technically capable talent but the best-suited candidates."

2. Pipeline and Succession Planning

Meeting with client-serving partners and other leaders across the firm, the ISC leader of this process reassessed current promotion pipeline development initiatives and succession planning processes at the firm, in particular focusing on the opportunities for talent differentiation at the individual level.

3. Coaching, Mentoring and Sponsorship

Building on EY's history of mentoring and coaching, the work in this area focused on a broader, more inclusive approach to supporting career progression and talent development. "We need to move beyond tactics that are focused solely on leveling the playing field for women or visible minorities. The programs have been hugely helpful, but they're limited and exclude the broader community of potential leaders," says Shea, who explains that the committee member in this area explored different ways the firm can deliver meaningful equitable coaching, mentoring and sponsorship activities built on a more inclusive model focused on individual strengths.

4. Markets and Growth

From the start, Henry has been vocal in connecting the "people" factor to the firm's overall market success and ability to grow. "Our clients, and the markets in which they—and we—operate, are increasingly diverse," he explains. "Our work teams and processes will be most effective when they reflect a similar breadth and depth of background, global experience and skills." The ISC team zeroed in on several specific work streams, from client development activities, to account team assignments and succession plans, to revenue planning, where the principles of diversity, inclusiveness and human equity can be built directly into the EY processes.

5. Leadership Accountability

Improving leadership accountability in the firm was deemed mission-critical for the project right from the start. In addition to proposing strategies for more deeply embedding human equity in partner goals and staff communications, the committee member responsible for this area of focus implemented the Equitable Leader Assessment (ELA) among partners and senior leaders. The ELA (see Chapter 10) is designed to provide leaders with candid feedback from colleagues as well as a structured process to support the development of behaviors in key areas related to diversity, inclusiveness and human equity.

"Part of our goal is to encourage the shift away from corporate metrics in our leadership assessment toward a greater emphasis on leadership behaviors, that's where we'll see the real impact of a different way of defining capabilities," explains Lynn Wilson.

Within a year of being established, the ISC had been convening regularly and had invested upward of 2,000 hours in developing its overall approach to the initiative and breaking down an enormous project into manageable phases. Each of the committee members had analyzed his or her area of focus and boiled it down to an achievable, clearly articulated theme and associated goals. The next step was constructing detailed action plans that would serve as the road map for the following months of research, consultation, analysis and implementation.

"It's important to know we have our CEO's ear on this, and that heightens the need for a very focused, pragmatic and results-based approach," explains Pereira, EY's inclusiveness and flexibility leader. "It also demands that we build alliances and understanding at every level of the firm, for we need the breadth of perspectives and insights that our people can share. That collaboration and consultation will also ensure we uncover the leading practices we already live, and be better able to share them across functions and business units."

WHAT'S NEXT?

By the end of 2012, the team's action plans had been approved by the firm's Canadian executive team and fully supported at the Americas and global levels. The first half of 2013 would be spent on implementation, working closely with the broader D&I team across the firm and leveraging other EY and external resources when necessary. Their activities included:

- Implementing the work plans of the five key work streams
- Rolling out the ELA process to more than 60 market segment leaders across the firm
- Investing a greater emphasis than ever on promoting the advantages—and best routes toward—partnership. This comprises a significant effort to increase the commitment to equitable sponsorship of high-potential leaders in the organization. It had emerged in the initial stages of the ISC's work that, more than ever, effective sponsorship and the development of valuable business-development skills were deemed to be the most important elements in propelling outstanding performers to seek partnership. A more concentrated effort on this front became a priority within the context of the ISC's work.
- Implementing a pilot project in the area of succession planning. Aligning with an initiative of the Americas People Team, the Canadian EY team would identify 10 high-potential partners for a development process for leadership positions.
- Shaping the "golden threads"—those core attributes for success at EY—by working closely with leadership across the firm, and collaborating with the recruiting team to map out how this approach would be integrated into the recruiting process seamlessly and effectively.

Along the way, the EY team in Canada would continue to work with its Americas counterparts, sharing information and liaising on leading practices.

Meanwhile, Ernst & Young continues to work externally on developing its human equity approach to the business. Externally, the firm's leaders frequently author articles and other thought leadership on the business case for a broader definition of diversity, and remain active as participants and sponsors of cross-industry events and working groups on these topics.

"We see an immense opportunity here not just to revolutionize the way Ernst & Young conducts and grows our business, but also to create a tidal wave of new thinking across the Canadian business landscape," explains Henry. "We're determined to be Canada's first 'number 4'— and the more people and organizations that can join us in that journey, the better."

LESSONS LEARNED

Looking back over Ernst & Young's journey from the early 1990s to now, in what is arguably its most ambitious evolutionary phase yet, EY leaders are quick to point out lessons learned along the way:

- Accountability and executive sponsorship are key.
- Leaders and participants are most effective when they understand their own frames of reference and unconscious biases, and they are able to flex their thinking and style.
- Formal programs make a difference, yet the culture is what drives the level of business-unit and individual ownership and engagement.
- "Policing" people's actions drives compliance, not necessarily effectiveness and full understanding.
- For success, a commitment to people needs to be a personal priority.
- The journey and business case must make sense to every employee.
- You have to walk before you run—but don't walk a marathon. It takes too long.
- Courage must triumph over conservatism.

One of the strongest characteristics of Ernst & Young is its commitment to effective measurement. The firm looks to have effective measurement beyond representation and have data for all four categories of the Equity Index—that is, quantitative, qualitative, leadership behavior and external. The organization has taken a leadership role in updating the human equity assessment, which will be highlighted in Part 3.

PART THREE

MEASURING HUMAN EQUITY

Chapter 9

ARRIVING AT THE HUMAN EQUITY ASSESSMENT TOOL

Recent research conducted by the Society for Human Resource Management indicates that while three out of four Fortune 500 companies have diversity programs in place, only slightly more than half measure their program's results. In the absence of measurement it is impossible to know how much progress an organization is making toward creating a work environment that will be able to attract and retain the best person for the job. Moreover, if outcomes are not properly measured, diversity efforts may cost organizations a great deal of time and money without creating sustainable change. Metrics or indicators of progress reinforce the idea that this work is tied to core business objectives and over the long term contributes to organizational effectiveness and sustainability. The groundbreaking work of the Trinity Group (I and II) represents a key contribution to the development of a systematic measurement tool aimed at assessing an organization's progress toward the development of a workplace that aspires to achieve human equity. Today, with the help of the tool that ultimately came out of the work of the Trinity groups and others—the Human Equity Assessment Tool (see Appendix)— one can conduct an assessment of an organization's progress along the Equity Continuum and properly measure its journey toward inclusion and ultimately human equity.

The importance of measuring human equity became clear to me only after the publication of *Diversity at Work* in 1996. Back then, I hadn't fully anticipated how organizations would respond to the Equity Continuum that I explained in the book. In those days, when clients asked me where their organizations were on the continuum, my response was, "Your people will tell you." The reality was, I didn't really have a good answer to their question because there was no objective way of measuring progress on the continuum.

One of our largest clients at the time was IBM. Within a year of the publication of *Diversity at Work*, the organization had appointed its first director of diversity, Laurie Harley. A few years earlier, I had conducted extensive diversity awareness training for all of the company's 10,000 Canadian employees. During this training the employees were introduced to the continuum and asked to rate IBM. They assessed the company as a 2.1 on the continuum.

Satisfied with the baseline number of 2.1, Harley was looking for a framework to move the organization forward. She quickly gained the support of her executive team to set a goal for the company: to achieve a Level 4 by the year 2000. In her words:

> IBM Canada had already made significant investment in diversity programs prior to establishing an executive diversity position in 1996. Leaders had a good sense of the importance of recruiting and retaining a diverse workforce and were influenced by a corporate focus that involved global initiatives directed at women, visible minorities and people with disabilities. But diversity was still viewed as "stand-alone" and clearly owned by HR. In Canada, HR was evolving as a strategic organizational partner, driven by the war for talent, but diversity lacked many characteristics needed to align it with overall business strategies. And at the top of that list was the need for more rigorous measurement.[1]

---

1. From an internal IBM document by Laurie Harley to justify supporting Trinity I.

Harley needed to answer two key questions: "How do we get to a Level 4 on the Equity Continuum? And how will we know when we've reached our goal?"

Harley wanted to know a lot more about the characteristics of a Level 4 organization—specifically, the policies, practices and attitudes that would distinguish it from those at levels 1, 2 and 3. She wanted to find data she could use to look for gaps in policies and practices, and from there, build strategies and action plans to get to their five-year—year 2000—goal. As we were to discover, setting the goal was one thing; designing the road map to get there was quite another.

Shortly after the IBM experience, I was in South Africa, meeting with another major client, South African Breweries (SAB). Like IBM, SAB had become enamored with the continuum and announced it wanted to be at Level 4 within two years. They proudly displayed an internal communication featuring the goal of Level 4 as its headline. With the commitment already in print and distributed to all staff, this client wanted to know what specific things the organization should be doing, and how would they measure progress along the way. I remember thinking to myself, "I wish I knew."

I knew that the questions IBM and SAB were asking were the right ones. But at that time I had no answer other than that a 2 was further ahead than a 1, and a 3 was more advanced than a 2, and a 4 was somewhere between 3 and 5. Hardly a satisfying or scientific explanation. We simply had no tools that would allow us to plot progress along the Equity Continuum. There were no standards to point to, internal or external benchmarks by which to effectively measure progress. And more and more, organizations needed these benchmarks and methods of measurement if they were to move beyond the realm of "We think we are making progress" to "We know we are."

TRINITY I: THE DIVERSITY ASSESSMENT TOOL

Then, in 1997, a group of diversity practitioners from a dozen blue-ribbon Canadian organizations came together with a single mission: to improve the way they measured diversity. They formed an informal network that became known as the Trinity Group. (The name has no religious connotation. It comes from the location where the group met regularly: Trinity Square, in Toronto.) The group's mission was to develop a software tool to measure diversity in the same rigorous way ISO standards measured quality. The Trinity argument was, "Where we are with diversity in the 1990s is exactly where we were with quality in the 1970s." In the 1970s, many organizations desired this ethereal state called quality, but until ISO was created, no one knew what inputs led to the output of quality. Such was the case with diversity in the 1990s. Everyone wanted the final output of a diverse workplace, but what practices and processes actually led to that output? This was the mission of Trinity.

Over the years, membership within the Trinity I Group and the Trinity II Group has changed, but the core mission has not. Trinity's initial mission was to develop a methodology that could be used to assess progress within its own organizations, that would balance ease of use with rigor and detail, and enable external benchmarking with other organizations.

The Trinity Group (Trinity I)

1. IBM Canada
2. Ernst & Young
3. Bell Canada
4. Northern Telecom
5. Motorola Canada
6. DuPont Canada
7. Bank of Nova Scotia
8. Canadian Imperial Bank of Commerce
9. National Grocers Company
10. Ontario Public Service Commission
11. Canadian Bar Association
12. University of Western Ontario

Trinity set out on a three-phase project: (1) a review of the available information on best practices and diversity measurement; (2) the creation of a diversity standards implementation model; and (3) the development of a tactical implementation tool that would systematize diversity initiatives according to the model.

The Trinity Group hired the Research Unit for Work and Productivity at the University of Western Ontario's Ivey School of Business, led by Dr. Julie Carswell for the first phase. In its February 1998 report, the Research Unit confirmed the Trinity Group's experience—that although measurement was frequently underscored as an important component of the diversity management process, there were no specific evaluative criteria that organizations could use. Measurement tools simply didn't exist. They were able, however, to demonstrate that the Equity Continuum offered a framework to assess organizational policies and practices at each point on the scale. And there was more. The researchers' report pointed to a potential link between a corporation's performance in diversity and its business performance overall: although it had not been proven, they hypothesized that some corporate diversity practices might link to business outcomes such as improved productivity, customer satisfaction, profitability and retention of talent.

Building on the research report, the Trinity Group set out to identify different criteria that could be used to benchmark an organization's position on the Equity Continuum—in other words, to describe in a standardized way what organizations operating at each level of the continuum look like. The result was a detailed matrix (see page 202) consisting of a series of statements that linked key processes and practices to each level of the continuum.

Although the matrix was an important outcome, it still didn't represent a formal assessment tool. For that conversion, the Trinity Group turned to Caribou Systems, a software company with expertise in creating comprehensive measurement software for environmental practices. Over the next year, Trinity worked with Caribou Systems to develop the Diversity Assessment Tool (DAT). The DAT was a sophisticated, comprehensive piece of software that included a series of probing questions about workplace practices and processes by which anyone can get beyond the "how do we feel" perspective into the "how do things really work around here" vantage point. The DAT dissected practices such as recruitment, training and development, and processes such as commitment and measurement, down to a nuts-and-bolts diagnosis of any workplace. Its arrival on the scene in the fall of 1999 marked a milestone in the efforts of the Trinity Group to turn their vision into reality.

The Diversity Assessment Tool: Canada and Beyond

Discussions about the development of a diagnostic and measurement tool attracted the attention of other groups in Canada and abroad. Not too long after the tool was created, researchers Julie Rowney and Gloria Miller from the University of Calgary's Faculty of Management began the Diversity: Research, Measurement, Action project. The objective of the project was to use the Equity Continuum to create a common framework for understanding diversity and a snapshot to assess diversity management practices. "It is hoped," the researchers wrote, "that organizations will identify their place on a continuum from zero to five, ranging from little or no initiatives and understanding regarding diversity to one of complete integration throughout the organization's processes and procedures. Where organizations have not reached the highest category, namely five, they can utilize the findings of this research to create action steps to reach the next level."[2]

The project team identified nearly 200 companies, each employing more than 250 people, to participate in the project. These organizations represented a cross section of industries, including agriculture, finance, food distribution, health and education, oil and gas, professional services, transportation, tourism and utilities. The researchers sought to gather information from three levels in the organization: executives with strategic responsibility for diversity; managers or supervisors with direct responsibility for implementing diversity; and team or group members with responsibility for working in diverse groups.

---

2. Julie Rowney and Gloria Miller, Leadership Diversity Advisory Committee of the Faculty of Management, University of Calgary, 1998.

The findings from this project represented one of the first times the continuum was used strategically to measure progress using a standardized measurement template. It also confirmed the state of the nation in the area of diversity. The project concluded that approximately 50 percent of organizations were classified as being between a 0 and 1. There were 20 percent of organizations between a 1 and 2 and 17.5 percent of organizations between a 2 and 3. The project found no organizations between a 4 and 5, which left 12.5 percent between a 3 and 4, that is, somewhere between diversity and inclusion. These results were somewhat different from my initial guesses cited in Chapter 2.

All of this dovetailed with the Canadian federal government's launching, in 1999, of the Task Force on a Representative Public Service (eventually renamed the Task Force on an Inclusive Public Service), described in Chapter 2. This task force, led by Dr. Janet Smith, sought to answer the question, "What would it take to create a culture of inclusiveness—an environment where people were valued *because of* their difference, not *in spite of* their difference—and a corporate culture that demonstrated respect for difference, not merely tolerance?" The focus of the task force went well beyond the concept of diversity, which dealt merely with having a representative organization, evolving the conversation to creating a work environment where each person was valued because of his or her unique strengths, talents and abilities.

This idea of creating a work environment where each *person*—as opposed to each *group*—was valued was a subtle but profound shift. Up until then, programs such as employment equity, affirmative action and equal opportunity had focused on the underrepresentation of historically disadvantaged groups. The move beyond the group to the individual was a significant change in approach and set the stage for envisioning work environments that value the uniqueness we all bring to the workplace. In other words, it set the foundation for human equity.

The task force built on the Trinity Group's Diversity Assessment Tool to create a more refined tool that could be used by both the public and private sectors, a tool accessible via the then-new mode of communication known as the Internet.

The challenges of measuring diversity were not unique to North America. Given the demographically complex and changing workforce in Europe, corporations there were beginning to respond to the compelling business connections and opportunities diversity could bring. Graham Shaw, then project manager for Gaining from Diversity, an initiative launched in 1997 by the European Network for Social Cohesion, met with members of the Trinity Group and discovered a common interest in identifying best practices that could be translated into a set of standardized measurements.

The Diversity Assessment Tool became a vehicle to share Trinity's work with organizations in Europe and see if the instrument was valid across geographies and cultures. Ultimately, the Trinity Group's work on measurement came to be recognized as a global standard that can be used to create a shared understanding of diversity, allowing organizations to assess where they are on the Equity Continuum, how far they have come and where they need to go.

The European Network on Social Cohesion recognized that they had to go into this new territory with their eyes wide open. The group had specific questions about diversity, such as:

- How do we convince European business and government that diversity is a strategic business imperative and must be approached with a workable strategic implementation framework?
- Can we develop or find strategic implementation tools that can help build successful diversity practices?
- Can we identify metrics to monitor progress to indicate levels of improvement related to diversity?
- Is it possible to create common standards of diversity across sectors, organizations and jurisdictions to allow benchmarking at local, national and global levels?

The European group used the work of Trinity to complete a benchmarking project in 2001–2002. The project was very similar to the Diversity: Research, Measurement, Action project. The primary difference was that it allowed organizations in several European countries to approach diversity from a business perspective using a common framework and language.

As Dr. Julie Carswell, the tool's original architect, says of the whole Trinity experience:

It was an exciting time from a research perspective. There were some, but not many, academic publications focused on enhancing difference in the workplace and most of that research was qualitative in nature (focused on case studies and describing organizations that were considered to be progressive in terms of embracing and advancing diversity). In contrast, there had been few attempts to systematically quantify an organization's approach to diversity, inclusion and human equity—a glaring absence of a tangible tool that organizations could use to benchmark themselves and evaluate their progress toward creating an inclusive and equitable workplace. As a group of organizational psychologists with a measurement background, we couldn't have been in a better place—being able to create, innovate, and fill a practical need. We understood what was out there from an academic perspective on the topic of workforce difference and recognized that this qualitative content needed to be "morphed" into a quantitative measurement tool. With input from the Trinity Group we were able to ensure that the tool resonated with corporate experience and best practice by having this consortium provide input and assistance with the development of content. As a researcher it was the perfect marriage of science and practice.[3]

It is hard to overstate the impact of Dr. Smith's Task Force on an Inclusive Public Service, which moved the discussion beyond the group to the individual. It has come to represent the defining feature of moving from a Level 3 to a Level 4 on the continuum.

---

3. From an e-mail to Trevor Wilson by Dr. Julie Carswell commenting on her experience with Trinity I.

The Structure of the Diversity Assessment Tool

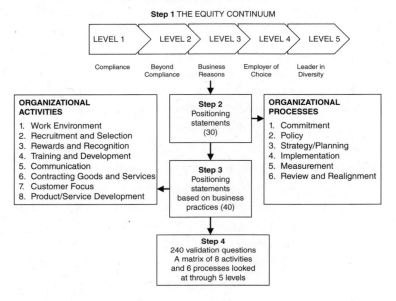

The Trinity Group, the Centre for Business and Diversity, the European Network for Social Cohesion and the Task Force on an Inclusive Public Sector all made important contributions to measurement along the Equity Continuum. In 1997, we set out to find the answer to the question, "How will we know when we get to a Level 5?" A few years later we had a tool to measure diversity and inclusion in the same rigorous way that ISO 9000 measured manufacturing quality.

There were important lessons learned from this journey. They were:

- Issues of equity and inclusion have an international appeal.
- The concept of the Equity Continuum is transferable across borders and can be applied regardless of the external legislative environment.
- A detailed organizational assessment can provide an effective way to analyze gaps in processes and practices and be used to identify and prioritize opportunities for improvement and measure progress over time.

- A consistent instrument can provide useful normative data for external benchmarking.
- Measurement is at the heart of any effective strategy of moving along the continuum.

TRINITY I: AN INSIDER'S PERSPECTIVE

by Laurie Harley

Here is my attempt at capturing the "feelings" around the original Trinity Group experience. They come from two perspectives:

1. The environment in IBM Canada as I started, in 1996, in the new position of director of diversity and workplace programs, and our progress over the next four years.
2. The Trinity Group process that provided the opportunity to build and leverage a diverse team of human resources, research and technical talent in search of a common goal.

Measurements were critical for a couple of reasons: first, corporate culture valued metrics (if it couldn't be measured and tracked, it couldn't be that important); second, measurement helped to define the problem, which, in turn, defined the solution. The traditional diversity measurements based on representation statistics fell far short of the standard required and clearly did not define the underlying challenges required for solutions.

So, as a brand new leader of diversity, I looked for external expertise and that search led me to Trevor Wilson. Trevor was a familiar face around IBM as he had been engaged several years earlier to conduct awareness training with all IBM employees. During those sessions, participants were asked to position IBM on TWI's Equity Continuum based on their perceptions of

(continued)

where the organization was on its journey to a fair and equitable workplace. That meant we had a "high-level" baseline statistic and a metric that managers and employees were familiar with. Establishing a goal of reaching Level 4 on the continuum by 2000 would be challenging but achievable, we thought. However, there was one major problem. There was no road map of how to get to Level 4 and no systematic description of the characteristics of organizations operating at that point on the scale. Without that benchmark, how would we know if we had reached our goal? I posed that question to Trevor, and, as they say, "the rest is history." Trevor recognized the need for a more rigorous instrument using the existing continuum framework and reached out to his clients and subject-matter experts to fill the gap.

The resulting initiative became known as the Trinity Group, a label that emerged as participants realized they needed an identity. The group met regularly at Bell Canada's offices in Trinity Square in Toronto and the location was adopted as the group's name.

When Trinity started, there were several forces at play in corporate environments that influenced our work. First, there was a growing body of research on best practices not just in North America but in Europe. Links to local as well as global research would become a high priority, starting with a partnership with the Research Unit for Work and Productivity at the University of Western Ontario. Organizations were also demonstrating that a focus on quality could take "soft" topics that had historically not lent themselves to measurement, and produce reliable standards. Learning from the quality model became a priority. And finally, there was an emerging need for easy access to tools in electronic formats. Trinity's goal would not only be to document standards but to produce a quality software tool. And that turned out to be a very aggressive goal for an informal group of practitioners who had never worked together before and whose sole motivation was to improve the way they integrated and measured diversity. The journey would be long, taking more than two years to complete, and engage researchers, software developers and diversity experts in Canadian public and private sectors as well as in Europe and South Africa.

When I look back on the Trinity experience, I often think if we'd known what lay ahead before we started, the initiative might never have happened. For the core group members, Trinity became a "second job" that had to be accommodated into already busy schedules. What kept us going was the challenge of the task, the priority we placed on a successful outcome in our own organizations, and the group experience itself.

The Trinity Group was literally a mini-experiment in inclusion. The team was diverse, with a wide range of experience, skills and talents—men and women who were leaders in their own organizations but who had no "position power" in the ad hoc group. We learned together to generate and share creative thoughts, to play to our individual strengths and to stay the very long course to achieve our goals. It was a truly rewarding team experience! In retrospect, I wonder if we would have been more effective with the advantages of today's technologies and social networking. Perhaps Trinity II will offer some interesting insights on how group dynamics have changed over the decade.

TRINITY II: THE HUMAN EQUITY ASSESSMENT TOOL

Early in 2012 the foundation work set by the Trinity Group was picked up by its successor group, Trinity II.

In January of that year, one of the original Trinity members was looking for a way to benchmark its 70 offices around the world in the area of diversity and inclusion. This was an organization that had moved beyond diversity in North America but recognized that from a global perspective their other international offices had yet to even consider diversity. They asked me if it was possible to use the Diversity Assessment Tool to complete the initial global benchmarking. I explained that that tool was out of date: it didn't take into account either the concept of inclusion developed by the Task Force on an Inclusive Public Service or our concept of human equity.

We discussed the idea of resurrecting the Trinity Group to update the tool to incorporate inclusion and human equity. We went back to the Trinity member organizations to see if they would be willing to participate in a project to update the DAT to create a Human Equity Assessment Tool. We also looked to bring in industries or sectors that had not been represented in Trinity I. The result was the creation of the Trinity II Group in April 2012.

The Trinity II Group

1. Canadian Imperial Bank of Commerce
2. Ernst & Young
3. Stikeman Elliott LLP
4. Ontario Public Service Commission
5. Ministry of the Attorney General
6. Home Depot
7. Mount Sinai Hospital
8. General Motors

We also invited someone to represent the not-for-profit sector, which had been missed by Trinity I. The Trinity II Group included partners from the original 1997 project—CIBC and Ernst & Young—as well as Dr. Janet Smith (by then retired from the Task Force on an Inclusive Public Service) and Laurie Harley (retired from IBM), who acted as project advisors. Susan Rogers, who had retired from Xerox, and Noelle Richardson, who had moved on to the Ministry of the Attorney General's office, also participated in the process as advisors and consultants. The group also included several new partners.

Based on the belief that the creation of standards "can inspire continued innovation toward totally inclusive and equitable environments for all," Trinity II's mission was to refine and update a robust measurement tool that quantitatively assesses an organization's progress in diversity, inclusion and human equity so that we can accurately develop standards that allow for benchmarking internally, externally, as well as within and between various industries and jurisdictions.

Trinity II built on Trinity I's intention to develop a methodology that could be used in various industries and jurisdictions to assess progress along the Equity Continuum. They looked to learn from the lessons of Trinity I to create a methodology that would balance ease of use with rigor and detail, and enable external benchmarking with other organizations using the same measurement template. Its focus was to update the process and practice definitions in the Diversity Assessment Tool to reflect the relatively new areas of inclusion and human equity. They used the matrix shown in the table below to guide their work.

At first, the group focused on process. The group set up six task force teams to look at:

- Commitment
- Policy
- Strategy and Planning
- Implementation
- Measurement
- Review and Realignment.

Once the process areas were updated, separate task forces were created to look at the following areas:

- Work Environment
- Recruitment and Selection
- Accountability and Recognition

Key Questions to Guide Trinity's Practice/Process Inquiry

Question	Level 1	Level 2	Level 3	Level 4	Level 5
What is their commitment?	To comply	To do the right thing	To have a business case for diversity	Inclusion, which moves beyond diversity	To achieve human equity for all
What do they want?	To avoid negative consequences of non-compliance	To be seen as socially responsible	To realize the ROI business benefits of diversity	An inclusive environment where each person's talents, regardless of group, are tapped into	Total human capital optimization
Who owns/who leads?	Legal or HR department	Internal advocates	Chief diversity officer supported by diversity infrastructure	Chief inclusion officer supported by skilled people leaders	Chief talent and leaders in the organization
What do they do?	Respond to audits or complaints	Demonstrate corporate social responsibility	Demonstrate the link between diversity and bottom-line outcomes	Practice talent differentiation through a diversity lens	Practice a positive psychology approach to management for talent optimization
How do they measure?	Representation of target groups	Representation and external image	Quantitative and qualitative metrics: the Equity Index	Leadership behavior referenced by quantitative/ qualitative/external	Job/talent fit using talent differentiation tools
What would make them stop?	Compliance or external drivers go away	Public interest or internal advocates change	Business case changes are no longer valid	Change in core values related to people	All employees in jobs where they achieve self-actualization and are judged solely by the content of their character

- Learning and Development
- Communication
- Contracting of Goods and Services
- Service Delivery
- Program/Service Development.

A separate task force was struck to complete a consistency check to ensure that assumptions were carried through the entire tool. At the time of publication, the updated tool is being field-tested in the various Trinity II organizations.

In the appendix of this book you will find the diagnostic questions that are in the updated Human Equity Assessment Tool (HEAT). The entire tool is available online; however, if you want to get a quick preliminary assessment, you can fill out the Equity Continuum Scorecard in the appendix. The scorecard contains eight questions that serve as a proxy to the entire Human Equity Assessment process. The eight questions were identified by conducting a correlation analysis of the 240 questions in the HEAT and finding those questions that are the best indicators of movement along the continuum. You can access your Scorecard Report via the Equitable Leader website (www.equitableleader. com). (Turn to page 301 to see how you can save $100 on ELA Assessment Tools.) An example of an Equity Continuum Scorecard Report is also provided in the appendix.

Chapter 10
THE EQUITABLE LEADER ASSESSMENT

This chapter provides a comprehensive overview of the Equitable Leader Assessment process, including detailed instructions on how to access the Equitable Leader Self-assessment available at www.equitableleader .com. I have also included a brief overview of the Equitable Leader Self Report and the full Equitable Leader Report.

There are three components to the Equitable Leader Assessment process:

1. The ELA Self-assessment
2. The ELA Colleagues Assessment
3. The ELA Report.

It is recommended that the entire process be conducted annually in an organization to use the data as a leadership accountability mechanism.

THE ELA SELF-ASSESSMENT

The ELA Self-assessment is an important part of a leader's development in that it measures an individual's perspective of his or her behavior on equitable and inclusive leadership practices. Each leader completes a web-based ELA questionnaire comprising 40 questions in the eight core competency areas. These eight leadership competencies have been shown to be those most relevant to the achievement of inclusion and human equity in the workplace.

If you have not already done so, I encourage you to visit the Equitable Leader website (www.equitableleader.com) and complete your free Equitable Leader Self-assessment. (Turn to page 301 to see how you can save $100 on ELA Assessment Tools.) In this chapter you will find an interpretation of results and an overview of the Equitable Leader Self Report, which you will receive after completing your ELA Self-assessment.

As you interpret your results it is important to remember that these results are based only on your perceptions of your work behavior compared to other leaders' perceptions of their behavior in the eight competency areas outlined in Chapter 7. As a result, you may be above, at or below the TWI self norm. This will give you an important start on your journey to becoming a more equitable leader. If you want to verify your perspective of yourself, you are encouraged to have a handful of your work associates complete an ELA Colleagues Assessment, which is also available on the Equitable Leader website. This will allow you to validate how you have scored yourself.

When you receive the report from your self-assessment, notice where you scored yourself significantly above the TWI self norm. You can initially verify your self score by looking at the behaviors of top performers in the body of the report. Identify behaviors that can confirm your perceptions and determine if there are other behaviors you may have missed that could further improve your effectiveness in this competency.

Next look at the competencies where you scored yourself below the TWI self norm.

Refer to the "Actions to Consider" section of the report to improve your effectiveness in these areas. Once again it is strongly recommended that you gather further feedback on your behavior by having your associates complete the ELA Colleagues Assessment. This is really the only way to verify whether the score you have given yourself is accurate.

Your score on a given competency reflects your perception of your current effectiveness in the eight areas. If you decide to take action to improve your effectiveness on a particular competency using the ELA

The Equitable Leader Self Snapshot

	Accommodation	Change Management	Commitment to Diversity	Dignity and Respect	Equitable Opportunity	Ethics and Integrity	Knowledge of Diversity	Openness to Difference
Your Self Norm	3.20	3.80	3.80	4.00	4.00	3.40	3.60	3.60
TWI Self Norm	4.12	3.64	3.69	4.33	4.39	4.36	3.33	3.70

ELA Rating

Personal Action Plan at the end of the report you can expect your scores to improve within six to nine months. You should view your first report scores as a baseline and in a constructive frame of mind. As you read your report, continually ask yourself, "What can I do to make myself a more equitable leader?"

Let's take a closer look at each competency by looking at a typical self report.

The Equitable Leader Snapshot

The most important part of your ELA Self Report is the ELA Snapshot (see the Equitable Leader Self Snapshot figure above). This graph is a summary of how one leader scored herself in the eight areas compared to the TWI self norm, which is made up of more than a thousand leaders from a global data base who have completed the ELA Self-assessment. Let's assume that the chart above is your own, and use it as an example of how to read the snapshot.

The first thing to notice in this report is where you have scored yourself lower than the external norm. In this example it would be five areas: accommodation, dignity and respect, equitable opportunity, ethics and integrity and openness to difference. The next step is to turn to these areas in the report and review the definition of the competencies and actions of top performers. Ask yourself which actions you are demonstrating on a consistent basis today and which actions are areas for improvement. For example, in the snapshot above the competencies showing the biggest gaps are ethics and integrity and accommodation. There are also gaps in dignity and respect and equitable opportunity, but nowhere near the significance of the other two areas.

Isolating the questions where you have marked yourself low in the self-assessment can help provide an understanding of areas you may need to strengthen and will help when you fill out the Equitable Leader Personal Action Plan. As you review each area of your self report where you have scored below the external norm, you can use these statements to help you isolate areas for growth.

Let's look at each area in more detail.

I. **Accommodation** (Definition: A leader or manager who demonstrates
    creativity when solving problems and adaptability when responding
    to the needs of different employees.) This competency is sometimes
    known as *workplace flexibility*. It is meant to test the leader's creativity
    when solving problems, and adaptability when responding to the
    needs of various employees.

    The current self norm for the accommodation competency is
    4.13 out of 5. If you scored yourself significantly higher than the
    norm in this area, it is likely because you are willing to think outside
    the box, rather than always staying with "tried and true" solutions. In
    other words, you are able and willing to explore different and maybe
    new ways of tackling old problems. This does not mean that you
    always develop these ideas yourself. You may get input from others
    on ways to create an innovative approach and have the ability to
    determine how the new method stacks up against the old. This will
    prove most important when looking at work and life balance issues.

    If you scored yourself lower than the norm, you may need to
    look at adapting your management style so that it is more aligned
    with the motivation of your direct reports. As noted in Chapter 6,
    some people come to work simply because it is a job, others come
    to build a career, and yet others see their work as a calling. Different
    people are motivated by different things. Human equity calls for a
    management approach that will speak to the uniqueness of each
    team member, rather than a one-style-fits-all approach.

    One of the best ways to improve your score in the area of accom-
    modation is to improve your understanding of the total benefits of
    accommodating the needs of various members of your team. For
    example, one North American leader found that allowing those who
    did not celebrate the typical statutory holidays, most of which are
    typically based on the Christian calendar, to work on those days and
    take their own significant days off had an overall benefit of increasing
    coverage in the department. In a similar fashion, accommodations for
    some employees often have unintended benefits for others—think

of power-assisted doors, which were designed to help those with physical disabilities.

If you seek to improve your performance in this area, consider asking other team members what more you (or the organization) can do to best support their needs and allow them to use their unique talent. Leaders and managers who score above the norm in accommodation tend to be most comfortable making decisions when they know all the facts. They will be proactive in seeking out information about how to best accommodate employee needs.

As you review your results, think about the following statements to better understand the depth of the competency.

- I am comfortable in situations that are not "clear cut" or that involve some degree of ambiguity or uncertainty.
- I tend to explore new approaches to solving problems rather than sticking with "tried and true" solutions.
- I am willing to accommodate the diverse needs of my employees in order to ensure that they are able to perform to their full potential.
- I adjust my leadership style (e.g., participative versus directive) depending on the situation.
- I actively seek out information about the best way to accommodate the needs of diverse employees.
- I acknowledge and value the opinions of others when making decisions.

2. **Change Management:** (Definition: A leader or manager who contributes to the development of an organization that values diversity and inclusion through the implementation of effective change management practices.) This competency is sometimes referred to as "pushing the envelope." This area is meant to test the leader's contribution to developing an organization that values inclusion and human equity through the implementation of effective organizational change practices.

    The current self norm for this competency is 3.64 out of 5. If you scored yourself higher than the norm, then you believe that you challenge the status quo and are willing to champion new human equity initiatives. You are likely to identify sources of resistance to change and are realistic in recognizing that most people tend to resist change. You may be likely to facilitate the change process, but an additional challenge may be getting those who resist to participate in the change strategy. Fostering their active participation in the change process will allow you to identify what their concerns may be and at the same time enhance their cooperation with the proposed change.

If you rated yourself lower than the norm in this area, you may want to evaluate where inclusion and human equity fall on your list of priorities. Have you truly looked at the business case? Analyze why or why not, and whether these areas are built into your existing roles and responsibilities or if competing priorities or even lack of interest have pushed these areas to the bottom of your list.

One way to improve your score in this area is to seek input from your staff on ways you can take a more active role in fostering inclusion and human equity in your business unit or organization. Another best practice in this area is developing a list of barriers to change (whether in the form of attitudes, processes or practices), developing an inventory of available resources that will encourage change initiatives, and formulating a plan to address the identified barriers using available resources.

As you review your results, think about the following statements.

- I actively communicate and consult with others to achieve the vision of diversity and inclusion at this organization.
- I actively contribute to policies and processes that support diversity and inclusion within this organization.
- I set challenging yet achievable goals related to increasing diversity and inclusion within this organization.
- I take responsibility for making progress toward diversity and inclusion-related goals.
- I make a priority of implementing changes that support diversity and inclusion.

3. **Commitment to Diversity and Inclusion:** (Definition: A leader or manager who enthusiastically endorses and participates in programs to create and support diversity and inclusion in the workplace.) This area is sometimes referred to as "enhanced interest." The old saying about ham and eggs comes to mind: the pig is committed, while the hen is interested. This area is meant to test the leader's enthusiastic endorsement and participation in initiatives to create and support inclusion and human equity in the work environment.

    The current self norm for this competency is 3.69. If you scored yourself higher than the norm, you probably seek out, encourage and promote diversity, inclusion and human equity initiatives. You are likely applying a positive psychology approach to your work and encourage others, creating enthusiasm by continuously communicating the value of inclusion and human equity.

    If you rated yourself lower than the norm in this area, consider increasing your level and profile of support for diversity, inclusion and human equity initiatives. Start by improving your understanding of how a work environment that acknowledges, supports and utilizes the talent of all employees is critical to superior performance and business results.

    One best practice in this area is simply adding inclusion and human equity as a standing item on meetings with staff. You can use this time to speak about your personal experience with inclusion and human equity or to discuss how your understanding of these issues has progressed. Also ensure that employees have access to information about the progress toward the goals of the inclusion and human equity program, and always provide employees with the opportunity to provide input into the goals and process to reach them. Those who are committed make a concerted effort to seek out ways to develop the culture of inclusion and human equity and practice it in their team and work unit.

    As you review your results, think about the following statements to better understand your score.

- I would come forward publicly and say that there is a strong business case for supporting diversity and inclusion.
- I act as a role model for others in dealing with people from diverse groups.
- I take an active role in creating a culture that supports diversity and inclusion in this organization.
- I openly discuss my support for diversity and inclusion.

4. **Dignity and Respect** (Definition: a leader or manager who creates a work environment that encourages dignity and respect, where the opinions and contributions of all team members are valued.) This area is the most important of the eight competencies. It is meant to assess how much the leader creates a work environment where the opinions and contributions of all team members are valued, not just tolerated.

    The current self norm for this competency is 4.33. If you scored yourself higher than the norm in this competency, you are likely to consistently foster open and transparent communication and recognize fellow workers as individuals, addressing them in an attentive and respectful manner.

    If you rated yourself lower than the norm, consider becoming more conscious of your language at work. You may also want to seek feedback on the degree to which your behavior and language are inclusive and sensitive to the listener. Seek input on how to create a work environment that supports open and honest communications. Ensure that your employees have access to information that could have an impact on them and flag issues that could be barriers to creating a more equitable and inclusive work environment.

    Assess yourself on the so-called dirty dozen behaviors, detailed in Chapter 3. Ask others if your humor is sometimes insulting or sarcastic. Begin to notice if you frequently interrupt others or treat them as if they were not present (for example, by working on your smartphone while they are speaking). Determine if you ever resort to verbal or nonverbal threats, intimidation or public shaming.

One of the best practices in this area is to embrace positive psychology interventions related to authentic leadership. This area builds on the leadership models by historic figures such as Gandhi, Mandela and Alexander the Great, all of whom provided positive leadership to address problems confronting their communities. The leader who embodies dignity and respect both "owns" his or her personal experiences (e.g., thoughts, emotions or beliefs) and acts in accordance with his or her true self (behaves and expresses what he or she really thinks and believes).

Dignity and respect is an area where leaders generally mark themselves higher than their colleagues rate them. As I mentioned earlier, I believe this is because leaders possess a certain hopefulness about this competency; that is, it is something that most people feel they should be doing. However, the authentic and equitable leader does not coerce others but demonstrates his or her values, beliefs and behaviors to serve as the role model in the development of associates—a positive spin on Emerson's "What you do speaks so loudly I can't hear what you say."

As you review your results, think about the following statements to better understand your score.

- I do not make stereotypic statements about members from diverse groups.
- I listen to the views of both men and women equally.
- I am conscious of my language to ensure that I do not exclude specific groups.
- I take action to address situations when inappropriate comments or jokes are made.

5. **Equitable Opportunity** (Definition: A leader or manager who makes employment decisions such as promotion, placement on projects, and team development solely on the basis of merit and skill.) This competency is sometimes referred to as "fairness." As with dignity and respect, this is a key competency in the area of diversity, inclusion and human equity. It is meant to assess if a leader bases employment decisions on objective criteria rather than allowing favoritism or biased assumptions.

The current self norm for this competency is 4.39. If you scored yourself above the current norm, you are likely to provide team members with opportunities to work on assignments that reflect their knowledge, skills and intangible abilities (see the SHAPE V discussion in Chapter 6).

If you rated yourself lower than the norm in this competency, it may be because you base employment decisions on subjective or biased criteria. This would lead to an inequitable distribution of assignments, which will be evident in the team you have built. When assigning tasks or selecting people for a job, look to choose candidates based on their knowledge, technical skills and innate strengths, passion, attitude, personality, virtues and life experience. Also look to avoid situations where some individuals are favored for reasons unrelated to merit, e.g., he or she graduated from the same school as you, say, or plays the same sport.

Best practices in this area relate strongly to rigorous talent differentiation and positive psychology management. As such, leaders who are rated high in equitable opportunity focus on developmental opportunities for their staff that build on unique talents and strengths, rather than focusing on the usual employee development model of fixing weaknesses or deficits.

Another best practice relates to the equity or fairness of policies and practices. Equitable leaders ensure that the policies and practices related to employment decisions are relevant to the discussion of merit. Some criteria, such as seniority provisions, may no longer align with the identification of best talent and will be challenged by the equitable leader.

As you review your results, think about the following statements to better understand your score.

- I do not let employees' lifestyle choices (e.g., married versus single, children versus no children) influence hiring and promotion decisions.
- I base employment decisions (e.g., hiring, promotion) solely on merit (i.e., the best person for the job).

- I assign projects and work based on an individual's skills and abilities.
- I give both men and women the opportunity to work on high-profile projects.
- I make an effort to identify and foster the skills, abilities and potential of all team members.
- I ensure that both men and women have the opportunity to succeed in this organization.
- I have a high regard for the feelings of every person I work with.

6. **Ethics and Integrity** (Definition: A leader or manager who embodies the principles of fair and ethical conduct and demonstrates honesty, reliability, responsibility and constancy in his or her daily work life.) This very important area is meant to assess if a leader is taking accountability for his or her behaviors, and places a high value on principled and honorable conduct.

   The current self norm for this competency is 4.36. If you rated yourself higher than this norm, then you are likely guided by your moral compass rather than solely relying on the organization's rules and regulations. You are likely an excellent moral role model for others who may look to you for advice or guidance. Leaders who are scored high in this area demonstrate honesty, reliability and responsibility, and have strong alignment between their actions and words. Leaders who rate themselves high in this area often demonstrate what Aristotle called practical wisdom—the will to do the right thing with the skill to figure out what the right thing is.

   If you rated yourself lower than the norm in this area, ask yourself if you are open in your dealings with others and consistently provide your colleagues with relevant, accurate and reliable information. Explore whether you honor your commitments to coworkers, clients and business associates, including deadlines, promises and meeting times.

   A best practice in this area is to complete the VIA assessment, a psychological assessment available online at www.viacharacter.org, created and administered by the VIA Institute on Character started in 2007. The mission of the VIA Institute is to "discern the basic elements of personality that are universally thought to be the pathways to fulfillment, satisfaction and flourishing." The VIA assessment is designed to identify an individual's profile of character strengths (see Chapter 6 for more on this). Being aware of your character strengths and virtues allows you to better demonstrate consistency between your actions, behaviors and words, which can impact on ethics and integrity.

As you review your results, think about the following statements to better understand your score.

- I am open in my dealings with others and provide people with relevant, accurate and reliable information.
- I take full responsibility for my own actions and for the actions that I initiate in others.
- I honor my commitments to coworkers, clients and other business associates.
- When making decisions, I consider the impact that my actions will have on all persons affected.
- I demonstrate consistency between my words and actions.

7. **Knowledge of Diversity and Inclusion** (Definition: A leader or manager who engages in behaviors that reflect a general understanding of the meaning of diversity and inclusion, and who demonstrates knowledge of best practices and relevant legislation related to diversity and inclusion.) Those who rate themselves higher than the norm in this area have a high degree of understanding surrounding issues of diversity, inclusion and human equity. They would be able to explain the evolution of diversity to inclusion and then to human equity. They could explain the difference between legislated and litigated equity, as well as the business impact of human equity in the workplace.

The current self norm for this competency is 3.33, the lowest of the eight. Leaders who rate themselves higher than the norm in this area demonstrate fluency around these issues, as well as knowledge of best practices.

Those leaders who rate themselves lower than the norm may consider enhancing their awareness and understanding about diversity, inclusion and human equity. These leaders could benefit by drawing on a data base of diversity, inclusion and human equity resources. One particularly effective tool is the web-based site Ted.com, which offers some amazing short talks on a multitude of topics, including areas surrounding diversity, inclusion and human equity. Here's a listing of some of the best Ted.com talks related to these areas:

- Chimamanda Adichie: The Danger of a Single Story
- Daniel Pink: The Surprising Science of Motivation
- Barry Schwartz: Using Our Practical Wisdom
- Martin Seligman: Positive Psychology
- Elizabeth Lesser: Take "the Other" to Lunch
- Shawn Achor: The Happy Secret to Better Work

As you review your results, think about the following statements to better understand your score.

- I keep abreast of up-to-date knowledge relevant to diversity and inclusion.
- I display an awareness of the values and customs of different ethnic groups.
- I convey an understanding of the relationship between a diverse workforce and enhanced business outcomes (e.g., productivity, innovation, profitability).
- I am able to speak knowledgeably about legislation surrounding fair hiring practices.
- I work closely with the human resources department to ensure up-to-date knowledge of key legislation relevant to diversity and inclusion.
- I act as a resource other people can come to for diversity and inclusion information and advice.
- I speak knowledgeably about the impact of fair and inclusive hiring practices.

8. **Openness to Difference** (Definition: A leader or manager who demonstrates a positive attitude toward others who are different from

himself or herself. This includes actively seeking out opportunities to learn about cultures and lifestyles that are different from one's own.) This area is designed to help the leader assess his or her tolerance and acceptance of those who are different from them.

The current self norm for this competency is 3.78. If you scored yourself higher than this norm, you are likely empathetic dealing with a wide range of individual issues and concerns. You are also more attuned to potential problems between individuals or within teams because you may be more aware of interpersonal issues before they arise. If you are above the norm you likely make an active effort to interact and develop relationships with all types of employees regardless of gender, sexual orientation, class, education, occupation, culture, race, age or any other characteristic unrelated to merit. Those above the norm actively build highly diverse teams with people who have complementary SHAPE V characteristics (i.e., traits they don't have), which allows them to build synergy in the team.

If you have scored yourself lower than the norm, then you may not display an openness to differing opinions, approaches and perspectives. Leaders below the norm may exhibit early judgment without confirming perceptions with evidence or considering situations from multiple perspectives.

As you review your results, think about the following statements to better understand your score.

- I express interest in opinions and ideas that are different from my own.
- I take the initiative to learn about issues that are important to diverse groups of people.
- I am able to empathize with diverse groups of people (i.e., see a situation as they see it, feel what they're feeling).
- I seek opportunities to collaborate with persons of diverse characteristics from my own (e.g., age, ethnic background, etc.).
- I listen to and value the differing views of all team members and encourage each person to share his or her opinions.

THE EQUITABLE LEADER PERSONAL ACTION PLAN

Once you have identified those areas where you have rated yourself below the norm and identified the possible areas that could be improved through the questions, then you are ready to fill out the Equitable Leader Personal Action Plan, which is at the end of your report.

The Equitable Leader Personal Action Plan is a place to write down your most crucial one-year goals based on the results of your self-assessment. This action plan helps you identify what is most important to develop your Equitable Leader Competencies. We recommend that you set one-year goals for the areas where you have scored yourself below the norm and put this number in the area marked "Goals." It is important to put a numerical, quantitative goal in this box to ensure that progress is measurable. We recommend you revisit these goals every quarter over the year to assess your progress and chart your movement. It is easy to get distracted by competing priorities, which will inevitably show up at work.

The next step is to consider things you could start doing, stop doing and continue doing. All progress starts with telling the truth. Identify the first things you need to start doing. The place to start is in the developmental advice that can be found in the "Action Steps to Consider" area of the report for each competency. These action areas are based on the best practices of the top 10 percent leaders discussed in Chapter 7. Reviewing these actions is an efficient way to determine how to improve in the competency that you have identified as an area for growth.

For example, if you have identified ethics and integrity as an area for growth based on your self-assessment, and know you have scored yourself below the norm, you may set a goal to be at the norm within a year. Using the snapshot from earlier in this chapter, that would mean your year-long goal would be a 4.36. Using the top performer behaviors and the statements listed earlier from ethics and integrity, you should be able to complete your action plan. For example, let's say you have identified an issue as it relates to following through on commitments. Using the Action Steps to Consider under the ethics and integrity area, you could identify a follow-up "tickler" system that can be used to track

The Equitable Leader Personal Action Plan Worksheet

What do I commit to START, STOP and CONTINUE doing?

	GOAL	START	STOP	CONTINUE
EQUITABLE OPPORTUNITY Making employment decisions (e.g., promotion, placement on projects, development) regarding team members on the basis of merit and skill				
ETHICS AND INTEGRITY Embodying the principles of fair and ethical conduct and demonstrating honesty, reliability, responsibility and constancy in one's daily work life				
KNOWLEDGE OF DIVERSITY AND INCLUSION Engaging in behaviors that reflect a general understanding of the meaning of "diversity and inclusion" and demonstrating knowledge of best practices and relevant legislation related to diversity and inclusion				
OPENNESS TO DIFFERENCE Demonstrating a positive attitude toward others who are different from you, including actively seeking out opportunities to learn about cultures and lifestyles that are different from your own				

The Equitable Leader Report™

your commitments made to coworkers. The "stop" and "continue" areas can be identified using the same process.

Once you have completed the start/stop/continue portion of the plan, consider which resources are available to help you achieve your goals. In the appendix we have listed some excellent resources related to the implementation of inclusion and human equity. But you should also consider online workshops related to the area of the competency, as well as mentors and coaches who can support you in improving your behavior.

It is important to think about how you will monitor your progress toward each goal, considering both the short- and long-term indicators you can use to evaluate movement. For example, you may decide to do a "pulse check" ELA Self-assessment, or some other kind of monitoring, halfway through the year. If you are working on ethics and integrity you may begin to monitor the percentage of commitments you complete each week.

While the ELA Self-assessment is a good place to start on the journey to becoming an equitable leader, the only real way to accurately determine your actual behavior is to complete a full 360-degree review using the ELA Colleagues Assessment.

THE ELA COLLEAGUES ASSESSMENT

The ELA Colleagues Assessment is a companion piece to the self-assessment. It validates the leader's self scores and provides an objective perspective of the leader's behavior in the workplace using a 360-degree type methodology. The ELA Colleagues Assessment is an important part of a comprehensive feedback process and the way to find the highest and lowest 10 percent leaders. In the Colleagues Assessment, up to eight colleagues are asked to provide candid and constructive feedback for the leader on the eight core competencies of the equitable leader. Each colleague is asked to complete an ELA Colleagues Assessment questionnaire that consists of 40 statements regarding the eight competencies.

In order for the 360-degree exercise to be effective, it is beneficial that the colleagues asked to provide the ratings be assured of complete confidentiality and anonymity. There are several ways to do this, but one of the most effective is to have at least half of the colleagues chosen by a third party. This prevents the leader from choosing a list of colleagues who could be biased toward or against him or her and encourages a much more objective evaluation. One CEO we worked with requested his entire senior leadership team evaluate him. This meant more than 35 individuals provided a colleague assessment and prevented the possibility of the CEO being able to ignore the results because of bias among the evaluators.

Ultimately, like any other 360-degree evaluation, the ELA is based on the objectivity of the data. If you choose eight of your closest friends, you are likely to get a very strong report. If you choose eight of your worst enemies, you will probably get the opposite. We suggest that at least five colleagues are necessary for a valid 360-degree report.

The full 360-degree Equitable Leader Assessment provides leaders with candid developmental feedback in the eight competency areas. It is a multidimensional assessment that enables leaders to identify how their colleagues rate them, compare their self-assessment to those of other leaders contained in a normative data base, and compare their colleagues' assessments to other leaders in a normative data base. By looking at the eight behavioral competencies, the ELA provides additional value by going beyond the ELA Self-assessment results.

The Equitable Leader Assessment is based on the premise that leadership behavior is a vital component to effective organizational change. The old saying that "individuals don't quit the organization, they quit their boss" is consistently reinforced by employee engagement survey data. Developing leadership competency to move toward inclusion and human equity moves beyond the identification of skills one needs to manage diversity.

The equitable leader seeks to create equitable and inclusive work environments where people feel valued, respected and engaged. Equitable leaders seek to develop a work environment and atmosphere of mutual trust, support and respect, where people feel they have a place at the organizational table that really matters. The equitable leader ensures that employees are valued because of, not in spite of, their differences, so that all people are recognized and developed, and their talents are routinely tapped into. Equitable leaders believe that human equity—that is, maximizing on human capital—is the most sustainable route to better employee engagement and improved business outcomes. They understand that human equity doesn't just mean putting people first but that it also leads to increased profitability, improved efficiencies and productivity, reduced costs, improved talent differentiation and increased employee engagement, resulting in reduced unwanted employee turnover and retention of high-potential talent.

Developing leaders who understand the complex issues of inclusion and human equity is vital to an organization's movement along the continuum. While it may be an organization's reputation that attracts its employees, research shows that it is the relationship that employees have with their managers and leaders that determines their level of productivity and how long they will remain with an organization. The ongoing challenge for many organizations has been in distinguishing and developing leadership behaviors that encourage high-performing employees to remain at an organization and to perform to their fullest potential.

THE EQUITABLE LEADER REPORT

The data collected from the ELA is captured and customized into a 30-page Equitable Leader Report, which includes benchmark comparisons using normative data from my company, TWI Inc. The TWI normative data is collected from more than 1,000 organizational leaders from the United States, Canada, Europe, Asia and Africa. All of these leaders have completed the ELA Self-assessment and Colleagues Assessment over the past decade and their data has been used to build these global norms, which are updated regularly. The Equitable Leader Report also includes a normative comparison for the aggregate colleagues score, which is made up of more than 8,000 colleagues who have rated their respective leaders on the eight competencies.

The Equitable Leader Report provides a quantitative record for leaders to identify and develop their competencies related to diversity, inclusion and human equity. From the report, leaders can identify

The Equitable Leader Snapshot

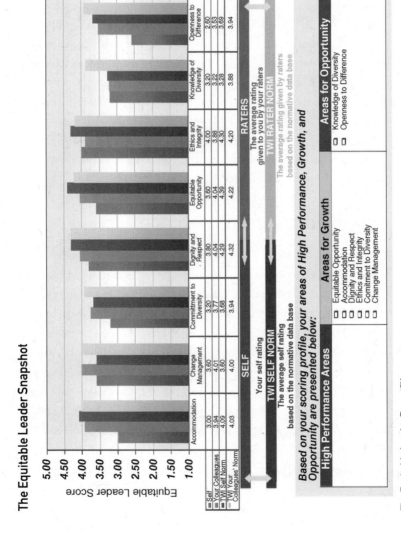

Equitable Leader Score

	Accommodation	Change Management	Commitment to Diversity	Dignity and Respect	Equitable Opportunity	Ethics and Integrity	Knowledge of Diversity	Openness to Difference
Self	3.00	3.60	3.20	3.80	3.60	4.00	3.20	2.60
Your Colleagues	3.94	4.01	3.77	4.04	4.04	3.88	3.22	3.53
TWI Self Norm	4.09	3.60	3.68	4.29	4.39	4.30	3.28	3.69
TWI Your Colleagues' Norm	4.03	4.00	3.94	4.32	4.22	4.20	3.88	3.94

SELF
Your self rating

TWI SELF NORM
The average self rating based on the normative data base

RATERS
The average rating given to you by your raters

TWI RATER NORM
The average rating given by raters based on the normative data base

Based on your scoring profile, your areas of High Performance, Growth, and Opportunity are presented below:

High Performance Areas

Areas for Growth
☐ Equitable Opportunity
☐ Accommodation
☐ Dignity and Respect
☐ Ethics and Integrity
☐ Comitment to Diversity
☐ Change Management

Areas for Opportunity
☐ Knowledge of Diversity
☐ Openness to Difference

The Equitable Leader Report™
© 2009 TWI Inc. All Rights Reserved

high-performance, growth and opportunity areas as compared to the average of their colleagues' assessments, relative to the TWI norms.

Each report includes an Action Planning Guide and guidance on how the leader can improve his or her results in each of the eight core competencies.

The Equitable Leader Report includes a "snapshot," an example of which is shown on the previous page. This snapshot summarizes the leader's self score in the first bar, the colleagues' score in the second bar, the TWI self norm in the third bar and the TWI colleague norm in the fourth bar. By comparing bar 1 (self score) to bar 3 (self norm), and bar 2 (colleagues' score) to bar 4 (colleagues' norm), we have an opportunity to assess a leader's effectiveness in the world of work. The snapshot also provides the leader with his or her high-performance areas, areas for growth and areas of opportunity.

BENCHMARKS AND BEST PRACTICES

Effective measurement, evaluation and reporting should be a major component of any human equity intervention. Measuring results and reporting on achievement will ensure that the organization continues to reach its human equity goals through proven progress. There is an established link between effective measurement, accountability and successful implementation of human equity. One of the key benefits of the ELA is that it is a tool that allows for accurate tracking and objective assessment of aggregate changes in leadership behavior. Many organizations have found that the combined averages of all their leaders on the ELA form an effective baseline that allows them to evaluate progress on a regular basis. This ELA framework will enable your organization to benchmark internally as well as externally against the normative data base maintained by TWI.

Another feature of the ELA is the ability to identify internal best practice leaders and managers. There is a common misperception that best practices are always found elsewhere. The ELA provides the added advantage of identifying internal best practice leaders who score higher than the external norm in the eight competency areas. Once identified, these high-performing leaders become an important resource to help develop competencies for other leaders who have scored below the norm and may require practical, hands-on guidance in particular areas.

CASE STUDY: ONTARIO MINISTRY OF LABOUR EQUITABLE LEADERSHIP ASSESSMENT

by Shelley James

> . . . And would some Power the small gift give us
> To see ourselves as others see us!
> It would from many a blunder free us,
> And foolish notion:
> What airs in dress and gait would leave us . . .

In his famous poem "To a Louse," Robert Burns wishes we had the ability to "to see ourselves as others see us."

For most of us, that's a noble yet challenging "developmental" exercise. But for managers, it's nearly impossible, when you consider the complexities of leading today's diverse workforce. Nevertheless, it's vital for improving employee engagement, filling the talent gap and enhancing business results.

Why?

If, as a manager, you don't understand how you're being perceived by all the employees you supervise, how do you know if you're leading them equitably? As a member of a leadership team, how is your contribution to building a respectful and vibrant workplace special and unique, and how do these skills translate personally into career aspirations for improvement and progression? Becoming a more perceptive, responsive and informed manager benefits your employees, your organization, your clients and your own personal and career growth.

(continued)

Treating people fairly isn't the same as treating them equitably. That's why the Ontario Ministry of Labour (MOL) has embarked on a journey to spur organizational change.

"Before 2008, diversity and inclusion concepts weren't integrated in our business practices, nor, I'd say, into how we approached our role as an employer across the Ontario Public Service," says Julie Bussieres, a business advisor in the ministry's Organizational Effectiveness Branch.

"It is not enough just to have a variety of different people in your workplace. There must also be an environment that values, celebrates and leverages those differences," says Noelle Richardson, the former chief diversity officer for the Ontario Public Service (OPS) Diversity Office.

Shelly Jamieson, a former secretary of cabinet, notes that "we recognize that racism and discrimination exist in the OPS, just as they unfortunately do in our broader society. Acknowledging a problem is the first step in tackling it. And we are doing both."

Each ministry was tasked with devising its own action plan to advance diversity and inclusion within the organization. The efforts of the Ministry of Labour on this front are making a difference inside the ministry and winning praise inside and outside the OPS.

It's the only ministry that has made a long-term commitment to annually assess its managers on their equitable leadership skills.

"It was a business imperative, both for our employees and for the people we serve," says Deputy Minister of Labour Cynthia Morton.

"Our mandate is to promote safe, fair and harmonious workplaces, so we really need to be leading the charge when it comes to promoting diversity and inclusion."

"When we go on a job site or try to assist workplace parties, our employees need to be able to understand and break through any cultural or linguistic barriers that may prevent vulnerable workers or employers from knowing their rights and responsibilities," Morton says.

In addition, she says, having a diverse and inclusive workplace is something that's essential for workforce planning.

"With the skills shortage resulting from an aging, retiring workforce, we have to be an employer of choice to attract the best and the brightest in order to compete with the private sector. We have to be an employer who values and respects diversity and reflects it in everything we do," she says.

The MOL's vision is to create a diverse and inclusive organization that delivers excellent public service, and supports all employees—including managers—to achieve their full potential. A task easier said than done.

To be successful, the ministry needed to engage its change agents: management!

"We launched a three-year diversity action plan that created opportunities for all staff to participate in designing and implementing new strategies for promoting equity and inclusion. A key part of our plan has been to help managers become fair, equitable and inclusive leaders because their actions and behaviors set the tone and the momentum across the ministry and across the regions," Morton says.

The ministry's strategic goals were to:

- Embed diversity objectives and outcomes into ministry policies, programs and services.
- Build a healthy workplace free from harassment and discrimination.
- Reflect the public it serves at all levels of the MOL workforce.
- Respond to the needs of a diverse population.

(continued)

To create and sustain real culture change, she says, "Our managers, including myself and the senior team, had to walk the talk. But they couldn't do that without the right tools and support."

Enter Trevor Wilson and His Team at TWI Inc.

The ministry issued a request for proposals to three consulting firms who specialized in diversity services. TWI Inc. won the competition.

"The company was selected because they're one of Canada's leading firms in the field of diversity and human equity," says Janis Bartley, director of the ministry's Organizational Effectiveness Branch (OEB).

"The process that they use to assess equitable leadership competencies was an ideal fit for our needs, and has proven to be a critical part of the ministry's journey of change and awareness.

"If we were really going to effect change, we needed to understand where we were as individual leaders as well as collectively as a senior management team, with regard to the diversity question. We needed to understand the internal and external barriers, develop strategies, set goals and measure success," she says.

The OEB, with the support of the deputy, used a staged developmental change process, created by TWI and researchers at the Western School of Business, called the Equitable Leader Assessment (ELA).

The ELA is a performance management tool that should be used annually to measure an individual's and an organization's behaviors and competencies that are consistent with inclusive and equitable leadership. These competencies are also related to business outcomes such as improved productivity, increased customer satisfaction, improved retention and increased business results.

The tool begins by setting benchmarks and goals with the deputy for leaders, to measure against and work toward.

Senior managers were evaluated first, followed by middle management.

They were evaluated on the range of competencies, identified by TWA and the researcher, as essential for equitable leadership:

1. **Openness to Difference:** demonstrating a positive attitude toward others who are different; actively seeking out opportunities to learn about cultures and lifestyles that are different from their own.

2. **Equitable Opportunity:** making employment decisions regarding team members (e.g., promotion, project staffing, development) on the basis of merit and skill.

3. **Accommodation:** demonstrating creativity when solving problems and adaptability when responding to the needs of different employees.

4. **Dignity and Respect:** creating a work environment that encourages open/transparent communication, where the opinions and contributions of all team members are valued.

5. **Commitment to Diversity and Inclusion:** enthusiastically endorsing and participating in programs to create and support diversity in the workplace.

6. **Knowledge of Diversity and Inclusion:** engaging in behaviors that reflect a general understanding of the meaning of "diversity" and demonstrating knowledge of best practices and relevant legislation.

7. **Change Management:** contributing to the development of an organization that values diversity through the implementation of effective change management practices.

8. **Ethics and Integrity:** embodying the principles of fair and ethical conduct and demonstrating honesty, reliability, responsibility and constancy in one's daily work life.

(continued)

The ELA asked the ministry's 40 senior managers and 90 middle managers to rate themselves on those eight competencies. Then their peers and direct reports were asked to assess the managers using the same markers. The results were then compared with each other and against industry and OPS norms.

Morton says, "We needed everyone to understand our business case and that the ELA wasn't a punitive evaluation, but one meant to identify high-performance areas and areas for growth.

"However, managers were also advised that after several years of using the ELA to better understand their strengths and areas for growth, if growth was not evident, the results of the ELA would become a part of a their performance plan to ensure progress and advancement of all managers' skills and competencies.

"Individual managers would be rewarded for being champions; weaker team members would be supported through education, awareness, training and mentoring to become equitable and respectful managers," she explains.

The Deputy Minister also set some goals for the ministry.

"It was really important for us to have something to work toward. Creating a diverse, inclusive, equitable and accessible organization isn't a destination, it's a journey," she says.

The ELA is a confidential tool. Raters are asked a series of questions about their colleague's work-related behaviors, including:

Does your colleague . . .

- Express interest in other people's ideas?
- Prefer to interact with those similar in age, ethnic background, etc.?
- Actively communicate with others to achieve the vision of a diverse organization?
- Willingly accommodate the diverse needs of employees to ensure they are able to perform to their full potential?
- Base employment decisions solely on merit?

- Display an awareness of the values and customs of different ethnic groups?
- Give both men and women the opportunity to work on high-profile projects?
- Assign projects based on an individual's skill and ability?
- When making decisions, consider the impact those decisions will have on all persons affected?
- Create work teams with diverse membership?

"The questions the ELA asks are questions we need to be asking, that many employers are not asking," says Joel Gorlick, a manager in the ministry's Employment, Labour and Corporate Policy Branch.

He has taken the ELA three years in a row and says, "The questions pinpoint gaps between the way you see things and the way staff perceive things with regard to ethics and integrity, dignity and respect, and so forth, and that's really useful."

The Results

TWI Inc. compared responses with those from managers' self-assessments, then measured them against standards for leaders in the public and private sectors. Each manager received a report identifying his or her high-performance areas, areas for growth, or areas of opportunities. For each competency they received a score from 1 to 5.

Filomena Savoia, regional director in the ministry's Operations Division, says, "I wasn't apprehensive about being evaluated in that way. I see the feedback as a great tool to help you improve your management style. It makes you more 'self-aware' of issues."

(continued)

"To be honest, I'm always a little nervous, yet interested in hearing other people's perception of me as a leader," says Sophie Dennis, assistant deputy minister of operations. "But the ELA is really helpful because it would be even harder to get that feedback directly from someone you work with every day."

The aggregate report of the baseline results gathered in 2010 showed that the ministry was performing at Level 4 (with Level 5 being the highest).

The last ELA was conducted in November 2012. It revealed the following high-performance areas:

Managers . . .

- Being able to speak knowledgeably about legislation surrounding fair hiring practices.
- Not tolerating other people making inappropriate jokes or comments.
- Actively seeking out information about the best ways to accommodate the needs of diverse employees.
- Working closely with human resources to ensure up-to-date knowledge of key legislation relevant to diversity.
- Not preferring to interact with others who are similar to oneself with respect to age and ethnic background, etc.

The lowest scoring indicators were:

Managers . . .

- Taking full responsibility for one's own actions and for the actions that one initiates in others.
- Basing employment decisions (e.g., hiring and promotion) solely on merit.
- Assigning projects and work based on an individual's skills and abilities.

- Not tending to delay the implementation of changes that support diversity.
- Being conscious of one's language to ensure that one does not exclude specific groups.

While the ministry has made incredible progress addressing the issues raised by the first ELA, there still remain some areas for growth.

"Although we have made significant improvements on all the competencies, the assessment also shows that we still have work to do to achieve our goals in many key areas," the deputy says.

All managers attended a half-day workshop, facilitated by the consultants, to discuss their results.

"It's like driving a Volkswagen Bug: once you have one, you always see one on the road," says Dennis. "It has made me a better person, and a better leader. As a ministry, we make better decisions and we are a better ministry for it."

Her division is responsible for administering the province's Occupational Health and Safety Act and Employment Standards Act.

She credits the ELA for helping to sensitize her divisional leadership in meeting the needs of vulnerable workers.

"We've adjusted our recruitment strategies, so we are now looking in places for talent we haven't in the past, like putting ads in ethnic newspapers, speaking to different ethnic groups and explaining the work that we do," she says.

"We have an obligation to protect the vulnerable and if there's a language barrier we can't do that effectively. We can't get their feedback about workplace hazards and employment standards violations," she says. "So now we're hiring people who can speak other languages and using translators on site visits."

(*continued*)

"Today, we strive to embed diversity and inclusion concepts into just about everything we do," adds Bartley. "We use an 'inclusion lens' in our policy development, results-based planning, program development and recruitment."

Beyond the focus on the managers as leaders, the ministry's action plan reached out to all staff and all regions of the province. To achieve buy-in and a good response rate, the MOL used a variety of internal communication tools to get its managers and employees on side. This was—and remains—an area of ongoing focus to ensure that staff members see real results and a consistent commitment to diversity as a priority of the ministry.

The ministry also established an inclusion and diversity council, made up of employees who volunteered from across the organization, to drive and sustain the change process.

First on their agenda was to develop a business case for diversity.

"To mainstream diversity and inclusion, incorporate it into all aspects of our business, we really needed to be able to show each and every employee 'what's in it for them'," says Tom Zach, the council's founding chairperson and the ministry's director of marketing and communications.

"We created a diversity portal on the MOL Intranet and produced a video, featuring a variety of employees making the case for diversity."

The crux of the ministry's business case centered on four key facts. The following business case for diversity was posted on the ministry's Intranet and all managers were asked to share and discuss it with staff during branch meetings:

Business Case for Diversity

I. The Need to Address the Talent Gap

With a retiring workforce ahead, MOL must be an employer of choice for new professionals from the global talent pool as well as existing OPS employees. MOL will be better positioned to recruit top talent from a diverse population and compete with the private sector to fill the skills shortage with employees who will choose inclusive employers.

In the next five years:

- 26 percent of all MOL employees will be eligible to retire.
- 42 percent of MOL senior managers will be eligible to retire.
- 37 percent of MOL managers will be eligible to retire.

2. Diverse Teams Produce Better Results

Capitalizing on diversity will help us generate new ideas on improved services and service delivery and increase productivity to provide better public services.

- Research shows that diverse teams (that is, people from different fields of expertise, cultures and perspectives) are much more productive than homogeneous teams.
- Diverse teams may see the same problem differently, which can lead to better solutions. Diverse teams produce better results.

3. Our Workforce Should Reflect Ontario's Diversity

Understanding various perspectives will allow us to better understand and proactively respond to the needs of the communities and clients that we serve.

- By 2017, visible minorities will make up almost 29 percent of the population.

4. An Inclusive Culture Will Foster Employee Engagement

Research shows higher employee engagement, reduced absenteeism and improved retention in inclusive organizations.

(*continued*)

The ministry also launched a diversity mentorship program that paired senior managers with staff from target groups. The program gave assistant deputy ministers and directors an opportunity to learn from mentees about the issues, experiences and challenges they may face in the workplace because of their background, disability or sexual orientation. In turn, mentees had access to senior leaders and their experience and perspectives on how to succeed in the public service.

"I learned a lot from my mentee," says Maria Papoutsis, director of the Health and Safety Policy Branch. "It was an incredible learning experience. It helped open my eyes to issues and barriers I wasn't aware of."

Where the MOL Is Today

- Since the 2010 baseline, all MOL leadership scores have gone up for both the self and colleague ratings.
- MOL leaders now rate above the external TWI leadership norm (leaders in private companies) for all eight areas.
- The leaders now rate above the OPS external norm (OPS managers) on all eight areas.
- The MOL highest 20 percent leaders still rate significantly higher than the external TWI norm.
- The MOL lowest 20 percent have substantially improved their scores, based on colleague perception, since 2010.

There is a substantially reduced gap between the way the lowest 20 percent see themselves and the way they are perceived by their colleagues, which signals an improvement in self-awareness.

But there's still a slight gap between the goals that the deputy originally set and the ministry's overall scores.

These are with respect to:

- Accommodation
- Equitable opportunity
- Dignity and respect
- Ethics and integrity.

"I set our goals high for a reason, because if you aim for the moon, you reach the stars," she says.

How does she plan on closing the gap?

"I think we can do a number of things that involve playing to our strengths," she says. For instance:

- Leverage high-performance managers.
- Provide mandatory training and development opportunities.
- Hold managers accountable.
- Include diversity and inclusion commitments in all performance plans.
- Work together as a team to find solutions.

Over the past three years, many employees have noticed a systemic change in leadership styles, says Bussieres.

This was reflected in the organization's last employee survey, she says.

Results showed the MOL had an inclusion index of 74.3 out of 100, in comparison to the OPS average of 72.5. And its employee engagement index measured at 73.4, while the OPS average was 69.2.

"Our managers are definitely more aware of how they're being perceived by their direct reports and understand what competencies they need to work on.

"Perception is reality," she says.

Robbie Burns would certainly agree.

Conclusion: The *Why* of Human Equity

> *Without talented, engaged employees and effective leaders to lead them, businesses will have trouble executing strategies and driving business growth.*
>
> —Conference Board of Canada, 2012[1]

One of the best arguments I have heard recently was in a Ted.com speech called "How Great Leaders Inspire Action" by Simon Sinek. Sinek is an author best known for popularizing a concept he calls "the Golden Circle." He joined the RAND Corporation in 2010 as an adjunct staff member, where he advises on matters of military innovation and planning. Sinek makes a compelling case that if you can clearly articulate *why* you are doing something, the *what* and the *how* are easy. However, without a compelling why, a great how or what (which may include a plan, abundant resources, excellent tools and superior product) will not lead to success. The bottom line of the speech is: "People don't buy what you do, they buy why you do it." That is, they buy your purpose, your cause, your belief. Sinek points out that Martin Luther King, Jr., didn't attract 250,000 people to the National Mall because he said "I have a plan." They showed up because he had a dream.

---

1. Rebecca Ray, The Conference Board Inc., "CEO Challenge Reflections: Human Capital Practitioners Respond," Executive Action 387 (September 2012): 2.

Sinek's speech caused me to think about the *why* of human equity. According to research done in 2011 by the Conference Board of Canada and the Conference Board Inc., in New York, global CEOs have ranked human capital as their second greatest challenge, just behind innovation, which is also intricately linked to human capital. It would appear that the long-awaited war for talent, put on hold during the depths of the global financial/economic crisis (which now seems to be coming to an end in parts of the world), has reemerged as a pressing issue for executive leadership. In high-growth economies such as India and China, human capital is listed as the number one challenge, ahead of issues such as global economic risk, cost optimization and even customer relationships.

As stated in Chapter 4, when we talk about human capital, the challenge can be broken into three areas:

1. The need to attract high potential talent in an increasingly competitive labor market.
2. The need to retain top talent in an increasingly competitive labor market.
3. The need to engage top talent at a time when more than 40 percent of employees are somewhat or completely disengaged.

What is driving the importance of human capital and human equity is the unrelenting reality of demographic changes in the North American workforce, especially in relation to leadership.

The "Demographic Changes in Leadership" figures (on the following page) show TWI Inc.'s typical client today. Many are facing the realities of the looming baby boomer retirement, where one-third of the workforce becomes eligible for retirement within the next decade. This is having a huge impact at the senior executive level: in some organizations, 75 percent of leaders are eligible for retirement. When they look to the usual feeder groups for succession planning, 50 percent of them are also ready to exit the workforce.

A recent *Economist* article puts the demographic reality into perspective: "According to Manpower, 46% of senior human-resources executives surveyed in the company's latest global annual survey said

Demographic Changes in Leadership

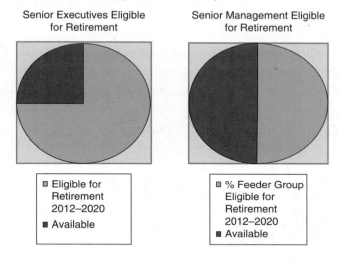

Senior Executives Eligible
for Retirement

Senior Management Eligible
for Retirement

▣ Eligible for
Retirement
2012–2020
■ Available

▣ % Feeder Group
Eligible for
Retirement
2012–2020
■ Available

that their talent gap was making it harder for their firm to implement its business strategy. Only 27% said they felt their business had the talent it needed."[2]

The primary *why* of my first book, *Diversity at Work*, was to position diversity as a business issue, to encourage people to look beyond diversity as a legislated or corporate social responsibility issue and position it as a business issue related to organizational effectiveness outcomes such as improved employee engagement, increased productivity and enhanced profitability.

Today, the idea of approaching diversity as a business issue is passé. In fact, many leaders are interested in the proof of the business case. I believe the diversity fatigue epidemic discussed in Chapter I is partly from the lack of solid evidence that diversity has had a major impact on bottom-line business outcomes, as was promised. This is even though 75 percent of Fortune 1000 companies have a diversity initiative and the business case for diversity has been embraced enthusiastically by most politically correct senior executive leaders. Despite all of this, empirical support for the business case is scant. Some evidence exists to support the general idea

2. "Got Talent? A Special Report on the Future of Jobs," *Economist*, September 2011.

that positive outcomes can result from having a diverse employee population, but just as much research indicates that the impact of traditional diversity initiatives can have a negative impact on organizations. Diversity in some organizations has led to a divisive, victim-oriented mindset that concentrates on correcting past wrongs for specific groups.

And so, at this 25th anniversary of diversity, it is time to take a sober second look at the promise of diversity. It's time for us to use some down-home Dr. Phil common sense and ask, "How's it working for us?" We need to ask, "If we continue on this road, are things likely to be much better in a decade or two decades or a century?"

So what are we to do? After 25 years, is it not too late to abandon ship, even if it is not exactly seaworthy? Is it possible to change direction? Millions, perhaps billions, of dollars and hundreds of thousands of people hours have been spent trying to find the Holy Grail of diversity. Where do we go from here?

Enter the *why* of human equity. It is time to move beyond diversity to human equity. It is time to move beyond the group focus of diversity toward the individual perspective of human equity. It is time to focus on talent differentiation rather than on group differentiation. It is time to focus on maximizing the unique abilities of each person rather than confining them to membership in a specific group.

The goal of this book is not to convince everyone in the business world who may need human equity to embrace it. Rather, its goal is to help everyone who believes human equity is needed in today's world to understand it. At the core of Sinek's Golden Circle is the *why*. The *how* of the Golden Circle is reflected in parts 1 and 2 of this book, which recount how human equity came out of the original diversity work done almost 20 years ago. We revisited the Equity Continuum and the work related to measuring progress, and also explored the essential role of leadership and the eight core competencies of an equitable leader. As well, we looked at the concept of positive psychology, which promises to revolutionize the way we manage people. It is my contention that human equity is the first management concept to be presented from a positive psychology paradigm, replacing the typical deficit management model that focuses on correcting employee weaknesses, rather than playing to employee strengths. I introduced the reader to the SHAPE V Talent Model, which seeks to expand the typical picture of talent by looking at an individual's intangible traits, such as his or her passions, attitude and character.

The final segment of the book, Part 3, dealt with the *what* of human equity. It explored the measurement tools: the Equitable Leader Assessment and the Human Equity Assessment Tool.

Today's work environment is one that includes globalization, unprecedented technological change, drastically changing demographics and an abundance of differentiated employment contracts. Never has there been a more important time to harness all employees' talents. Never has there been a more important time to use human equity and to maximize on human capital. Never has there been a more important time to create equitable leaders who understand the human equity advantage.

Afterword: My *Why* of Human Equity

Shortly before I graduated from university in the early 1980s, I heard a survey result that scared the hell out of me. Apparently, 90 percent of people hated their job. Hated! I swore to myself that I would not be in that number. Within two years of that earnest but silent pledge, I was smack in the middle of that 90 percent, working as a teller supervisor at one of the largest commercial banks in Canada. Not only did I hate my job, but I was also awful at it. "How did this happen?" I would ask myself regularly. "Where did I go wrong?"

I spent about two years in this living hell before escaping to do something else. But looking back, I can see that those two years of suffering started me on the path to understanding human equity; it was when the *why* of human equity started to manifest for me. I say "started" because it would take almost 30 years for the full picture of human equity to unfold, including the 20 years my colleagues at TWI and I spent with the idea of diversity. It has been a slow gestation, almost like putting together a 10,000-piece jigsaw puzzle, with only a handful of pieces being provided every year from 1987 to 2011, when the final piece was provided and I could see the whole picture.

Those first two years of my career initiated a search that continues to this day. The search had me seek out ancient great thinkers and teachers, challenging self-development courses and sacred manuscripts. It had me travel around the world in an attempt to understand what really matters in life and why so many people are unfulfilled in their work.

I have had two midlife crises. The first was actually a pre-midlife crisis, I suppose, since it happened when I was 27 years old. It was prompted by my confronting the "bill of goods" that I had unconsciously bought into during my university years. The unquestioned belief was that if you went to the right school, got a reputable degree, found a worthy spouse, bought a nice house with a white picket fence and a few cars, and had a couple of kids, you would be happy. I followed this checklist with great fervor. By the time I was 27, I had pretty much completed the list.

One night in particular stands out for me. It was around 2 a.m. I walked down the stairs of my very nice suburban home, with my beautiful wife sleeping upstairs and my first child safely in his crib. I remember thinking, "You have done it. You have completed the entire checklist." Oh sure, I could get another car, or have another child or even buy a nicer house, but by and large I had checked everything off the list. The frightening part was that when I looked inside myself, I realized that there was no happiness. Where was this happiness that I had been promised? How did I miss it? Where did I get ripped off? That was the beginning of a crisis for me—and the first piece of the human equity puzzle.

The search for happiness started with finding what life was really about beyond that checklist based mostly on material things. And so I started to search for my purpose. It was that search that led me to three quotations that would have a profound effect on me. To me, these three quotations represent the essence and the *why* of human equity.

Our deepest fear is not that we are inadequate. Our deepest fear is that we are powerful beyond measure. It is our light, not our darkness, that most frightens us. We ask ourselves, "Who am I to be brilliant, gorgeous, talented and fabulous?" Actually who are you not to be? You are a child of God. Your playing small doesn't serve the world. There's nothing enlightened about shrinking so that other people won't feel insecure around you. We were born to make manifest the glory of God that is within us. It's not just in some of us; it's in everyone. And as we let our own light shine, we unconsciously give other people permission to do the same. As we are liberated from our own fear, our presence automatically liberates others.

—*Marianne Williamson*, A Return to Love[1]

To me, this quote represents much of what human equity is about. In most of my life, fear has been present. It was present when I entered the workforce, it was there during my first job, it was there when I left that job, it was there when I got married, it was there when I had my first son, it was there when I had my first daughter, it was there when I went through divorce, it was there when I wrote my first book, it is here now. It is relentless and ubiquitous. It visits regularly and frequently leads to another common foe: procrastination. I suspect I am not the only one who has this type of relationship with fear. It is the primary reason that it has taken 17 years to write this second book.

But then the quote takes us beyond fear to point to the possibility for something else—"our light." A light that has been put in each one of us. A light so brilliant and fabulous when accessed that it can actually change the world. Most people don't spend too much time thinking of themselves in these terms, but that does not mean they don't have this light. It may simply mean they have yet to see it. And until that time they play small. They live partially, instead of fully self-actualized.

The quote ends with hope, the hope of finding our light. And as we find it and live it, we unconsciously become a role model for others. We live out of happiness instead of worry, we live out of hope instead of fear, we show up in the world as the passionate, impactful creative beings that we already are even though we may not know it. By accessing our light we defeat fear and prepare ourselves for the promise encapsulated in the second quote:

---

1. Marianne Williamson, *A Return to Love* (New York: HarperCollins, 1992), 21.

To man has been given the job of emulating his maker—of becoming a creator, finding new and broader and better ways through which to express the creative force in him. His is the work of creating beauty, of bringing more of comfort, of joy and happiness into the world.

You are a son of God, a Creator; therefore creation is expected of you. You are to spread seeds not merely of human kind but of intellect as well. You are to leave the world a better place than you found it, with more of joy in it, more of beauty, of comfort, of understanding, of light.

Robert Collier, The Law of the Higher Potential[2]

Here we are offered the promise of creation. Rarely do we think of ourselves as creators emulating the source that created us all. But surely this is the case: we create and are capable of creation. We simply need to look at the plethora of inventions that continue to flow from these body/mind organisms called human beings—everything from the wheel, the chair, the atomic bomb, all the way through to the Internet. All inventions, including this book, were created through some person. I say "through" because I believe we are the channels for these ideas, not the source.

Perhaps one of the most impactful speeches I've ever heard was given by Archbishop Desmond Tutu. It was called "The Impotence of God." Tutu explained that we always talk about the omnipotence of God and how God can do everything. But rarely do we talk about the impotence of God. "God has no mouth," he explained. "He uses your mouth. God has no arms, he uses your arms. God has no body, he uses your body. You are co-creators with God."[3] And as co-creators, what are we here to create? As the last line of the Collier quote says, we are here to create something that will leave the world a better place than we found it.

---

2. Robert Collier, *The Law of the Higher Potential* (Kingsport, TN: Kingsport Press, 1947), 48.

3. Archbishop Desmond Tutu, interviewed by Sir David Frost, "God's Omnipotence and Impotence: Archbishop Tutu—The Frost Interview" (2013): www.youtube.com/watch?v=ySCkDwYaZIE.

Not too long ago I heard about a survey of 90-year-olds.[4] They were asked, knowing what they know now, how they would live their lives differently if they had a chance to do it all over again. Their answers fell into three themes:

1. Worry less
2. Risk more
3. Work on something that would live beyond them.

The "something" in this last point no doubt refers to something that would bring more comfort, joy, understanding or light. This is another piece of the *why* of human equity. This is what some people call legacy. One hundred years from now, will Bill Gates be remembered more for the billions of dollars he made at Microsoft or for giving away billions of dollars through his foundation? I suspect the latter.

The last is a declaration of how to live and also how not to live:

This is the true joy in life, the being used for a purpose recognized by yourself as a mighty one; the being thoroughly worn out before you are thrown on the scrap heap; the being a force of Nature instead of a feverish selfish little clod of ailments and grievances complaining that the world will not devote itself to making you happy.

I am of the opinion that my life belongs to the whole community and as long as I live it is my privilege to do for it whatever I can.

I want to be thoroughly used up when I die, for the harder I work the more I live. I rejoice in life for its own sake. Life is no brief candle to me. It is a sort of splendid torch which

---

4. Keith Boudreau (www.growthcoachnorthshore.com), "If I Could Go Back and Change One Thing," January 2011.

I have got hold of for the moment, and I want to make it burn as brightly as possible before handing it on to future generations.

—*George Bernard Shaw,* Man and Superman, *1903*

Being used for a purpose is an important part of understanding the *why* of human equity. For years I would say a prayer that ended with, "Let me become all you planned for me." If you take the theme of using the light from the first quote, the creative ability referred to in the second quote and the idea of being used for a mighty purpose in this last quote, you have the *why* of human equity.

But what of the option referred to in this third quote, of "being a feverish, selfish little clod of ailments and grievances complaining that the world will not devote itself to making you happy"—an option many choose to take? It is so easy to assume that the world revolves around us. But what if we are only part of something much bigger? What if we each have a unique and important contribution to make to this place? What if we had the courage to use our power to make this world a better place? Would we not want to have this light burn as brightly as possible before it is extinguished?

• • •

Every thirteen minutes another hundred people—members of the wealthiest and best-educated generation the world has ever known—begin reckoning with their mortality and asking deep questions about meaning, significance and what they truly want. When the cold front of demographics meets the warm front of unrealized dreams, the result will be a thunderstorm of purpose the likes of which the world has never seen.

—*Daniel Pink,* Drive[5]

---

5. Pink, *Drive*, 133.

My second midlife crisis began more than 20 years later, on June 11, 2005. While I was no longer wallowing in the unhappiness I felt at age 27, there was something else that had raised its head. Some refer to it as the flame of dissatisfaction, some call it halftime, some just call it the fear of getting old. I was being confronted with turning 50 and the realization that most of what, when I was young, I hoped my life would look like was unlikely to happen. I was past my prime and old age was looming fast. I was facing the fact that I probably had fewer years left on this planet than I had already used.

On that day a woman shared with me that she was "born again" at 50 and had started counting her age all over again. She explained that this meant she was only 5 years old, not the 55 years she looked. I thought this was a better way of looking at turning 50 than simply believing you were getting old. When I applied this idea to my own life, I realized that it was exactly nine months to the day before I would turn 50. In other words, this was the day of my second conception. On the date of my first conception, I wasn't conscious; however, I certainly was on this second one. This second conception allowed me the opportunity to witness the nine-month gestation period of a second, yet-to-be-lived life. I spent the following nine months looking deeply at what was next for me. It was a very difficult time. There were many questions and many visits to very dark places. At one point I wrote in my journal that I now knew how dark the womb must be.

Somewhere in this gestation period I came across two books by Bob Buford: *Halftime* and *Finishing Well.* Buford is a very successful businessman who had also lamented over getting old as he turned 50. He was explaining his dilemma to an 80-year-old man one day and the wise old soul pointed out to him that 50 was not old. It may have been old when people died at age 65, but it wasn't old today when people are expected to go to 80, 90 maybe even 100. In fact, he said, "If you go to 100, think of 50 as the halftime point in your life." Buford extended this line of reasoning into his concept of halftime. The halftime movement has since grown into a full curriculum of courses and online support groups that involves thousands of baby boomers and their spouses.

Halftime is based on the premise that life has two periods: the first half and the second half—just like in a soccer game. And just like in a soccer game, the second half need bear no resemblance to the first half. The book explains that the first half (up to age 50) is about getting. It is all about the list I was confronted with in my mid-20s. You get your house, you get your spouse, you get your job, you get your car, and the rest of your "stuff," which creates some level of material success and comfort. As another spiritual thinker, Neale Donald Walsch, writes of this transition from first to second half:

> Your younger years were never meant for truth teaching but for truth gathering . . . and you will be searching and experimenting and finding and failing and forming and reforming your truth, your idea about yourself until you are half a century on this planet . . . then you become a wiser one, an elder. . . . it is elders who know of truth and life. Of what is important and what is not. Of what is really meant by such terms as integrity, honesty, loyalty, friendship and love.
> —*Neale Donald Walsch*, Conversations with God, Book 3[6]

In other words, by the time you reach 50 you are ready for your second half, which is no longer about getting but about giving back. Your second half is about what you will leave behind—that is, being used by a mighty purpose. This second half is the half of your life reserved for purpose, significance and legacy.

In *Finishing Well*, Buford documents notable leaders who lived their second half quite differently from their first half. Apparently, this book led Bill Gates to leave Microsoft, where he had made billions of dollars for himself, to run the foundation where he will use some of this money to end diseases on the planet that have already been beaten in the developed world, educate every child by supporting education breakthroughs such

---

6. Neale Donald Walsch, *Conversations with God: An Uncommon Dialogue, Book 3* (Newburyport, MA: Hampton Roads Publishing Company, 1998), 34–35.

as the Khan Academy, and make technology available to every person. Talk about leaving the world a better place than he found it.

A few months ago, an old friend told me that after almost 23 years, he was two steps away from the CEO position in his company, a leading Fortune 500 organization. He explained that if he left his job today at 48, he could get 75 percent of his pension; if he stayed another two years, he would get 100 percent. I asked what his dilemma was. He went on to explain that he didn't think he could last another two years there. After more than 20 years at it, the work was no longer meaningful to him, and he doubted that he was making a difference. I told him it sounded like he was going through a midlife crisis and shared some of the learnings from my own seven years earlier, when I had discovered *Halftime*. Within months of our conversation, he voluntarily left his six-figure job, designed and negotiated a generous golden handshake package and had recommitted to his 25-year dream of becoming a minister.

In 2006, the first members of the baby boom generation turned 60. Somewhere between ages 50 and 60 is the time that people will begin to ask questions like, "When am I going to make a difference in my life?" and "What is my purpose?" Given that in the United States alone there are almost 80 million boomers, each day more than 11,000 people will hit this age of purpose. Human equity—with its emphasis on the unique abilities that each one of us has to offer—can play a major role in the transition of this group from the first to the second half.

Appendix

I: PERSONAL LEADERSHIP BEHAVIOR ASSESSMENT: ANSWER KEY

0 True: You may be a top 10 percent equitable leader.
1–5 True: You may be a bottom 10 percent equitable leader.
5–10 True: You may be a temporary boss-hole.
10–15 True: You may be a borderline certified boss-hole.
15 or more True: Certified boss-hole.

II: THE HUMAN EQUITY ASSESSMENT TOOL TEMPLATE

A year after the publication of *Diversity at Work*, a group of diversity practitioners from a dozen blue-ribbon organizations came together with a single mission—to improve the way they integrated and measured diversity. They formed an informal network that became known as the Trinity Group. Over the years, the core members of the group dedicated hundreds of hours to create a reliable measurement framework for diversity. The mission was finally completed in 1999 with the creation of the Diversity Assessment Tool (DAT). Trinity's initial vision was to develop a methodology they could use to assess progress within their own organizations, which would balance ease of use with rigor and detail, and eventually enable external benchmarking with other organizations.

Over the years, progressive organizations aspiring to move forward along the Equity Continuum began to use the Diversity Assessment Tool. This assessment tool is a survey of perceptions to measure both internal climate and to gauge external public and stakeholders' perceptions. The tool measures the five levels of the continuum through the lens of six organizational processes and eight practices, based on the original ISO framework for measuring quality. Shortly after the Trinity Group completed its work, the Canadian government's Task Force on an Inclusive Public Service adapted the tool to evaluate progress in diversity in its various departments.

In the summer of 2012 the Trinity Group reconvened to update the Diversity Assessment Tool to encompass the concepts of inclusion and human equity. The renewed Trinity Group included original members as well as sectors not represented in the first project. The result of the work of the renewed Trinity Group is the Human Equity Assessment Tool (HEAT). This enhanced measurement tool is described as a robust measurement process that quantitatively assesses an organization's progress in diversity, inclusion and human equity. The Trinity Group has partnered with a team of academics to use the tool to develop standards that allow for benchmarking internally and externally, as well as within and between various industries.

The template is divided into three stages:

Stage 1 provides a diagnostic overview, and allows the organization to assess its progress on the Equity Continuum at a high level using the Equity Continuum Scorecard. (See below.)

Stage 2 of the Human Equity Assessment Tool reviews the essential organizational processes necessary to create an equitable and inclusive environment.

Stage 3 evaluates what an organization actually does in terms of an essential practice, rather than its formal policies and procedures.

The online tool also includes a matrix of validation statements that are constructed to measure the five levels of the continuum against the six processes and eight practices, which comes to an aggregate of 240 statements that form the entire evaluation. Working through these three levels and using these statements will allow you to conduct an informal assessment of how far your organization is from a Level 5 on the continuum.

The Structure of the Diversity Assessment Tool

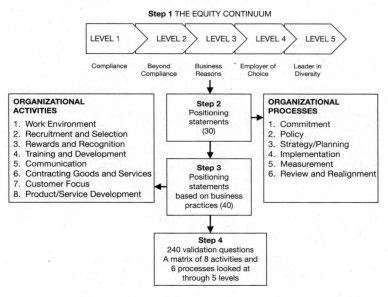

STAGE 1: THE EQUITY CONTINUUM SCORECARD

This tool can be accessed on the Human Equity Advantage site (www .equitableleader.com). It will allow you to get an initial assessment of where your organization is on the Equity Continuum. (Turn to page 301 to see how you can save $100 on ELA Assessment Tools.) These eight questions are a proxy for the 240 questions in the full Human Equity Assessment Tool. By taking a sample of your employees and having them answer these eight questions, you can receive a customized analysis report to strategize how to move to the next step on the continuum.

The Equity Continuum Scorecard

Complete the scorecard to help rate your organization's performance in the area of diversity and inclusion. The scorecard helps gauge where your organization sits on the Equity Continuum—a core measure of equitable and inclusive work environments.

To complete the scorecard, read each pair of phrases and rate your reaction on the scale provided.

	1 2 3 4 5	
We do not have a clear vision of our ideal work environment that incorporates equity and inclusion	☐ ☐ ☐ ☐ ☐	We have a clear vision of our ideal work environment that incorporates equity and inclusion
We do not have a compelling business case for diversity	☐ ☐ ☐ ☐ ☐	We have a compelling business case for diversity
Leaders do not understand, support or regularly communicate the business case	☐ ☐ ☐ ☐ ☐	Leaders understand, support and regularly communicate the business case
We do not have clearly defined goals and timetables to achieve an equitable and inclusive work environment	☐ ☐ ☐ ☐ ☐	We have clearly defined goals and timetables to achieve an equitable and inclusive work environment
We do not have qualitative and quantitative organizational data to understand our current work environment	☐ ☐ ☐ ☐ ☐	We have qualitative and quantitative organizational data to understand our current work environment
We do not have strategies and a well-defined road map to achieve our goals	☐ ☐ ☐ ☐ ☐	We have strategies and a well-defined road map to achieve our goals
We do not have an integrated measurement process that uses our human resources and organizational review practices to "prove" our business case	☐ ☐ ☐ ☐ ☐	We do have an integrated measurement process that uses our human resources and organizational review practices to "prove" our business case
We do not have an infrastructure to support our equity and inclusion strategies	☐ ☐ ☐ ☐ ☐	We have an infrastructure to support our equity and inclusion strategies

0	1	2	3	4	5
Organizations that Believe They Are Equitable	Organizations Driven by Compliance	Organizations Moving Beyond Compliance	Organizations Using a Business Case Approach	Organizations Practicing Integrated Diversity	Organizations That Are Inclusive and Equitable

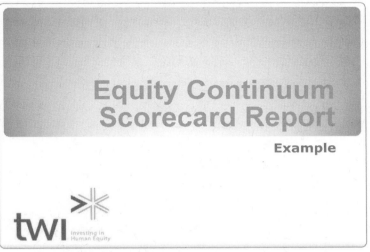

© 2011 TWI Inc. All Rights Reserved.

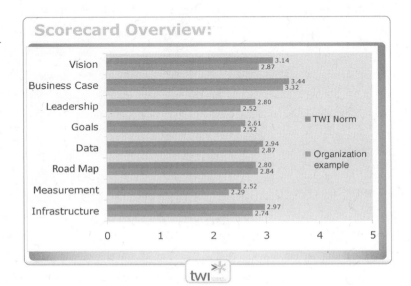

Range Scores: Organization Example

	Minimum Score	Maximum Score	Average	Consensus Index*
Vision	1	5	2.87	1.024
Business Case	1	5	3.32	1.423
Leadership	1	5	2.52	1.061
Goals	1	4	2.52	0.890
Data	1	5	2.87	1.088
Road Map	1	5	2.84	0.898
Measurement	1	4	2.29	1.006
Infrastructure	1	5	2.74	1.125
Continuum Score			2.75	1.100

* Higher numbers = less consensus

Scorecard: Highlights

Highest Scores	Highest Relative to TWI Norm
• Business Case	• Strategies and Road Map
Lowest Scores	Lowest Relative to TWI Norm
• Measurement Process	• Vision • Leadership and Communication
Most Variability	Most Consensus Overall
• Business Case	• Goals and Timetables

Overall EC Rating = 2.75	versus	TWI Norm = 2.90

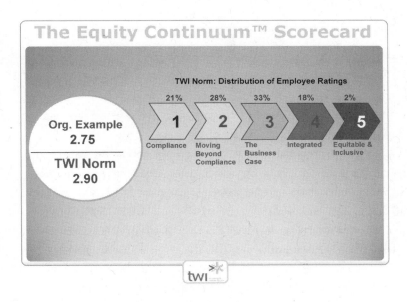

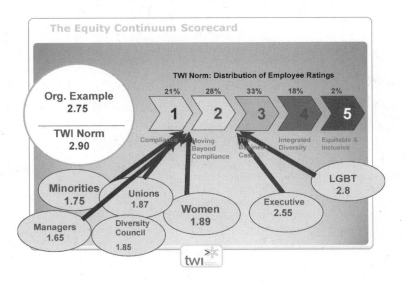

STAGE 2: PROCESSES

Definition: A sequence of interdependent and linked procedures that, at every stage, consume one or more resources (employee time, energy, money) to convert inputs (data, material, etc.) into outputs. These outputs then serve as inputs for the next stage until a known goal or end result (e.g., a Level 3, 4 or 5 on the continuum) is reached.

The process statements in the HEAT follow the ISO quality circle process model. If an organization is committed to becoming an equitable and inclusive work environment (a Level 5) it would first make a commitment to do so, which is followed by a policy to formalize the commitment and outline specific goals and outcomes to bring the commitment to life. The organization would then create a strategy and plan to achieve the desired outcomes articulated in the policy that is followed by the effective implementation of the strategy or plan. The next steps are to develop appropriate metrics to measure if the outcomes are being achieved. Based on the results of the measurements the organization would realign its strategy to achieve continuous improvement toward its vision of an equitable and inclusive work environment.

Commitment

Definition: To commit is to pledge yourself to a certain purpose or line of conduct. It also means practicing your beliefs consistently. Commitment ignites action. The necessary condition for commitment is having a sound set of beliefs and faithful adherence to those beliefs demonstrated through behavior. Possibly the best description of commitment is "persistence with a purpose."

Level 1
- A commitment is made to comply with legislated guidelines or other standards.

- Commitment flows from HR or the function responsible for compliance.
- Resources are allocated to meet these equity requirements.

Example: A written organization statement confirms the organization's commitment to compliance.

Level 2
- A commitment is made to go beyond compliance to correct injustices to historically disadvantaged groups because doing so meets the goal of corporate social responsibility.
- Commitment usually flows from a supportive manager.
- Resources are allocated for special equity projects and their promotion.

Example: The organization provides Brailled business cards and product information in alternative formats.

Level 3
- A commitment is made to diversity as a business issue that will bring benefits to the workplace and marketplace.
- Commitment flows from the organizational leaders.
- Resources are allocated for diversity initiatives in the workplace and investments made in targeted markets where a business case exists.

Example: The organization's leaders regularly focus on diversity as a benefit to the success of the business in internal and external communications.

Level 4
- A commitment is made by all members of the organization to create a diverse and inclusive work environment, where each person is valued and respected and individual talents optimized.

- This commitment is evidenced at senior leadership and management levels.
- Inclusion-related financial and people resources are allocated as a standard operating cost.

Example: The organization's leaders focus on moving beyond discussions of groups to the individual talent of each employee.

Level 5

- A commitment is made by all members of the organization to embrace and foster the practice of human equity, both internally and beyond the boundaries of the organization.
- The organization works with customers/clients, stakeholders, suppliers and communities that share their commitment to diversity, inclusion and human equity.

Example: The organization's leaders focus on maximizing the individual talent of each employee and rigorous talent differentiation from a positive psychology perspective.

Policy

Definition: A proposed or adopted course of action.

Level 1

- Policies are developed to respond to applicable legislated guidelines or other requirements.
- Policies are developed by HR or the function responsible for compliance.

Example: The organization's hiring policies are developed to comply with legislated guidelines or other requirements.

Level 2

- Policies are developed to go beyond compliance to correct injustices to historically disadvantaged groups and to promote corporate social responsibility.
- Policies designed to benefit target groups are developed by HR or the function responsible for compliance, with input from a supportive manager.

Example: Policies are developed to provide reasonable religious accommodation to employees of various religious backgrounds.

Level 3

- Policies are developed to implement diversity programs in the workplace and in targeted markets where a business case exists.
- Policies are developed with input from employees and approved by organizational leaders.

Example: Workplace policies focus on the elimination of systemic barriers; marketplace policies focus on achieving business advantage in target markets.

Level 4

- Policies integrate diversity and inclusion in all workplace processes and across all markets.

Example: Workplace policies focus on including each person based on his or her unique difference and contribution to the organization.

Level 5

- Policies are developed to promote human equity internally and also externally beyond the boundaries of the organization.
- Customers/clients, stakeholders, suppliers and/or community provide input to the development of policies.
- Policies are leading-edge and recognized as models of excellence.

Example: Workplace policies focus on implementing human equity to both internal and external stakeholders.

Strategy and Planning

Definition: A plan of action designed to achieve the major or overall aim of an established policy.

Level 1
- Plans are undertaken to comply with legislated guidelines or other requirements to avoid the negative impact of failure to comply.
- Plans are developed by HR or the function responsible for compliance.

Example: The organization develops a plan to respond to a negative audit finding and establishes hiring targets to increase the representation of designated group members.

Level 2
- Strategy and planning are undertaken to go beyond compliance, to correct injustices to historically disadvantaged groups and promote corporate social responsibility.
- HR or the function responsible for compliance, and a supportive manager, develop strategies and plans for special initiatives.

Example: The organization develops a recruiting strategy that features historically disadvantaged group member employees prominently in its promotional material.

Level 3
- Strategy and planning are undertaken to realize the benefits from diversity programs in the workplace and in targeted markets where a business case exists.

- Strategies and plans are developed with input from employees and approved by organizational leaders.

Example: The organization develops a strategy to ensure job descriptions and selection criteria are based on the principles of bona fide job requirements and merit.

Level 4

- Strategy is undertaken to support the integration of diversity and inclusion in the workplace with market needs, and therefore to leverage the business benefits of a fully optimized workforce.
- Diversity and inclusion strategies are supported by all levels of leadership and management and incorporate employee feedback.

Example: The organization develops a strategy to move beyond the group focus of diversity toward the talent focus of inclusion. This strategy is not the responsibility of one person or office; e.g., one organization states they have "150,000 inclusion agents of change."

Level 5

- Strategy and planning are the driving force of embedding human equity throughout the organization and the broader community.
- Input from customers/clients, stakeholders, suppliers and the community is sought in order to achieve this.

Example: The organization develops a strategy to maximize on human capital and move each employee toward self-actualization. This human equity strategy is integrated into every feature of human resource management, such as recruitment, selection, promotion, training, development, discipline, etc.

Implementation

Definition: Implementation is the carrying out or execution of a strategy or plan. As such, implementation is the action that must follow any preliminary thinking in order for something to actually happen. The word *deployment* is sometimes used to mean the same thing.

Level 1

- Equity programs are implemented that comply with legislated guidelines or other requirements.
- Required programs are initiated by HR or the function responsible for compliance.

Example: The organization provides training to all employees on accessibility for people with physical disabilities as required by legislation.

Level 2

- Programs are implemented that go beyond compliance to correct injustices to historically disadvantaged groups and promote corporate social responsibility.
- HR or the function responsible for compliance, and a supportive manager, initiate programs that benefit target groups.

Example: The organization forms a diversity team to organize workplace events that celebrate cultural differences.

Level 3

- Diversity programs are implemented in the workplace and in target markets where a business case exists.
- Programs have the support of organizational leaders.

Example: The organization implements a women's networking initiative to help increase business development opportunities for female clients/prospects.

Level 4

- Diversity and inclusion principles drive the implementation into all aspects of policies, processes, programs and services to ensure that each person is valued and respected, and individual talents optimized.

- All employees consider themselves responsible for creating a diverse and inclusive environment.

Example: The organization implements individually focused development programs to empower each person by virtue of their one-of-a-kind attributes.

Level 5

- Human equity principles are fully integrated into the implementation of all policies, strategies, processes, programs and services, internally and externally.
- The organization plays a leadership role in encouraging other organizations to do the same.

Example: The organization implements a human equity–focused immigrant selection process in collaboration with the federal government.

Measurement

Definition: Dimensions, quantity, or capacity as ascertained by a quantitative comparison to a standard with established properties.

Level 1

- The organization measures and reviews results as required by legislation to ensure compliance.
- Measurement is focused on representation of target groups as stated in the legislation.

Example: Federally regulated organizations are required to file an equal opportunity or employment equity document stating the number of women and minorities hired and promoted.

Level 2

- The organization measures and reviews results to go beyond compliance, determine impact on historically disadvantaged groups and promote corporate social responsibility.

Example: The organization creates an annual Corporate Responsibility Report highlighting its work in the LGBT community.

Level 3

- The organization maintains qualitative and quantitative measurements on key diversity initiatives in the workplace and in target markets where a business case exists. Measurements include employee engagement surveys, leadership assessments (such as the ELA), external reputation benchmarking, as well as representation and retention of selected groups. These metrics are gathered on a regular basis and are reviewed and assessed by organizational leaders.

Example: The organization establishes an annual review of leadership behavior using the Equitable Leader Assessment.

Level 4

- The organization develops and maintains a qualitative and quantitative measurement framework to assess the integration of diversity and inclusion principles into all policies, processes, programs and services.
- Relevant results are shared with leaders and employees to help ensure that each person is valued and respected and individual talents optimized.

Example: The organization holds quarterly human capital reviews to ensure that talent is being fully optimized.

Level 5

- The organization develops and maintains a qualitative and quantitative measurement framework to assess the integration of human equity principles into all policies, processes, programs and services.

- Relevant measures are shared externally with customers/clients, stakeholders, suppliers and the community.

Example: The organization holds quarterly human equity sessions with clients and other key stakeholders.

Review and Realignment

Definition: A formal assessment or examination of progress with the intention of instituting change if necessary.

Level 1

- The organization reviews and realigns plans in response to external audits or specific external requirements as required by legislation or other requirements to ensure compliance.
- HR or the function responsible for compliance undertakes reviews as required.

Example: The organization responds to an audit finding that employees with disabilities are unable to access training programs by reviewing the accessibility of its training facilities.

Level 2

- The organization reviews and realigns plans to go beyond compliance, determine impact on historically disadvantaged groups and promote corporate social responsibility.

Example: The organization responds to a review that identifies the underrepresentation of women at senior positions by launching an external search for a highly visible senior position to be filled by a female hire.

Level 3

- The organization undertakes regular, in-depth reviews of diversity initiatives in the workplace and in target markets for which a business case has been made.
- There is a process to realign based on direction from organizational leaders.

Example: The organization's three-year diversity strategy is reviewed by the executive committee using a diversity scorecard.

Level 4

- The organization systematically reviews culture, individual performance and processes and realigns in the workplace and marketplace based on direction from all levels of management and employees to ensure alignment with diversity and inclusion principles. Comprehensive action plans are created in response to results of the review.

Example: The organization conducts a leadership assessment using the ELA and links to the annual employee attitude survey by department to identify the highest and lowest performing leaders.

Level 5

- The organization systematically reviews and realigns internal and external activities to ensure alignment with human equity principles. Action plans are created in response to the results.
- Relevant review and realignment findings are shared externally with customers/clients, stakeholders, suppliers and the community.

Example: The organization reviews external customer satisfaction surveys with internal employee engagement surveys to quantify how much improvement in employee engagement impacts on improvements in customer satisfaction.

Work Environment

Definition: Factors related to employee satisfaction, fairness of HR policies and practices, climate for diversity and inclusion. Includes assessments and procedures for health and safety, harassment/discrimination, workplace violence and flexible work arrangements, self-care and dependent care, management and leadership ("directing mind") guidance.

Level 1
- Work environment issues are addressed so the organization can comply with minimum workplace standards.
- Initiatives are undertaken by HR or the function responsible for workplace health and safety and are usually in response to a specific problem or complaint.

Example: The organization has a written statement that informs employees of its commitment to a workplace that is free from harassment.

Level 2
- Work environment initiatives are launched to support the organizational goal of corporate social responsibility by ensuring a safe, healthy and well-functioning workplace.
- The organization supports flexibility programs where convenient for the organization on an ad hoc basis.
- Initiatives are undertaken by HR or the function responsible for workplace health and safety.

Example: The organization introduces an alternative working arrangement for a specific department to address the needs of working mothers; the initiative is sponsored by a supportive manager.

Level 3
- A comprehensive work environment policy is put in place for business reasons, including employee engagement and increased productivity.

- Benchmarking, employee feedback and best practices are utilized in the development of work environment policy.
- Organizational leaders understand and support the business case.

Example: The organization's leaders visibly promote and participate in flexible work arrangements; they launch a task team to recommend changes to the organizational culture and work environment that will help achieve the business case.

Level 4

- All members of the organization are expected to create a diverse and inclusive work environment, where each person is recognized and developed, and individual talents maximized.
- This commitment is evidenced at the senior leadership and management levels by valuing and recognizing each person and through the allocation of diversity- and inclusion-related financial/people resources as a standard operating cost.

Example: The organization creates sponsor/mentor impact sessions to assess the progress of high potential/high performance candidates.

Level 5

- All members of the organization are expected to embrace and foster the practice of human equity in the work environment, both internally and beyond the boundaries of the organization.
- The organization works with clients, suppliers and other stakeholders who are also committed to achieving diversity, inclusion and human equity.

Example: The organization shares human equity best practices with clients and other stakeholders.

Recruitment and Selection

Definition: Initiatives related to enabling the organization to identify, attract, recruit and select the best talent. Includes monitoring representation of groups, workforce census data, employment systems reviews, interviewer and recruiter training and processes, job posting systems and succession planning.

Level 1

- Recruitment and selection activities meet applicable legislative or other requirements. Initiatives are undertaken by HR or the function responsible for compliance.

Example: Efforts focus on trying to increase the overall number of under-represented target group members in the organization.

Level 2

- Recruitment and selection initiatives are undertaken to promote the organizational goal of going beyond compliance.
- The organization fulfills its corporate social responsibility to correct past injustices by recruiting and hiring from historically disadvantaged groups.
- Initiatives are undertaken by HR and a supportive manager.

Example: The organization creates a highly visible position and recruits a qualified member of an underrepresented group to fill it.

Level 3

- A diverse workforce is recruited and selected for business reasons. Recruitment and selection efforts attempt to eliminate employment barriers to hire and promote the best-qualified applicants.
- Organizational leaders understand and support the business case of a workforce that reflects the diversity of the talent pool and customer base.

Example: The organization's CEO highlights its diversity recruiting as a key focus area in the annual planning process and links it to building the talent pool needed to achieve business objectives.

Level 4

- Inclusive recruitment and selection initiatives are fully integrated into the organization and support the strategic business advantage of optimizing diversity and inclusion. Selection criteria emphasize knowledge, skills and abilities of individuals, and are linked to organizational competencies.
- The organization addresses biases throughout the recruitment and selection process, both individual and systemic.

Example: The organization introduces SHAPE V recruitment tools into outreach and selection process.

Level 5

- Inclusive recruitment and selection initiatives are fully integrated into the organization and support the strategic business advantage of optimizing human equity.
- The organization demonstrates leadership by promoting human equity, diversity and inclusive recruitment and selection beyond the boundaries of the organization (e.g., customers/clients, stakeholders, suppliers, industry peers and community).

Example: The organization conducts a Golden Thread analysis and realigns its recruitment and selection process to incorporate intangible traits such as character virtues.

Accountability and Recognition

Definition: Accountability and recognition are viewed by organizational leaders as key to an equitable and inclusive employment system. Quantitative, qualitative, external and leadership goals are set to hold leaders accountable. Accountability mechanisms are established for leaders' and employees' behavior. The organization rewards people managers for developing and retaining best talent. Consistent performance, promotion and recognition criteria are applied and merit-based compensation and recognition programs are evident. Initiatives related to customer satisfaction and accessibility of customer sites are evident (these include accessibility reviews and a credible process to deal with customer complaints).

Level 1

- Accountability and recognition programs comply with applicable legislation and other requirements.
- Reward structures are developed by HR or the function responsible for compliance in response to specific problems or complaints.

Example: The organization responds to an audit finding that designated group members are not adequately represented in awards programs. It establishes goals and a mechanism to monitor the number of awards given to designated groups.

Level 2

- Accountability and recognition programs are designed to address past injustices and to support the organization as socially responsible.
- Members of historically disadvantaged groups may be found in high-profile roles in the organization.
- Programs are developed by HR with the assistance of a supportive manager.

Example: The organization introduces a highly visible management award to recognize managers who achieve their representation goals.

Level 3

- Accountability and recognition are viewed by organizational leaders as key to a diverse and equitable employment system.
- Accountability and recognition based on merit are the foundation for attracting and retaining diverse talent.

- The organization rewards managers for attracting and retaining diverse employees, and develops consistent performance, promotion and recognition criteria to promote this goal.

Example: The organization implements quarterly reviews with leaders to review the impact of accountability and recognition on hiring, performance management and retention.

Level 4

- Accountability and recognition are aligned with business goals and are integrated into the organization at all levels to achieve the strategic benefits of a diverse and inclusive workplace for all.
- Employee feedback is applied to measure progress and design new accountability and recognition programs.

Example: The organization introduces an inclusion index to guide its talent optimization program.

Level 5

- Accountability and recognition programs extend beyond the boundaries of the organization to promote human equity with its customers/clients, stakeholders, suppliers and community partners.
- The organization requires its external stakeholders to demonstrate a shared commitment to diversity, inclusion and human equity.

Example: The organization introduces inclusion and human equity measures as part of its external contracts with suppliers.

Learning and Development

Definition: Building knowledge, awareness, understanding, skills, behaviors and competence through experience, exposure, education, coaching, mentoring, sponsorship, unique ability career planning, annual performance plans and employee feedback through a 360-degree process.

Level 1

- Learning and development opportunities are provided in accordance with legislated or other compliance requirements.
- Learning and development initiatives are undertaken by HR or the function responsible for training and development compliance.

Example: The organization responds to an audit finding by requiring HR to develop a training program to help prepare designated groups for advancement.

Level 2

- Learning and development opportunities are used to promote the organization's corporate social responsibility to correct past injustices.
- Learning for historically disadvantaged groups is offered on an ad hoc basis. Data on underrepresented groups is used to analyze career movement.
- Initiatives are driven by HR and a supportive manager.

Example: The organization supports external non-profit groups to develop specialized training programs to assist people with disabilities to gain employability skills; as part of its community relations, the organization hires summer interns from the program.

Level 3

- There are business reasons to support learning and development as a mechanism to break down systemic barriers.
- Foundation principles are established for a diverse and inclusive employment system that are performance based and that influence hiring, development, compensation and termination.

- Opportunities are offered to address individual and group skill gaps, and plans are put in place to increase skill levels.

Example: The organization introduces formal and informal mentoring programs that are open to diverse employees to ensure equitable access to developmental opportunities.

Level 4

- Learning and development opportunities focused on diversity and inclusion are fully integrated into the organization and support the strategic business advantage of a high-performance workplace.
- They are inclusive and accommodate employees' unique needs; e.g., counseling is provided equitably for individual career development.
- Programs are based on skill and merit, and measurements are designed to link to business goals; managerial competencies are assessed to ensure they are inclusive. Individuals take ownership of their career development and provide input to learning and development initiatives.
- Leaders believe that the organization will succeed to the extent that each employee reaches his or her full potential.

Example: An inclusive education curriculum is introduced to move individuals beyond diversity to inclusion.

Level 5

- Learning and development opportunities focused on human equity are fully integrated into the organization and support the strategic business advantage of a high-performance workplace.
- Learning and development opportunities focus on fostering diversity, inclusion and human equity beyond the boundaries of the organization, e.g., with customers/clients, stakeholders, suppliers and community, to extend the organization's leadership. Opportunities focus on supporting the organization's reputation as an "employer

of choice for all" and new initiatives or changes are made as a result of ongoing internal and external feedback.

Example: The organization introduces human equity courses designed to grow its high potential/high performance employee base.

Communication

Definition: Communications include internal, external, informal, formal and all formats, e.g., social media, imaging, branding, posted statements, external sponsorships, recruitment advertising, targeted marketing, integrated communications plans, town hall meetings, team meetings and Intranet and Internet presence.

Level 1
- Communication is undertaken to comply with applicable standards or in response to a non-compliance event.
- Information is developed and distributed by HR or the function responsible for compliance.

Example: The organization responds to a compliance audit by having HR reissue a communication to all managers and employees stating its employment equity policy.

Level 2
- The communication plan is developed to support and promote the organization's corporate social responsibility to correct past injustices; maintaining a positive external image is central to the communication plan.
- Communications are developed by HR or the function responsible for compliance and a supportive manager.

Example: The organization showcases its corporate social responsibility initiatives through articles in HR journals and speaking engagements at external conferences.

Level 3
- The communications plan is a means to promote and support diversity as a business issue with bottom-line impact.
- Organizational leaders are key to the development and delivery of the plan.

Example: The organization's leaders hold regular town hall meetings with employees and reinforce why diversity is an important workplace and marketplace issue.

Level 4
- Communications support the strategic business advantage of diversity and inclusion.
- All communications use inclusive language and formats.
- There is continuity and consistency of communications at all levels of the organization. Diverse opinions and diversity of thought are valued and encouraged.

Example: The organization introduces a video series to explore various elements of inclusion.

Level 5
- Internal and external communications support the strategic business advantage of human equity.
- Diversity, inclusion and human equity communications are shared beyond the boundaries of the organization (e.g., customers/clients, stakeholders, suppliers and community) to extend the organization's internal practices.

Example: The organization publishes a white paper on human equity within its industry.

Contracting of Goods and Services

Definition: Initiatives related to the tendering and contracting of goods and services. Can include programs related to contract compliance, supplier diversity and development programs, targeted set-asides, supplier recognition, supplier measurement and inclusive supplier outreach.

Level 1
- The tendering and contracting of goods and services complies with legislated guidelines or other requirements.
- Contracting of goods and services is handled by the group responsible for contract services.
- Additional contract requirements may be included in reaction to negative feedback.

Example: The organization has a standard requirement in all its requests for proposals asking potential vendors to certify they comply with legislation or other requirements.

Level 2
- The tendering and contracting of goods and services goes beyond compliance to include historically disadvantaged groups where possible.
- Additional requirements are included in contracts for highly visible initiatives or to be seen as leaders in corporate social responsibility.
- Contracting is undertaken by the group responsible with input from HR or the function responsible for compliance and a supportive manager.

Example: The organization informs suppliers that they will have preferred status if they indicate in their bid how they will include designated group members in the provision of their goods and services.

Level 3

- The tendering and contracting of goods and services includes specific diversity components where they are linked to the business case.
- Organizational leaders view targeted contracting as strategic to success in markets focused on diverse groups.
- New contracting requirements are identified and implemented by the responsible group with input from the employee diversity team.

Example: A supplier development program is implemented for women-owned businesses.

Level 4

- The organization integrates diversity and inclusion considerations at all stages of tendering and contracting goods and services.
- Mechanisms are in place to evaluate and ensure that tendering and contracting processes are inclusive and result in supplier diversity.

Example: The organization assesses the impact of inclusion initiatives in the tendering and contracting process.

Level 5

- The organization leverages its best practices in contracting of goods and services to extend human equity principles beyond the boundaries of the organization.
- The organization actively reaches out to a diverse pool of suppliers and does business only with those who share their commitment to diversity, inclusion and human equity.

Example: Human equity principles are used to determine contractor choices.

Program/Product/Service (PPS) Development

Definition: Initiatives related to customer satisfaction and accessibility of customer sites. Includes customer satisfaction for target markets, accessibility reviews and processes to deal with customer complaints. Initiatives related to consultation with customers/clients, stakeholders, suppliers and community on program/product/service design for target markets based on input.

Level 1

- Program/product/service development complies with legislated guidelines or other requirements. It is undertaken by the groups responsible for program/product/service development, who consult with HR or the function responsible for compliance.
- Unless driven by external requirements, there is little or no specific differentiation of products or services for diverse customers.

Example: The organization develops a plan to respond to a human rights complaint that it has failed to make reasonable changes to a product to accommodate persons with a disability.

Level 2

- Program/product/service development promotes the organizational goal to go beyond compliance and maintain a positive external image.
- Design features for diverse customers are included in the development of some highly visible program, product or service; they are included as a result of positive or negative feedback that impacts corporate image.
- Program/product/service development is undertaken by the groups responsible with input from HR or the function responsible for compliance and a supportive manager.

Example: The organization consults with a well-known advocacy organization to adapt a product that has been identified as not accessible; the endorsement of the advocacy organization is showcased in its product advertising.

Level 3

- Diversity features are included in program/product/service development where a business case has been made.
- New program/product/service development occurs as a result of market research and in consultation with specific communities of interest, including diverse employees.
- The organizational leaders understand and support the business reasons for program/product/service design that embraces diverse customers.

Example: The organization designs a unique product to meet the needs of women customers.

Level 4

- Program, product and service development is inclusive and addresses the diverse needs of all target markets by integrating diversity and inclusion practices into all workplace and marketplace processes.
- Processes are continually re-evaluated and redesigned to be inclusive and address the unique perspectives and needs of employees, customers/clients, stakeholders, suppliers and communities.

Example: The organization updates its website to ensure full accessibility using inclusive technology, and solicits wide-range feedback on products.

Level 5

- Human equity principles are fully integrated into product, program and service development.
- The organization is a leader externally in promoting diversity, inclusion and human equity in program/product/service development.

Example: The organization sponsors an independent website to promote best practices in human equity.

Customer Focus/Service Delivery

Definition: The practice of identifying the customers, products/services, quality characteristics, and performance measures that are most important to successful service delivery.

Level 1
- The organization's customer focus complies with legislated, bid or contractual requirements.
- It is undertaken by the sales/marketing group, who consult with HR or the function responsible for compliance.

Example: The organization maintains a record of the number of customer complaints it receives from designated group members and forwards it to HR for review.

Level 2
- Customer focus promotes the organizational goal to be socially responsible and maintain a positive external image.
- Plans are developed in response to customer complaints or anticipated concerns that could negatively impact the organization's image; focus is on programs that avoid customer dissatisfaction.
- HR or the function responsible for compliance, and a supportive manager, attempt to anticipate customer issues and advise on action plans.

Example: The organization includes a question in its customer satisfaction survey on its effectiveness in being socially responsible.

Level 3
- Diversity is viewed as a key factor in customer satisfaction and profitability in market segments for which a business case has been made.
- Organizational leaders understand and support initiatives that target opportunities in diverse markets; they see a diverse workforce as a

link to the marketplace and actively seek ideas from employee groups on how to improve customer satisfaction and grow market share.

Example: Metrics examine diverse buying patterns in key market sectors to validate the business case. The organization implements a marketing strategy to attend major external events that attract target groups and adapts promotional material to appeal to the target group.

Level 4

- Diversity and inclusion principles are integrated into the organization's customer/client outreach, service and satisfaction initiatives in relevant market sectors.
- Ongoing processes monitor and track customer feedback from diverse groups and communities to inform and achieve business objectives and overall customer/client service strategies.

Example: Customer service strategies are based on input gathered by inclusive focus groups and services, using audience response technology.

Level 5

- The organization promotes human equity beyond its boundaries by sharing its best practices with customers/clients, stakeholders, suppliers and the community.
- The organization is committed to being a leader in customer/client service by recognizing, understanding and meeting the unique needs of each individual.
- The organization is viewed as a leader in diversity, inclusion and human equity and is committed to maintaining its leadership as a vendor of choice for all.

Example: The organization sponsors an annual conference to promote human equity for customers, clients and stakeholders.

Glossary

Designated or protected groups   The groups of people who are designated for employment equity or equal opportunity purposes because they are underrepresented in the labor force or concentrated in lower-wage-earning occupations. The four designated groups in Canada are women, visible minorities, persons with disability and Aboriginals. In the United States, the protected groups include men and women on the basis of sex; any group that shares a common race, religion, color or national origin; people over 40; and people with physical or mental handicaps. The Equal Employment Opportunity laws were passed to correct a history of unfavorable treatment of women and minority group members.

Diversity   A term coined in the 1987 Hudson Institute *Workforce 2000* report in reference to the presence of a wide range of human qualities and attributes within a workforce or organization. Diversity is often looked at as "a difference that can impact on equitable treatment." It encompasses primary dimensions such as gender, age, ethnicity, culture, race, ability/disability and sexual orientation. It may also include secondary diversity dimensions such as language, family status, place of origin, socioeconomic class, education and religion. Diversity is approached from a group perspective.

Employment equity   A term coined in 1984 by Justice Rosalie Silberman Abella, commissioner of Canada's Royal Commission on Equality in

Employment, to describe a distinct Canadian process for achieving equality in all aspects of employment for designated equity groups. This term was meant to distinguish the process from the primarily American affirmative action model, as well as to move beyond the equal opportunity measures available in Canada at the time. Employment equity focuses on identifying and eliminating systemic barriers in an organization's employment procedures and policies for designated equity groups, and replacing them with positive policies and practices. It also focuses on ensuring appropriate representation of "designated equity group" members throughout the workforce. Employment equity is approached from a group perspective.

Equality   Refers to the practice and belief of treating people the same—that is, so the same rules and practices apply to everyone, regardless of individual needs or differences.

Equity   Refers to fairness; treating people equitably means recognizing differences in order to treat people fairly and take different approaches based on identified differences.

Human equity   A term coined in 2005 by Trevor Wilson in an article called "The Human Equity Advantage," published in *CMA Management* magazine. Human equity emanates from the field of human capital, which is defined as the intangible assets employees bring to the workplace. Human equity is about maximizing human capital and human potential. Human equity means focusing on the unique and intangible assets each employee brings to the workplace. It builds on the individual perspective of inclusion and focuses on talent differentiation strategies, innovation and diversity of thought, finding the right fit between the employee and the job, and a positive psychology approach to management that focuses on maximizing individual strengths. Human equity is approached from an individual perspective.

Inclusion   A term coined in 1999 by Dr. Janet Smith of Canada's Task Force an Inclusive Public Service. Smith argued that although a corporate culture may have a demonstrated commitment to diversity, it may not be inclusive. An inclusive environment values individual differences. In an inclusive environment, each person (rather than each group) is valued, recognized and rewarded for his or her unique contribution. An inclusive organization seeks to recognize each person and allow that person to develop and routinely exercise his or her talents. In an inclusive environment, people are valued because of, not in spite of, their differences. Inclusion is approached from an individual perspective.

Index

DATE DUE
